D0581698

THE COMPACT TIMELINE OF

AVIATION HISTORY

Two generations of frontline fighters: a modern US Air Force F-16C Fighting Falcon flies alongside a World War II vintage P-51 Mustang.

THE COMPACT TIMELINE OF
AVIATION HISTORY

A. A. EVANS AND DAVID GIBBONS

WORTH PRESS

To Jeremy Gambrill (1948–2002)

First published 2008 by Worth Press Ltd.,
The Manse, 34 South End, Bassingbourn, Hertfordshire,
SG8 5NJ, UK
info@worthpress.co.uk

British Library Cataloguing in Publication Data
A catalogue record for this book is available from the British Library

ISBN10: 1-903025-74-5
ISBN13: 978-1-903025-74-1

Acknowledgments The publisher and authors wish to extend their thanks to Jeremy Gambrill and Derek Wood for their advice and suggestions in the preparation of this work. *The History of Aviation* chapter written by Jeremy Gambrill.

Publisher's Note Every effort has been made to ensure the accuracy of the information presented in this book. The publisher will not assume liability for damages caused by inaccuracies in the data and makes no warranty whatsoever expressed or implied. The publisher welcomes comments and corrections from readers, emailed to worthpress@aol.com, which will be considered for incorporation in future editions. Every effort has been made to trace copyright holders and seek permission to use illustrative and other material. The publisher wishes to apologize for any inadvertent errors or omissions and would be glad to rectify these in future.

Designed and produced by
DAG Publications Ltd., London.
Printed and bound in China.

Key to Abbreviations			
AH	Austria-Hungary	INT	International
AR	Argentina	IS	Israel
AUS	Australia	IT	Italy
F	France	J	Japan
BR	Brazil	NZ	New Zealand
CA	Canada	PO	Poland
CHI	China	RU	Russia
CZ	Czechoslovakia	SA	South Africa
FIN	Finland	SK	South Korea
G	Germany	SP	Spain
GB	Great Britain	SW	Sweden
HO	Holland	SWI	Switzerland
IN	India	US	United States
		USSR	Soviet Union

Illustrations Arpingstone: A300, Canberra, Dassault Falcon, Embraer ERJ 135, Gloster Javelin, Boeing 747 rooftop. Dmottl: BA609, Rafale, Il-86. G. Paktor: Airbus A380. Indian Ministry of Defence: Tejas. US Air Force: A-10 Thunderbolt II, A-1E Skyraider, B-25 Mitchell, B-26 Marauder, B-29 Superfortress, B-36 Peacemaker, B-58 Hustler, C-46 Commando, C-47 Skymaster, C-82 Packet, Camel, F-100 Super Sabre, F-104 Starfighter, F-22 Raptor, F-35 Lightning II, F-86 Sabre, F-94 Starfire, Focke-Wolf 190, Fokker DVII, P-12, KC-135, Macchi C.200 Saetta, Messerschmitt Me 163, Messerschmitt Me 262, MiG-19, MiG-21, Mirage 2000, N1K2-J Shinden Kai, P-26 Peashooter, P-38 Lightning, P-40 Tomahawk/Kittyhawk, P-47 Thunderbolt, P-80 Shooting Star, PBY Catalina, RQ-4A Global Hawk, S2F-1 Tracker, Sikorsky H-5, Sikorsky S-58. US Department of Defense: A3D-1 Skywarrior, A4D-1 Skyhawk, A-6 Intruder, A-7A Corsair, AGM-86 (ALCM), An-12 Cub, An-124 Condor, AV-8B Harrier, B-1B Lancer, B-2B Spirit, B-52 Stratofortress, Buccaneer, C-130 Hercules, C-141 Starlifter, C-17 Globemaster, C-5 Galaxy, CH-46 Chinook, CH-46 Sea Knight, CH-53 Sea Stallion, DHC-4 Caribou, Enola Gay, Etendard IV, Exocet/Super Etendard, F-101 Voodoo, F-102 Delta Dagger, F-104 Starfighter, F-105 Thunderchief, F-106 Delta Dart, F-117 Nighthawk, F-15 Eagle, F-16 Fighting Falcon and P-51 Mustang, F-16 Fighting Falcon, F-35 Lightning II, F-4 Phantom II, F6F Hellcat, Grippen, Il-76 Mainstay, Jaguar, Ka-25 Hormone, Mi-24 Hind, Mi-8 Hip, MiG-23, MiG-25, MiG-29, Mirage F-1, Mirage III, OV-10A Bronco, P-38 Lightning, P-51 Mustang, S-3A Viking, SA 341 Gazelle, SA.330 Puma, Sea Harrier, Sea King/Commando, Shackleton, SR-71 Blackbird, Super Etendard, Super Puma, T-16 Badger, T-38 Talon, T-4 Goshawk, Tornado, Tu-95 Bear, UH-1 Huey, UH-60 Blackhawk, V-22 Osprey, Victor, YUH-60A Black Hawk. US Navy: F-14 Tomcat, F-18 Hornet. PageantPix: Airbus A300-600, Albatross, Antonov An-12, Apache, Argosy, Augusta A109, AWACS E-8, Betty, Boeing 247, Boeing 314, Boeing 707, Boeing 747, Britannia, C-54, Camel, Caravel, C-Class S-23, Chinook, Comet, Concord, Constellation, Dakota, Dornier Do X, Douglas DC-10, DR-1, Flying Fortress, Ford Tri-Motor, Fw 190, Hellcat, Hind, Hindenburg, Horsa, HP42, Hunter, Hurricane, IL-76 Mainstay, Ju-52, Lancaster, Lightning, Lockheed Martin 130, Me 109, Meteor, Mi-8, MiG-17, MiG-21, Nieuport 28, R101, Sea Harrier, Sikorsky S-76, Skyship, Spitfire, SR-71, Stratocruiser, Super Mystere, Transall, Tu-104, U-2, Viscount, Vulcan, Zeppelin, Zero. NASA: Tu-144 Conordski. Other illustrations are from the Derek Wood collection and from certain individual manufacturers. While every effort has been made to trace copyright holders and seek permission to use illustrative material, the Publishers wish to apologise for any inadvertent errors or omissions and would be glad to rectify these in future editions.

Front endpaper: *A Bleriot monoplane on display at the National Museum of the United States Air Force.*

Back endpaper: *The X-35A, Lockheed Martin's Joint Strike Fighter concept demonstrator, which will be manufactured as the F-35 Lightning II single-seat multi-role combat aircraft, which represents the very latest generation of fighter aircraft. The B variant will be a short takeoff and landing version, enabling it to operate from aircraft carriers.*

Contents

Featured Aircraft

CONTENTS

Below: *A Quantas Boeing 747-400 airliner comes in to land at London's Heathrow airport – just above the roofs of Myrtle Avenue. Heathrow, one of the world's busiest airports, desperately needs anther runway, but there is much controversy about this, especially in view of the airport's close proximity to the outskirts of London. This photograph shows why.*

Introduction

A little over a century ago, Orville Wright took to the air in man's first powered heavier-than-air flight. Ballooning and gliding were already established; but fitting an engine to a man-carrying aerial device gave that vital element of control – to fly at will and in any direction.

From small beginnings, the aviation industry grew to revolutionize world communications – it is a commonplace to say that the world has shrunk, but for most of humanity it is literally true. A tourist can fly from Europe to Australia, on the other side of the world, in half a day; businessmen commute across the Atlantic; and warplanes have delivered bombs and missiles across vast oceans from distant continents. In the era of globalization, aviation sits at the very heart of the world economy.

This book presents a detailed chronological panorama of more than a century of aviation history, listing the significant events in the development of the airplane and the first flights of the many thousands of aircraft types that have taken to the skies – encompassing airliners, fighters, bombers, helicopters and lighter-than-air craft. More than eighty of the most significant of these aircraft are shown in more detail, with production details and full technical specification.

The book opens with a general history of aviation, and there are also sections providing concise biographies of more than seventy of the great pioneers of flying – pilots, designers, and innovators; details of the great fighter aces, listing their victories; and sections covering aircraft weaponry.

Aviation today sometimes does not give the outward appearance of rapid progress – a major airliner or warplane can take many years to plan, finance, develop and construct before that tense but magical moment of 'first flight', followed by months, even years, of testing and refining before it enters service. But that is to obscure the dramatic technical developments constantly taking place, as engines become more powerful and 'greener', control systems become 'fly-by-wire', and the military planemakers develop further radar-defeating 'stealth' designs. Over a century, speeds have increased from less than 100 miles per hour to more than 2,000. Aircraft have also got a lot bigger: contrast the tiny one-man Blériot monoplane that made the first crossing of the English Channel in 1909 with the mighty Airbus A380, capable of carrying some 850 passengers, which entered service in 2007.

One major factor affecting the world today is climate change, and the need to reduce carbon emisions involves the aviation industry especially. While the cost of oil has risen dramatically, pressure is on aircraft manufacturers to increase efficiency with 'greener' technology. Some even predict the end of the 'aviation boom'.

More such dramatic developments are inevitable in future decades, and it is probably as difficult for us today to imagine aviation in another century's time as it was for those great pioneers of the early 1900s in their propeller-driven wood and canvas biplanes. The only certainty is that aviation will continue to advance, impress and fascinate.

THE HISTORY OF AVIATION

Looking back to the beginning of the 20th century, it seems quite reasonable to consider that in the past hundred years or more the advent of manned flight was the most significant development to impact the world. It enabled humans to understand the real dimensions of planet Earth, allowed us to travel to anywhere we liked, to cross continents and oceans in hours rather than weeks, to set foot upon the moon. Commercial air transport has allowed the developed western world to see and understand the less fortunate, and to act positively to help in times of drought, famine or flood. It allows us to fly the seriously ill to a hospital; to spread seeds and fertilize thousands of square miles of barren land and to fight fires in remote areas of farmlands and forest. Military air power has, sadly, allowed one nation to heap devastation upon the citizens of neighbouring countries with relative safety but, on a more positive note it has enabled the deployment of deterrent forces which may well have prevented more serious conflicts from breaking out. Hopefully, the score will show that, since the Wright brothers staggered into the sky on December 17, 1903, aviation has been the cause of more good than harm. Thinking back to that monumental event, we will never know if those two great pioneers had any idea how significant their first manned flight would be.

The history books show that in about 1500 Leonardo da Vinci drew up a number of ideas in his series called 'Studies in Mechanical Flight', but historians believe that his ideas were never followed up. Monsieur Le Besnier, a French locksmith, certainly made an attempt in 1673, but sadly the magnificent Bartholomew-Laurence de Guzman did not. In 1709 he revealed plans for a 'flying device' that incorporated pieces of amber and a number of magnets to aid his descent, but it seems unlikely he too did more than put pen to paper. Eventually the honour of being the first aviator would go to a 'balloonist' but first of all a means of achieving 'lift' was required. Joseph Priestley, an English chemist, theorized on the practicalities of hydrogen, but it was Michael Montgolfier who first took to the sky when on November 21, 1783 he and his brother Jacques Étienne persuaded two volunteers to step aboard. Thus aviation was born.

'Balloonatics', 'aeronauts' or 'aérostiers' – whatever they were called, these remarkable men were true heroes. Consider for one moment the following account of a voyage by the Marquis de Arlande:

"I stirred the fire and took with a fork a truss of straw, which, no doubt from being too tight, did not take fire very easily. I lifted it and shook it in the middle of the flame. The next moment

***Left:** Blanchard's and Jeffries' balloon crossing of the English Channel in 1785 as depicted in a contemporary illustration. The Royal Navy – the 'wooden walls of England' – stood between the French armies and Britain during the subsequent wars. It would be more than a century before the threat from the air became a practical reality.*

I felt as if I were lifted up by my armpits, and said to my dear companion 'now we mount'!"

Clearly the noble Marquis and his unnamed companion shot up into the sky and his story continues.

"Then I heard another noise in the machine which appeared to be the effect of a rope breaking. I saw that the part of the machine that was turned toward the south was full of round holes, several of which were of considerable size. I then said, 'We must descend.' 'Why?' [asked his companion, who had not realized that the fire was spreading to the canopy of the balloon, which was alight in various places]. The moment we touched the ground I raised myself up in the gallery [basket] and perceived the upper part of the machine [appeared] to press very gently upon my head. I pushed it back and jumped out, and on turning myself toward the machine expected to find it distended, but was surprized to find it perfectly emptied and quite flattened."

Re-reading the journals of the day it becomes clear that these noble aviators risked their all with every ascent, not least because of public distrust of these wonderful flying machines. One account from 1783 tells of 100,000 people watching the ascent of a hydrogen-filled balloon from a field near the centre of Paris. The balloon travelled some fifteen miles and landed close to a small village. A journal records:

"After it alighted, there is yet motion in it from the gas it still contains. A small crowd gains courage from numbers, and for an hour approaches by gradual steps, hoping meanwhile the monster will take flight. At length one bolder than the rest takes his gun, stalks carefully to within shot, fires, witnesses the monster shrink, gives a shout of triumph, and the crowd rushes in with flails and pitchforks. One tears what he thinks to be the skin, and causes a poisonous stench, again all retire. Shame no doubt, now urges them on, and they tie the cause of the alarm to a horse's tail, who gallops across the country, tearing it to shreds."

However dangerous early flight might have been, it was not so hazardous as to dissuade the proud aviators from their mission. Monck

***Above:** Alberto Santos-Dumont was the first European to make a recognized, powered flight in 1906, but his earlier experiments were with lighter-than-air vehicles. Here he demonstrates his airship in the Champs Elysées, Paris.*

Mason, a contemporary observer, noted that in the first 1,000 balloon ascents only eight deaths were recorded, five of the victims being burned to death. The Montgolfiers and a host of other creative minds all endeavoured to be the first to fly in a controlled manner from one point to another, but getting a man up into the sky was always of minor concern when compared with the real conundrum: how to take off, fly to a chosen destination and land in safety? Balloons were fine provided that nature was on the side of the flier. As long as he had the conditions in which he could take off and he wanted to go where the wind chose to take him, then getting from A to B might be possible, though there was still the delicate matter of getting down in one piece.

The search for controllable flight went on. Work on gliders by Lilienthal in Germany, Pilcher in England, Chanute in America and others elsewhere in the world had served to indicate that if flight were to be practical, the real issue was providing the aviator with a means of controllable power. It was not until 1894 that a successful flight in a man-carrying glider was achieved, but true controlled flight could only be accomplished when a manageable form of propulsion could be found. Throughout the 19th century the search continued. In 1848, for example, came the Stringfellow model steam plane that, with an all-up weight of less than 9lb, managed a flight of 40 yards powered by its tiny steam engine. In America Dr. Samuel Pierpoint Langley had begun the construction of a series of power-driven models, the first of which flew in 1896, powered by a 1hp engine. Sadly his 'Aerodrome' hit its launching post as it was catapulted into the air and it fell into the Potomac river. Journalists who had been invited to witness this flight of his celebrated glider commented that he might have done better had he launched the craft upside down, so it might then have travelled up instead of down. Langley was not the only pioneer of aviation to have to live with a hostile press. Elsewhere, designs appeared for ornithopters, rowing boats that might paddle their way along and, of course, any number of remarkable attempts to re-create the wing action of birds in flight. Whilst it is all too easy now to laugh at the absurdity of contra-rotating 'spinners', air screws and multi-winged machines that look more like toast-racks than aeroplanes, we should never forget that the men who devized these incredible craft were each working in isolation with nothing to guide them but their ingenuity and their desire to fly. Today we take for granted that information can be exchanged at the press of a button. We have television, video, cameras and, of course, the internet to give us access to ideas, to show us the work of others that provide us with food for thought. But Jobert, Melikoff, Penaud, Moy, Kaufmann and countless others had only their imaginations to inspire them as they laboured to succeed.

Their biggest hurdle was a reliable power source. They needed one that was light enough

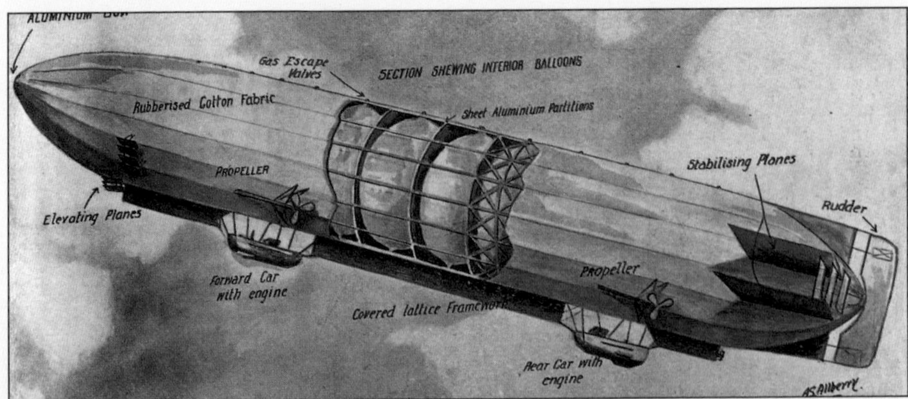

Above: *Contemporary cutaway of a Zeppelin-type airship, showing the subdivision of gasbags within the overall envelope. At the time these vast airships could carry loads – of passengers or bombs – far in excess of heavier-than-air craft. But they were vulnerable to the weather, and many of them perished in accidents on the ground.*

to be carried upon their flimsy machines and was more reliable than the first engines they were using, which were either electric or steam driven, neither of which could be made to work. Everything was on hold until the internal combustion engine had been invented. Meanwhile the balloonists carried on trying to develop a navigable machine. In Germany, Count Ferdinand von Zeppelin completed the plans for his first 'airship', the LZ-1, in 1893. A German commission pronounced his ideas to be "worthless" but undaunted he raised by public subscription the funds he needed to build his craft, and made his first flight in July 1900. The Zeppelin proved to be a bold step forward, but in the long run it wouldn't beat the world. Two young men who were hard at work in North Carolina, USA would win that honour.

American aviation pioneers Wilbur and Orville Wright were born in 1867 and 1871 respectively. Owners of a 'bicycling' shop, they built their first large kite in 1899 having learned of Lilienthal's glider flying in Germany. They then constructed their own glider and built a small wind tunnel to test their calculations on the dynamics of lift. The Wright brothers followed this up with a series of gliders until, in December 1903, they fitted an engine to their most recent model and took to the skies for the first powered flight, lasting 59 seconds. With Wilbur at the controls they set the pace for all to follow as America and the world went aeroplane crazy. 1906 saw the first aeroplane flight in Europe when Brazilian Alberto Santos-Dumont took to the skies in France in a flight of some 25 yards. In 1907 in the USA the Aerial Experiment Association was formed with founder-members including Alexander Graham Bell and Messrs Baldwin, Curtiss, Douglas, McCurdy and Selfridge.

From the very beginning, the Wright brothers believed that the future of the aeroplane was as a military machine. They knew that balloons had pioneered the way in providing platforms for observation high above the battlefield as early as 1794, when the French had used the *L'Entrepenant* to monitor troop movements in the battle of Fleurus. And on home soil the exploits of Captain John Randolph Bryan in the American Civil War were fresh in the mind. During the Peninsular campaign of 1862, he ascended in a tethered balloon to observe the movement of Union forces but, as he ascended, an unfortunate soldier caught his leg in the restraining cable and was hauled up in the air after the balloon. One of his companions slashed through the cable to free the soldier and in doing so set the balloon free. The wind carried the balloon toward the Union troops who unleashed all of their firepower upon the gallant aviator. He had to huddle in the observation basket for protection. To his relief the balloon stayed aloft and the wind backed around sending him toward his own lines. But the Confederates, having no means of identifying friend from foe, proceeded to attack his frail craft, which finally came to

Above: *The Wright Flyer and its successors were flimsy affairs, light enough to be manhandled on the ground with ease. Steering of the Wright aircraft in the air was by rudders and wing-warping, relatively easy to implement on wood and fabric flying surfaces; but subsequent development favoured the modern system of flaps and ailerons.*

Left: *The eight-cylinder engine that powered one of Curtiss's early aircraft.*

Below: *Rear view of the Wright aircraft showing the primitive, but lightweight, transmission system. It also shows the wing-warping wires for steering.*

Bottom: *Contemporary explanation of the Wright aircraft, showing its pusher design and canard nose wings.*

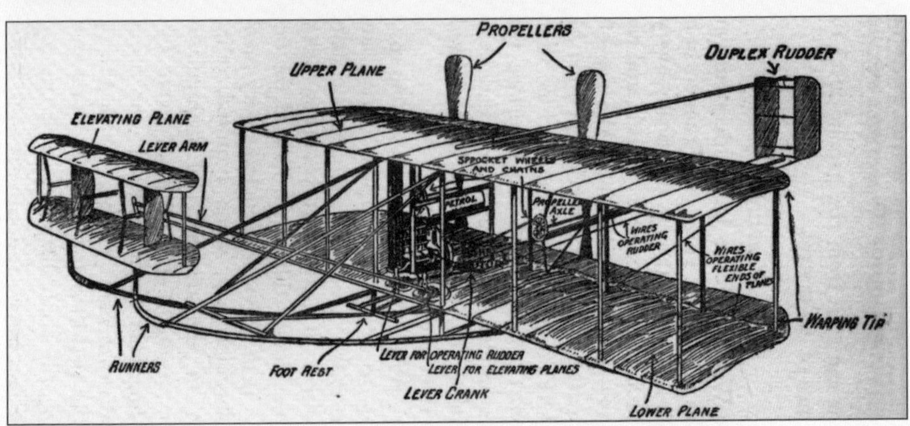

grief in the York River. Captain Bryan made it back to camp, but history does not record him taking part in any further exploits in the air.

So perhaps Orville and Wilbur were not too surprized when in a letter dated October 1905 the US War Department "recommended that the Messrs Wright be informed that the Board of Ordnance and Fortification does not care to formulate any requirements for the performance of a flying machine or take any further action on the subject until a machine is produced which by actual operation is shown to be able to produce horizontal flight and to carry an operator." What the War Board failed to accept was that the brothers had already achieved a flight of 24 miles, although it had not been observed. Sadly, the local press did, however, report the first flight of the Flyer No.2: its engine had failed to reach maximum speed and to the amusement of the gathered journalists, the biplane nose-dived off the end of its launch rail. Undaunted, Wilbur and Orville carried on with their developments and in 1908 the US Army was finally persuaded to support them. This they did with an award of $25,000 to fund an improved Wright Model A that could accommodate both a pilot and an observer. The Model B was delivered in 1909, though sadly not before a passenger was lost when Orville crashed during a test flight.

News of the Wright brothers' exploits in the air spread rapidly and in 1908 they made a series of spectacular flights throughout America and Europe with Wilbur piloting a Wright Model A that had been carried across the Atlantic by steamer. During their tour, Griffith Brewer accompanied Wilbur Wright on a flight and became the first Englishman to travel in a power-driven, heavier-than-air machine. That same year saw Wright make a flight of 36 miles in 1 hour, 31 minutes, 25 seconds, far exceeding any speed record previously achieved. The European pioneers quickly realized that the American machine greatly out-performed their own aeroplanes and so three brothers, Eustace, Horace and Oswald Short contracted with Wilbur to build six Wright Flyers on what was to become the world's first aircraft production line. The selling price was £200 each and they were sold to members of the Aero Club which included in its membership at the time the Hon. Charles Stewart Rolls and Sir Frederick Henry Royce. In 1906 these two formed Rolls-Royce Ltd., manufacturers of motor cars and aero engines.

The next landmark event in the history of flight came in 1909 when, for the first time, an aeroplane flew across the seas between two countries. It was Louis Blériot flying his own Blériot XI monoplane in a flight lasting 36½ minutes across the English Channel from England to France. Blériot, A. V. Roe and others were moving the new aviation technology along at speed. Whereas the early Wright types had to be launched from a fixed rail using a catapult device to gain added airspeed, they had moved on to construct planes that could take off and land on wheels rather than skids. This radical step added a new dimension to the aeroplane, which was no longer reliant upon fixed launch gear. The shape of the aircraft was changing too. Now the general design was to have a propeller at the front and a tailplane at the rear, whereas previously a front elevator had been favoured.

Blériot's flight, on July 25th, 1909, captured the imagination of the world and later that year more than a quarter of a million people were drawn to the first international flying meeting in Rheims, France. There were twenty-three flying machines at the show, flown by pilots from all over the world who competed for cash prizes in speed, distance and duration competitions. Records continued to be broken and in 1910 a Peruvian, Georges Chavez made the first flight over mountains when he flew his Blériot monoplane across the Alps.

Back home in the USA, the Wright brothers' belief in the power of the aeroplane as a war machine was coming true, although not in the way they had predicted. In their minds it had a crucial role to play as an observation platform. Traditionally, the army had deployed cavalry to determine the enemy's movements, but Orville and Wilbur believed their flying machines could do the same job faster and with less risk of casualties. But the military had other plans in mind. In June 1910, Glenn Curtiss first dropped bombs from one of his biplanes upon a dummy battleship marked out on Lake Keuka in New York State. In August of that year, Lieutenant Jacob Earl Fickel of the US Army fired a rifle from the passenger seat of a Curtiss machine at a target on the ground. It was in America, too, that a live bomb was dropped from a Wright biplane and a machine-gun was fired from a Wright Model B, in January 1911 and June 1912 respectively.

The pace of progress in the rest of the world was far from even. In Great Britain the War Office had pronounced that it would not carry out any further experiments with aeroplanes because "aircraft are useless for army purposes as it [was] impossible for anybody moving at more than forty miles an hour to see anything at all." Perhaps their judgement was in part driven by the experience of others? The US already had experience of wartime aviation in the Spanish-American War of 1898, though it was not a happy memory. On July 1 more than 8,000 American infantrymen were struggling through heavy undergrowth toward the Spanish forces dug in on San Juan Hill, which guarded the approaches to Santiago on the island of Cuba. The US decided to make use of tethered balloons for observation, so some 100ft above his comrades, Lieutenant Colonel Darby looked down and around from an observation balloon, searching for signs of the enemy. Through the thick canopy of the jungle he could see no evidence of the Spaniards – but

***Right:** S. F. Cody (1861–1913) was an American who built aircraft in England and is often confused with 'Buffalo Bill' Cody of Wild West Show fame. He made the first recognized powered and sustained flight in Great Britain. He died in a flying accident on Salisbury Plain.*

***Below:** Monsieur Blériot (at left) after his flight across the English Channel in 1909. He travelled 24 miles, and crash-landed, breaking the propeller and both wheels, but emerging himself unscathed and triumphant.*

they could see him. Reasoning that beneath the balloon there would be American troops, the Spaniards opened fire with an almighty barrage. A Colonel Woods, marching with his men, was heard to tell his commanders that Darby's mission was "one of the most ill-judged and idiotic acts" that he had ever seen. Many Americans died that day on San Juan Hill as a result of Darby's flight, although of course it was his commanders who made the decision that he should make the ascent. Despite this awful experience the US War Office could see the potential for the aeroplane in war, and history, of course, has proved them to be correct.

Records show that the first time an airplane was used in combat was on October 22, 1911 when Capitano Piazza, flying a Blériot monoplane of the Italian Air Flotilla, made a reconnaissance of Turkish forces on a flight from Tripoli to Azizia in North Africa. A few days later 2nd Lieutenant Giulio Gavotti dropped grenades on to the Turkish positions at Taguira Oasis, marking the arrival of the aeroplane as a machine of war.

Flying for sport continued apace. In the USA, in the summer of 1910, a young Canadian aviator J. A. D. McCurdy was preparing his own aeroplane for an historic flight from Key West to Cuba. Should he succeed this would be the longest flight to be accomplished over water, but as nobody knew if his mission could be achieved, he enlisted the support of the United States Navy. To provide a 'safety net' they stationed a torpedo-boat every ten miles along the route. McCurdy took off, climbed to a height of 1,000ft and, following the line of naval vessels, set off at his top speed of 50mph. Alone in his open cockpit, he headed toward Cuba. With ten miles to go, his aeroplane ran out of fuel. McCurdy had taken the advice of friends and equipped his aircraft with pontoons in case of just such an emergency, so he was able to land on the water without mishap. A US Navy destroyer picked up him and his aircraft within a few moments of his crash-landing and ferried him on to Havana. There he found President Gomez waiting to congratulate him, as McCurdy's was the first aeroplane to be seen in Cuba. The Toronto Star newspaper, back home in Canada, agreed the gallant aviator should receive their prize of $8,000 for so closely reaching his destination, and the following day McCurdy took off and flew over Havana a number of times to the delight of the local population. Although he had been forced to land earlier than planned, his was still the longest sea flight yet achieved. Nobody else would attempt the route until 1927, when the great aviator Charles Lindbergh flew the first airmail and passenger service between Florida and Cuba.

These truly were great days. By now the aeroplane was being considered as more than a rich man's toy, and serious thought was being given to the possibilities for commercial flight. On November 7, 1910 two packages of silk were carried from Dayton to Columbus, Ohio in a Wright biplane piloted by Philip Parmalee. The flight was carried out on behalf of the Home Dry Goods Store, who divided the silk into small pieces that were sold as souvenirs. Far away in India the first delivery of letters by air would shortly start. The Frenchman, Henri Pequet carried 6,500 letters across the Jumna River on February 18, 1911 and so carried the very first airmail. It would be another two years before the first paying-passenger took to the skies. On January 1, 1914, Anthony Jannus took off in his Benoist flying boat on the first scheduled flight, flying between St. Petersburg and Tampa, Florida. His passenger on that inaugural flight had paid $400 for the privilege, having beaten all comers in an auction. But the service closed after four months, there being too few people willing to brave the elements in an open cockpit for the half hour flight across Tampa Bay.

Across the Atlantic there was little thought of commercial flight as the nations of Europe locked horns in what would become known as the Great War or World War I. This would become a time of fantastic technological development as the protagonists sought to gain advantage by any possible means. But when the war began in August 1914, Germany owned the most powerful air force with 258 aircraft. Even so, the aeroplane featured low in the plans of the German High Command. In the enemy camp, the French force comprized 156 aeroplanes whilst the British power comprized 63 in the Royal Flying Corps, plus the Royal Naval Air Service with 39 land-borne aeroplanes, 52 seaplanes and 7 airships. Apart from their numerical strength, the German force was probably the best equipped, being powered in the main with the very advanced Mercedes engine. In the early days the aeroplane was used largely for reconnaissance, although the first official bombing mission took place on August 30, 1914 when German aircraft dropped five bombs upon Paris. Before the aeroplane could come into its own it would first have to convince the sceptics of its potential worth. Just as the US War Department had been dismissive of the Wright brothers' plans in 1905, so the British military commanders still had lessons to learn. In 1914 General Haig, who would go on to command British forces in France, declared to his officers "I hope none of you gentlemen is so foolish as to think that aeroplanes will be able to be usefully employed for reconnaissance in the air. There is only one way for a commander to get information by reconnaissance and that is by the use of cavalry." But as aeroplanes began to play an important role in military campaigns, the evidence became impossible to deny.

Thousands of machines were produced throughout Western Europe in factories including those of Fokker, Nieuport and the Royal Aircraft Factory. There was little time for development or test-flying, so the front-line service pilots were going to war in untried aeroplanes and learning by their often fatal mistakes quite what made the difference between the good and the downright dangerous. By the end of the Great War Great Britain would have lost 14,166 pilots. But almost 8,000 of these brave young men were killed while learning to fly, an indictment of both training methods and aircraft.

It was a simple step from the reconnaissance aeroplane to the bomber, with the observer becoming first the bomb-aimer and then the air gunner, with his aeroplane being equipped with a machine-gun mounted on a ring running around the rear cockpit. Several early machines were fitted with a forward-firing machine-gun, but since this was mounted on top of the upper wing of biplanes in order to keep the vulnerable propeller intact, it was impossible to aim it properly. The true fighter was only born when Anthony Fokker, a German designer, invented 'interrupter gear'. This synchronized the firing of the machine-gun with the rotation of the propeller, allowing the pilot to sight his enemy down the line of the aircraft nose. First seen on a Fokker Eindecker E.1 monoplane in the summer of 1915, the advantage to the German forces was enormous. For six months the French and British forces suffered heavy losses, having no defence against the new German fighters. After the war, it was learned that the British had rejected the design for their own interrupter gear in 1914 on the grounds of cost. How high was the price paid by the pilots and observers who sat helplessly seeing their machines shot out from beneath them by the enemy's superior technology?

World War I was the time for heroes; for the birth of the first 'aces': Ball, Bishop, Mannock and McCudden; the Americans, Lufberry and Rickenbacker; Boelke, Fonck, Guynemer, Immelmann and of course, von Richthofen, the legendary 'Red Baron'. The war was being fought over sea as well as over land. There were now seaplanes, floatplanes, torpedo-bombers and flying boats. The first aircraft carriers were at sea and the Allied forces were flying anti-

Above: *Though very manoeuvrable, the Sopwith Camel was a difficult fighter to fly. It was in service during the last two years of the war and is credited with more kills – over 1,200 – than any other fighter of World War I. It had a maximum speed of 120mph and mounted two fixed forward-firing Vickers machine-guns.*

submarine warfare missions against German U-boats. In 1918 the newly formed Royal Air Force flew its first heavy bomber mission, but, thankfully, the war was coming to a close. When the Armistice was signed to mark the end of World War I, the British forces totalled over 22,000 aircraft, the French had 15,000, the US had constructed almost 15,000 machines and there were some 20,000 aeroplanes in Germany. So much for the predictions of those War Departments who believed there would be no future for the aeroplane!

With the war over there were pilots and aircraft to spare. Bombers were converted to passenger and freight carriers, and commercial aviation went mad. In May 1919, Lieutenant Commander A. C. Read of the US Navy made the first solo crossing of the Atlantic, piloting a Curtiss flying boat via the Azores. Later that year, Alcock and Brown made the first non-stop crossing, in a converted Vickers Vimy. In

Left: *Manfred von Richthofen – most famous of fighter aces – in conversation with an army pilot while a mechanic checks the cockpit of a naval Albatros D.V. This may have been the aircraft in which he was wounded and forced to land on July 6, 1917.*

Right: *Vickers Vimy heavy bomber. It was in a converted Vimy that Alcock and Brown made the first non-stop crossing of the Atlantic in 1919.*

1922 Lieutenant James H. Doolittle flew from Pablo Beach, Florida to San Diego, California in a DH-4B, covering the 2,163 miles in 21 hours and thus achieving the first trans-continental crossing of the United States. In 1924 four Douglas World Cruisers left Seattle and flew around the world in 174 days, and in 1925 Henry Ford started the first regular air freight service, between Detroit and Chicago. In 1927 Captain Charles A. Lindbergh, in a Ryan, became the first man to fly solo across the Atlantic and that same year Pan American Airways set up their first service, flying between Key West and Havana, and so re-tracing the historic flight of J. A. D. McCurdy just seventeen years earlier.

Nothing better illustrates the impact of aviation upon the 20th century than the example of the postal service. In the USA an ambitious plan to create a transcontinental route was announced in 1919; by 1920 the complete route, 2,680 miles long, was in place and in service. Although flights initally took place by day only, night flying was inaugurated in 1924, by which time the transit time was down to 19 hours. In 1933, 3,489 tons of airmail was carried by the American system – more than on all the other airways of the world combined. And by then the US system included 20,000 miles of external routes which were operated by Pan American Airways, chiefly into Central and South America. The US postal system took a body blow when the Roosevelt Administration cancelled all internal air mail contracts in 1933, believing that many of them had been obtained illegally. For a time the services were flown by Army aircrew in military aircraft. Once the contracts were restored to public enterprize, by newly formed companies who had won contracts at considerably lower prices than before, the carriage of passengers and mail became commonplace and internal air travel was born.

Within a period of twenty years the airplane had empowered the movement of people and goods across vast distances in hours instead of days. Where before there was the train and the motor car, now, flying overhead at greater speeds and unhindered by the need for tracks and roads, flew aeroplanes. Gone were the wood, cloth and wire constructions of the '20s; now aircraft were being constructed in aluminium. They were streamlined, with retractable undercarriages, wing flaps and enclosed cockpits. They had variable-pitch propellers and were beginning to make use of the new technologies of radio direction finding and voice communications to improve their navigation skills.

But across the Atlantic, Europe was preparing to go to war again and this time there were no doubts about the role for the aeroplane in every aspect of warfare. When German forces attacked Poland, their spearhead weapon was the formidable Ju-87 Stuka dive bomber, an awesome sight and sound as it plummeted toward its target. Hard to defend against, Stukas were, however, vulnerable to even the slowest

Below: *Lindbergh's famous Ryan, 'Spirit of St. Louis', in which he made the first solo crossing of the Atlantic in 1927. The 25-year-old aviator made a tremendous impression in Paris, where he landed, and was awarded the Légion d'Honneur.*

Right: *The dramatic Hindenburg disaster of 1937 at Lakehurst, New Jersey ended the age of the airships. Impressive though they appeared, they were already being left behind by the rapid development of heavier-than-air craft. Nevertheless, airships were used by the US Navy in World War II for patrol duties and proved successful in anti-submarine work. Many ideas have been proposed for modern airships, but as yet with little result.*

Right: *The Puss Moth in which the Mollisons flew the Atlantic east–west in July 1933.*

Right: *It was in the three-engined Fokker 'Southern Cross' that Sir Charles Kingsford Smith, Charles T. P. Ulm, Harry W. Lyons and James W. Warner flew the Pacific in 1928. They made the crossing in three stages, from California via Hawaii and Fiji to Brisbane in Australia.*

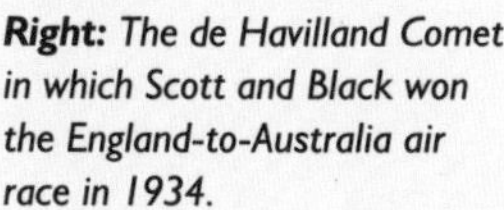

Right: *The de Havilland Comet in which Scott and Black won the England-to-Australia air race in 1934.*

***Above:** Boeing P-12s first flew in 1929 and were among the United States' principal fighters of the early 1930s.*

***Below:** Accompanying the US bomber formations during World War II, from July 1943, were Republic P-47 Thunderbolts, which were built in larger numbers than any other American fighter.*

fighter aircraft when flying to or from their target. Escort duties would be flown by many different types as World War II progressed, probably none more successfully than the P-51 Mustang. Once long-distance bombing became a priority, the purpose-built heavy bomber was required. The Russians had the Tupolev TB-3, the British their Avro Lancaster and the Americans their Boeing B-17 Flying Fortress. Purpose-built to fill a need, each was successful in fulfilling a specialist function. Gliders were required too. Towed behind converted bombers or transport aircraft, they contained men and materials destined for the battlefield. Perhaps their best-known campaign was in the D-Day attacks on bridgeheads in France that were held by German forces. It is hard to imagine now the horror of being a soldier forced to sit in an unarmed glider with no noise save for the whistling of the wind and the shriek of bullets and shells coming up to greet him.

Success in air-to-air combat required highly specialized aircraft. To this day there is disagreement about the real winners and losers. All experts agree that the American P-51 Mustang, the British Supermarine Spitfire, the German Messerschmitt Bf 109 and Fw 190, the Japanese Mitsubishi A6M Zero-Sen and the Russian Yakovlev Yak-3 were all outstanding fighter aircraft, but to compare one with another requires consideration of a multitude

of variable factors. In the 'Battle of Britain', for example, statistics show that the RAF's Spitfires and Hawker Hurricanes had the edge over the Messerchmitts. But the German aircraft needed to fly across the English Channel and back again as well as to dog-fight. How much more successful might they have been had they the fuel to stay and fight for as long as their opponents? Every aeroplane had its strengths and its weaknesses, and so there were massive efforts made by all the combatants to win the technical battle and develop superior airpower. The years between 1938 and 1944 saw a continual flow of new ideas and new solutions. The task was universal: identify the problem; examine possible answer; adapt to supply an interim 'fix' whilst developing a purpose-built solution as quickly as possible. Take the anti-shipping role as an example. Submarines and surface warships could meet and engage the enemy at sea, but only aircraft could meet the need to patrol vast areas, communicate news of any sightings and launch an immediate attack. To achieve all this they needed to be able to fly long distances, carry a heavy payload and defend themselves against attack from air and sea. At the start of the 'Battle of the Atlantic', the Germans could deploy the Fw 200 Condor. This was first flown in 1937 as a passenger transport, was converted to take on a maritime reconnaissance role and further developed as a mine layer. But, once it ran up against the superior long-range Beaufighters and Liberators, it could no longer be relied upon. The interim 'fix' appeared in the Junkers Ju 290, but this aircraft failed to perform adequately. Finally, the Me 410 Hornisse was deployed, a superb machine though too late and in too few numbers to influence the course of the war.

At sea, too, there were many new and innovative developments that would influence the outcome of the war. Torpedo- and dive-bombers, air-dropped mines and the ability to attack warships from the air were all continually improved. But the world's navies were far from defenceless. Cruisers, destroyers and even submarines could carry scout aircraft to extend their ability to patrol long distances, and perhaps, most dramatic of all, aircraft carriers developed the ability to launch massive pre-emptive strikes from across the seas, as the Japanese attack upon Pearl Harbor proved all too clearly.

In every aspect of World War II the airplane played a major role, indeed it can be argued that it was an aircraft of the US Air Force that finally brought the War to an end. On August 6, 1945 a Boeing B-29 Superfortress, the *Enola Gay*, dropped the first atomic bomb upon the Japanese city of Hiroshima. Colonel Paul W. Tibbets took off from Tinian in the Mariana Islands at 2.45 a.m. and finding the weather over his target to be favourable, he dropped the bomb at 8.15 a.m. Three days later a second atomic bomb was dropped, this time upon the city of Nagasaki, by another B-29, the 'Bock's Car', again of the 509th Composite Group, US 20th Army Air Force. After the war the United States Strategic Bombing Survey Forces estimated that, in round numbers, the Hiroshima bomb had killed 70–80,000 men, women and children and had injured about the same number. Certainly 4.7 square miles of the city had been destroyed along with over 80 percent of its buildings. On August 15, 1945 the Emperor announced that the Japanese government had accepted the Allies' peace terms and, officially, the war was at an end. It is debatable whether these two events did in fact force the Japanese hand, as was later claimed by the US government. By mid-May 1945 there was little left of Japanese air power, and USAAF B-29s flying on raids over the Japanese mainland encountered little resistance. Nagoya, Tokyo, Hamamatsu, Osaka, Kobe, Amagasi and Toyama were each repeatedly attacked with fleets of as many as 470 of the heavy bombers. On May 29, 1945 the firestorm caused in Yokohama by the raid of more than 450 Superfortresses destroyed some seven square miles of the city, and on August 1, 1945 over 99 percent of the built-up area of Toyama was destroyed in a single raid. And, significantly, the size and scale of the American air attacks resulted in Japanese radio broadcasts calling for the evacuation of 5,800,000 of the 6,000,000 residents of Tokyo on July 2, 1945, more than a month before the first atomic bomb would be dropped.

History records, however, that on July 26, 1945 the Allies called for the complete and total surrender of the Japanese saying, 'the alternative for Japan is complete and utter destruction', and the surrender duly came, to the relief of a world weary of fighting, death and destruction.

However, the Japanese had succeeded where no other force had. They had bombed the US mainland – albeit with little effect. During World War II Japan launched 30,000 small balloons carrying incendiary explosives, which were carried off across the Pacific by the prevailing winds. One landed in Montana and several reached the forests of Oregon. Sadly, this pathetic act did cause the death of a mother and child picnicking by a lake ,and their pointless deaths can, perhaps, serve as a final example of the futility of war.

As had been the case in 1919, aeroplanes and pilots were in abundance in 1945 and once again the focus fell upon civil aviation. There would be major changes from the pre-war picture, however. The days of the great flying boats were numbered as there were now concrete runways throughout North America and Europe, a legacy of the need to station military aircraft close to centres of population. Private flying sprang to popularity as in the US former pilots looked for ways to use their flying skills. Now the agricultural aircraft and the 'short-hop' passenger planes rolled out. The helicopter, too, came into its own. Born during wartime, its slow speed made it vulnerable in battle but behind the front lines its ability to land on almost any surface made it perfect for liaison and light haulage duties. Aeroplanes now made their mark in providing emergency services as fire-fighters, air ambulances and in police work. 'Executive' passenger services sprang up and new airlines were born, many fading away within weeks due to the cut-throat competition between operators scrambling for new business.

Perhaps the most radical developments came through the advent of the jet engine. Although the turbojet engine had been pioneered in 1937 by Frank Whittle in England, it was not until the German Me 262 appeared in operational service on July 10, 1942 that the world saw the vast potential available in jet power. In fact the German Air Ministry had originated a proposed jet aircraft as early as 1938, when it had authorized a twin-engined fighter designated the P.1065. But technical difficulties dogged the project. The first jet aircraft to be deployed by the Allies was the Gloster Meteor, but there are no records to indicate that the aircraft ever encountered its German rival in combat. It did, however, play an important role in combating the threat of the fearsome V-1 flying bombs. These unmanned impulse-jet powered bombs were flown against

***Below:** The P-38 Lightning was used in a number of different roles, including dive bombing, level bombing, ground strafing, photo reconnaissance missions and extensively as a long-range escort fighter when equipped with droppable fuel tanks under its wings.*

the British Isles from their launch bases on mainland Europe. Their engines were timed to shut down before the target was reached, allowing the weapon to glide on to its target, sometimes with devastating effect. It was only the Meteor that had the straight-line speed to catch up with a V-1, fly alongside until its wing tip was immediately beneath that of the missile and then 'flip' the enemy weapon to knock it off course. Not for the faint-hearted. However there was no defence against the other German secret weapon, the V-2. This, a rocket launched from a concrete pad, was the brainchild of Werner von Braun who, after the war, was to work at the forefront of the US space programme. Thankfully for the British, the weapon arrived in the German arsenal too late and in too few numbers to affect the outcome of the war.

But even as the war in the Pacific was reaching its conclusion plans were being laid for the further dramatic expansion in the civil aircraft market. The first proposal for a jet-engined commercial aircraft was produced in July 1945. It was to have two or more engines, cruise at over 450mph at a ceiling of 30,000ft and carry 14 passengers. By October the design specifications had been altered to enable the aeroplane to cross the Atlantic using four Ghost engines and carrying a payload of 82,000 lb.

At the end of 1945, the International Air Transport Association was officially established. To round off the year, it published statistics showing that 9,300,000 passengers had been carried on the world's scheduled airlines that year with an average of 13.7 passengers per aircraft.

In February 1946 a Pan-American Airways Lockheed Constellation made the first scheduled transatlantic flight, from La Guardia to Hurn airport near Bournemouth, England. It stopped in Newfoundland and Eire, carried 29 passengers and completed the journey in 12 hours and 9 minutes of flying time. This historic flight heralded the beginning of the end for commercial flying-boat services and on March 10, 1946 the British Overseas Airways Corporation (BOAC) announced the termination of their services to the USA. They had been flying three Boeing 314 flying-boats in partnership with Pan-American Airways but in the winter months, when the prevailing winds blew strongly from the west, the aeroplanes could not fly the North Atlantic route carrying a full payload. It was clear that the service would be unable to compete with the new American commercial landplanes. A little later in the year, in

***Below:** The beautiful and impressive Saunders-Roe Princess, the world's biggest metal flying boat and the world's largest pressurized aircraft. By the time it was built in 1952, the era of the flying boat was ending, and only one of the three machines built actually took to the air.*

May, the first scheduled passenger service opened between Britain and Australia. The journey took 5½ days in a Hythe flying-boat built by Short Brothers.

In Seattle, Washington the Boeing Airplane Company announced the first export sales of its commercial development of the C-97 military transport, which had in turn been developed from the highly successful B-29 Superfortress. The Stratocruiser, powered by four Pratt & Whitney Wasp engines, was destined to become a major landmark in the history of commercial aviation. BOAC ordered six of these new aeroplanes which they planned to add to the fleet of Lockheed Constellations which were being flown on the transatlantic route.

Meanwhile, development work went ahead on the jet airliner. The Ghost engine was further developed, and two prototype de Havilland DH-106 jets were ordered in September 1946. These paved the way for the world's first jet-engined passenger aircraft, the de Havilland Comet.

Records startled to tumble. Commander Thomas D. Davies and a crew of four flew a US Navy Lockheed Neptune 11,236 miles non-stop from Perth, Australia to Columbus, Ohio in 55 hours, 18 minutes. Powered by two Wright piston engines, the *Truculent Turtle*, leaving on September 29 and arriving on October 1, 1946 set a new distance record for flight in a straight line, but for how long would the record stand? Distance, speed, payload – these were the critical factors determining success. In the decades to come new factors such as take-off and landing distances would come into play, but in the immediate post-war euphoria everything related to power. The winner in the commercial world would be he who could fly farthest and fastest while carrying the heaviest payload.

In June 1947 American Airlines inaugurated a service between New York and Los Angeles, with a stop in Chicago. Flying Douglas DC-6s, the east-west journey time was to be 10 hours and 45 minutes. A few days later a Pan-American World Airways Constellation left La Guardia on the company's first round-the-world flight.

Every year saw progressively more air travellers, and on December 31, 1947, the International Civil Airline Organisation announced that 21,000,000 passengers had been carried on scheduled flights that year, and that the average number of passengers per aircraft was 16.6.

In 1948 a remarkable and unprecedented event took place, the Berlin Airlift. By the end of

Below: *The stylish Lockheed Constellation was the most successful airliner of its time, breaking new ground by introducing a pressurized fuselage. This allowed it to cruise at 20,000ft, far above the turbulence that previously made journeys by air uncomfortable. Some served during World War II as C-69 transports, and after the war improved versions remained in production until 1959.*

Right: *The 6,000lb thrust of the Bell X-1's rocket propelled Chuck Yeager to supersonic flight on October 14, 1947 – Mach 1.06, or 700mph.*

the Second World War relations between the Allies had deteriorated badly. Joseph Stalin had made demands upon his US and British partners for territories to be ceded to the USSR, and President Truman and Winston Churchill were united in their determination not to give way. All the indications were that confrontation between the former allies was inevitable. In the uneasy peace that followed the Germans' unconditional surrender on May 8, 1945, the Russian forces occupied the eastern half of Germany; the Americans and British were encamped in the west but also had forces in the city of Berlin. The artificial division was continued within the city with the Soviet forces in the east and the other nations, including a French contingent, located in the west of Berlin. To supply their forces, the western powers maintained a corridor through territory controlled by the Red Army. But it was an uneasy peace and through the succeeding years the USSR made a series of demands that these 'occupying' forces should leave. Matters came to a head on March 20, 1948 when Marshal Sokolovsky, Russian Military Governor in Berlin, walked out of a meeting of the Allied Control Council for Germany saying that the Western Powers had held a private

Below: *The impressive B-36 bomber, one of the last propeller-driven bombers in US service. Subsequent marks added four jet engines mounted in pods beneath the wings.*

Above: *The autogiro used a conventional nose-mounted propeller for forward motion and horizontal unpowered rotating blades for lift, unlike a helicopter in which the blades provide both lift and motion. Cierva's first attempts at this type were made in the 1920s, and he had succeeded by 1923. Avro produced autogiros in Britain, and they served in World War II, but not in combat roles.*

Below: *The Bell 47 made its first flight in 1945 and became the first helicopter in the world with full certification for civil flight. This model, dating from 1949, was the 47D-1, the first to carry three passengers and a 500lb payload. The US Army version was named the Sioux and saw casualty evacuation service in the Korean War.*

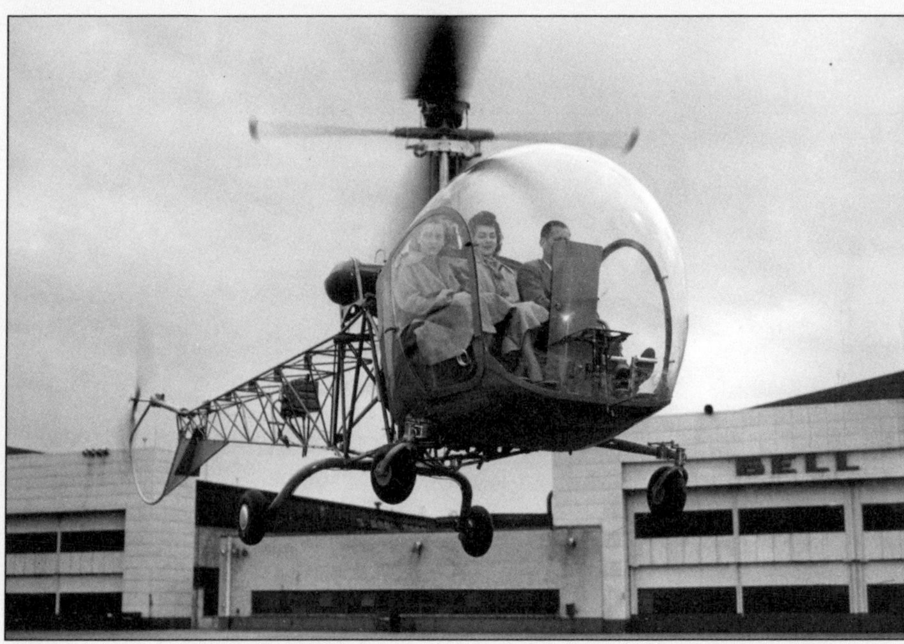

Right: *The Sikorsky H-5 was operated by the US Army, also being built under licence by Westland, who named it the Dragonfly. British European Airways used them for urgent mail delivery and the Royal Navy operated them from carriers.*

Right: *First flown in 1954 the US Army applied the name Choctaw to the H-34 helicopter. Capacity was 16 troops or 8 stretchers*

Right: *A Sikorsky UH-60 Black Hawk, the US Army's current standard troop transport helicopter, prototypes of which first flew in 1974.*

Above: *Lockheed F-94 Starfire, the first jet-powered interceptor in US Air Defense Command and also the first to make use of a drag parachute on landing.*

meeting and that the USSR should have been formally advised of the results of the meeting. Following this absurd event the Russian Military Government in Berlin informed the American, British and French authorities that they would be applying new and more stringent restrictions to the passage of goods along the 'Western Corridor' through Soviet-held Germany. In succeeding days the Russians closed down passenger rail access into Berlin from the west and later stopped barge transport on the River Elbe between the Russian and British zones. On June 26, 1948, claiming there were 'technical troubles' on the line, the Russians stopped all rail traffic between Berlin and the west. The American, British and French forces were cut off. No food or supplies could reach them. Two days later, on June 26, USAF twin-engined Douglas C-47s ferried in 80 tons of food in 32 flights operating out of their base at Rhein-Main, near Frankfurt. The Berlin Airlift had begun.

The Western Powers were having to feed not only their own forces but also the thousands of German refugees who were dependent upon them for everything. In total there were some

Above: *William C. Park, chief engineering test pilot at Lockheed, stands before the SR-71 in which he flew at more than Mach 3. The SR-71 Blackbird flew many operational spyplane missions and, remains the fastest conventional aircraft ever built.*

Above: *The 560mph B-47, contemporaneous with the B-36, was propelled by jet engines and introduced the modern shape of large jet aircraft – swept wings, swept tail surfaces, and engines mounted in pods on underwing struts. In 1948 trials began to extend the range of these early jet bombers by means of in-flight refuelling, a procedure that has subsequently become routine.*

2,100,000 people cut off and now wholly reliant upon supplies coming in by air. This was to become the most dramatic example of civil air cooperation ever seen, as the skies over western Germany grew thick with the continuing stream of transport aircraft bringing supplies to the beleaguered city. Food, coal, paraffin, petrol, diesel, building materials, clothing – even a steam roller and a number of 3½-ton girders needed to build a new power station were delivered. The USAF had some 200 Douglas C-54 Skymasters, the RAF had 40 Avro Yorks, 40 Douglas Dakotas and 14 Handley Page Hastings plus a collection of civil airliners that were pressed into service. Realising that the blockade would achieve nothing, the Russian Military Government in Berlin eventually re-opened the rail and road routes and on May 12, 1949 the blockade was formally lifted. In fact the USAF and the RAF continued to fly supplies into Berlin until the final flight made by in a RAF Hastings which, carrying coal, landed at Gatow, Berlin on October 6, 1949. The role of the aeroplane in providing humanitarian aid was now well and truly established.

In the post-war USA, private aircraft were now regularly joined in the skies by the fast-growing band of 'homebuilt' aircraft. These were either built from scratch or assembled from kits supplied by a host of innovative designers. But the vast bulk of private aircraft came from the factories of Beech, Piper and Cessna – three companies who would dominate the US market until a class action lawsuit in the mid 1960s totally re-shaped the business of constructing light aircraft. The first aviation insurance policy was written in 1924, but in the early days of private flying few owner/pilots bothered to insure themselves. The constructors, however, needed to have some security against claims of negligence or fault, and by the 1970s the rising costs of the insurance premiums would be cutting steeply into their profit margins. Far better to let the would-be pilot buy a partly built kit and take the liability onto his own shoulders.

Through the late 1940s, 1950s and 1960s, aircraft development was taking man up to and beyond the realms of anything that the early pioneers could even have dreamed might be possible. Consider speed for example:

✱ April 26, 1939: Fritz Wendel achieved an average speed of 469.14mph in a Messerschmitt Bf 109R, establishing a new world air speed record.

✱ November 7, 1945: Group Captain H. J. Wilson, RAF took the record up to 606.25mph in a Gloster Meteor.

✱ September 7, 1946: Group Captain E. M. Donaldson, RAF, again flying a Gloster Meteor averaged 615.81 in flights over a 3 kilometre course.

✱ August 20, 1947: a Douglas D-588-1 Skystreak research aircraft flown by Commander

Above: *A USAF F-104 Starfighter. The German Air Force was largest operator of this aircraft. It set a speed record of 1,404mph in 1958, but its performance as an air-combat fighter was less impressive. It turned out to be better in the roles of low-level attack and reconnaissance and also served in NASA's test fleet.*

Turner F. Caldwell of the US Navy averaged 640.74mph at Edwards Air Force Base in the Mojave Desert, California.

✱ August 25, 1947: flying in the same aircraft that had set a new record only five days earlier Major Marion J. Carl of the US Marine Corps averaged a speed of 650.92mph over the same 3km course.

Finally, the magic moment. On October 14, 1947, Major Charles E. Yeager became the first pilot to exceed the speed of sound, 760mph, in level flight. 'Chuck' Yeager made his historic flight to break the sound barrier in a Bell X-1 rocket-propelled research aircraft flown over Edwards Air Force Base, only 15 months after the Director-General of Scientific Research (Air) of the British Ministry of Supply had stated, "Flying at speeds greater than sound introduces new problems. We do not know how serious they are. The impression that supersonic aircraft are just around the corner is quite erroneous." By the end of December 1953 Major Yeager would fly at 1,650mph – approximately 2½ the times the speed of sound – at a height of 70,000ft in a Bell X-1A.

Not for the first time the powers that be completely failed to comprehend the ability of designers, engineers, constructors and pilots to make aeroplanes do what they had thought to be impossible. The new aircraft now emerging were dwarfing what the world had considered to be the awesome power of the wartime bombers. The Consolidated Vultee Aircraft Corporation's XB-36 made its first flight on August 8, 1946. With a wingspan of 230ft and a fuselage of 163ft, it was by far the world's largest bomber. Powered by six Pratt and Whitney pusher-type piston engines, it would be modified and upgraded and the final production version, the B-36D which first flew on March 26, 1949 required an additional four General Electric J-47 jet engines in underwing pods in order to get this massive beast airborne. Only a short time earlier, the magnificent Northrop XB-35 had taken to the skies. In a design that would be moth-balled until the emergence into the public gaze of the Northrop B.2 Stealth bomber in 1988, the Flying Wing was sensationally unlike any other aircraft the world had seen. Fourteen of the piston-engined heavy bombers were ordered, three of which would be converted to an eight-jet format and re-designated the YB-49. Three more would be re-configured to be powered by six jet engines. These were heady times as design after design rolled on to the runways. Elsewhere, in Los Angeles, North American Aviation were developing what would become the USAAF's first multi-engined jet bomber. Powered by four General Electric J-45 engines, the prototype XB-45 made its first flight from Muroc, California on March 17, 1947.

As aeroplanes were flying faster, so they were also flying higher. A de Havilland Vampire set a

Contrasting fighter shapes.

Right: *F-111 with variable-geometry wings, here shown in the lower speed mode where more lift is required than in the swept-back configuration required for high speed.*

Right: *A delta-wing French Air Force Mirage 2000C.*

Right: *Saab Gripen, Sweden's latest multi-role combat aircraft with its distictive wing canard design.*

Left: *The Lockheed C-141 'Starlifter' strategic transport entered service with the US Air Force in 1964. It has a four-man crew and can carry 154 troops or 123 paratroopers or 80 stretcher cases with eight medics; or, alternatively, more than 32 metric tons of freight.*

Far left and left: *The Lockheed C-5 Galaxy is a military transport aircraft designed to provide strategic heavy airlift over intercontinental distances. It is the largest American military transport and one of the largest military aircraft in the world, designed to carry outsize and oversize cargo. It entered service with the USAF in December 1969.*

new height record of 59,446ft in March 1948, shattering the pre-war record of 56,046ft set in a Caproni by Lieutenant Colonel Pezzi of the Italian Air Force in 1938. But on August 15, 1951 Major William Bridgeman, a test pilot for the Douglas Company, flew a US Navy Douglas D-558-2 Skyrocket to a height of 79,494ft. Two years later, on August 31, 1953, Colonel Marion E. Carl of the US Marine Corps, flying another Skyrocket which had been launched from a Boeing B-29 Superfortress at 34,000ft, took the altitude record to 83,235ft.

The world continued to re-arm. The USA, the USSR, Great Britain and France continued to develop first the atomic bomb and then the hydrogen bomb. Relations between the West and the USSR worsened and behind the 'Iron Curtain' the Soviets were engaged in a race that was every bit as ambitious as their western counterparts, to build new and more powerful weapons. Following the war many German scientists and engineers who had been engaged in pioneering projects in jet propulsion and rocketry for the Third Reich switched to working for their new Russian masters. Information about their activities was hard to find, but the story of the development of the remarkable MiG-15 became widely known in 1952. In 1946 the post-war British government had authorized Rolls-Royce to sell ten of its Nene jet engines to the Russians. The application of one of the West's finest engines to a radical swept-back wing design (produced, no doubt, with the assistance of former German engineering skills), allowed the MiG-15 prototype to fly by July, 1948. Within two and a half years from the receipt of the Nene engine, a high performance fighter, powered by this engine, was being produced in quantity and had been deployed into service.

All too soon the West would see these same MiG-15s in action, as military airpower was to about to be called upon again, this time in Korea. In June 1950 President Truman ordered the USAF to assist South Korean forces who were under attack from the north. In July the

Above: A Soviet Tupolev Tu-95 ('Bear') maritime patrol aircraft being buzzed by an RAF Lightning and its Victor refuelling tanker during the Cold War, when confrontations of this sort were continually tacking place in the skies above the North Sea.

United Nations agreed to send forces to support the South Koreans and General Douglas MacArthur was appointed as Supreme Commander of United Nations forces in Korea. The British, Australians, New Zealanders, Canadians and forces from many other nations were quickly caught up in the war, and it soon became apparent that Russian as well as Chinese forces were actively engaged alongside the North Koreans. Armistice negotiations commenced at Kaesong on July 10, 1951, and after the Korean War, on November 21, 1951, General Hoyt S. Vandenburg, Chief of Staff, USAF declared the MiG-15 to be 'a superior fighter to, and in many respects could out-perform our own F-86 (North American Sabre) the only plane in production today capable of challenging the MiG on approximately even terms'.

Before too long the skies over South East Asia would be filled with airpower again as war broke out in Vietnam, where the US Air Force undertook bombing on an unprecedented scale. In the Middle East – the Arab-Israeli Wars, the Iran-Iraq War and the Gulf War – the influence of air power on major conflicts was often decisive. Since 1945 military aircraft have been almost continuously engaged in one theatre of conflict or another. During that time every aspect of the world of aerospace has changed. Where once there had been innovative 'seat-of-the-pants' designers taking hammer to metal, now there are vast ranks of men and machines providing massive computing power to calculate every last detail before even a scrap of metal is touched. No room now for the brilliance of an Ed Heinemann or a Mikoyan or a Camm. Where the brilliance of test pilots was once the difference between success and failure, now the world rarely hears of

Above: *The revolutionary British Harrier II 'jump jet' capable of vertical take off and landing but with all the capabilities of a frontline fighter.*

Below: *The American F-35 Lightning II (Joint Strike Fighter) embodies the same concept. The latest generation of strike fighter under development, it first flew in 2000 and is manufactured as a conventional take off and landing aircraft and also as an STOL (Short Take off and Landing) version, both with stealth attributes.*

Above: *In-flight refueling – a KC-135 Stratotanker aircraft refuels F/A-18C Hornet Strike-Fighters.*

such pioneers as Peter Twiss or Chuck Yeager. And, where once a pilot took to the skies armed with nothing more than a compass, now satellites can pinpoint the moves of every aircraft in the air and a rescue team can be guided directly toward anywhere they are needed.

In the past half century we have seen magnificent new machines take to the sky. The Boeing 747, the AV8B Harrier, the F-16, the Su-29, Concorde, are just a few of many innovative new developments. We take flight for granted as we make plans for our business trips, our vacations, our need to get a package across the world in a matter of hours. We forget that the atmosphere is awash with satellites predicting our weather and carrying our messages. The collaborations now between governments, constructors and aircraft operators are the stuff that dreams would have been made of half a century ago. Who, in 1945, would have believed that Airbus Industries could exist thanks to the partnerships of the French, Germans, British and Spanish? Or that joint exercises between countries of the former Eastern bloc and NATO members would become commonplace?

As we look back to the birth of manned flight we should pay tribute to those whose skill, determination – and not a little measure of luck – made it possible for us to lead more peaceful and productive lives. And some final statistics: in 1956, just eleven short years after the end of World War II, the ICAO declared that 78 million passengers had flown in that year on the world's scheduled airlines, a vast increase since 1945. By comparison, in the year 2006 the world's skies were filled with 2,130,000,000 passengers! IATA predicts that this will increase to some 2,750,000,000 by 2011 – more than two billion people benefiting from the most radical technical development of the 20th century.

Below: *An Unmanned Aerial Vehicle (UAV) is piloted by someone on the ground, using a computer. The wars of tomorrow may well see aircraft such as this US Navy RQ-4A Global Hawk taking on the full combat role. With a cruising speed of 404 mph and a service ceiling of 65,000 feet, it can stay aloft for 34 hours. UAVs started life as small-scale projects for reconnaissance, often difficult to see from the ground; the Global Hawk is on a different scale altogether – more than 44 feet long with a wingspan of 116 feet.*

NAVY

The face of modern air transport:

Above: *The revolutionary Boeing 747, capable of carrying more than 400 passengers first flew in 1969. Introducing the wide-body concept, it represented a quantum leap in airline economics – costs per seat were slashed and long-haul travel made dramatically cheaper. One version can carry more than 560 passengers. One of Russia's answers to the 747, the Ilyushin Il-96-300, is a long-range, wide-bodied jet carrying up to 300 passengers. The vertical wing-tips help the lift:drag ratio.*

Below: *The successful European challenge to US domination of the air routes is mounted by Airbus Industries (see page 37), a continental consortium building a family of jetliners, each tailored to a specific market requirement. This is the A300-660 medium-range, wide-bodied airliner carrying 267 passengers.*

Top to bottom:
More of the Airbus Industries line-up: the A319 short-range, narrow-bodied jet, the smallest of the family with 124 seats; the A330 large-capacity, medium-to-long-range airliner carrying 335 passengers; and the latest, most spectacular airliner in the family, the A380. This is a double-deck, four-engine airliner, the largest in the world with versions able to carry more than 850 passengers. The first A380 went into service with Singapore Airlines in October 2007 on the Singapore-to-Sydney route.

TIMELINE OF AVIATION EVENTS BEFORE 1900

(BEGINNING WITH LEGENDS OF EARLY FLIGHT)

c.850 BC Legend of King Bladud of Britain's attempted flight with wings attached to his arms. Falls to his death on to Temple of Apollo

4th century BC Archytas of Tarentum's model wooden dove worked by 'a current of air … within it'

c.60 Actor at a feast of Roman Emperor Nero killed attempting flight possibly with feathered arms

c.875 Andalusian Abu'l-Kasim 'Abbas with feathered wings and body said to have flown 'a considerable distance'

c.1020 Monk Eilmer of Malmesbury, Wiltshire, UK, flies from the top of a tower with wings attached to his hands and feet; breaks only his legs

c.1420 Venetian Giovanni da Fontana's model dove powered by a rocket flies 100 feet

c.1505 Leonardo da Vinci's sketch of an ornithopter

1507 John Damian flies a short distance fro Stitling castle's walls with wings made of hen's feathers

1536 Denis Bolori uses spring-powered flapping wings to fly from Troyes cathedral, ending in a fatal crash

The Montgolfier balloon ascends.

1540 João Torto flies from Viseu cathedral in Portugal with two pairs of wings, but crashes when his eagle's-head helmet slips over his eyes

c.1589 Seven-year old John Williams at Conway, Wales, uses a long coat as wings but falls nastily on to a large stone

c.1600 Giovanni Francesco Sagredo wears wings based on those of a falcon at Venice

c.1640 An English ten-year old is placed in a winged chariot built from farm machinery and is said to fly the length of a barn

1647–8 Tito Livio Burattini in Poland flies indoors on an ornithopter fashioned like a dragon

17th century Adriaen Baartjens in the Netherlands uses bat-shaped leather wings to fly from Rotterdam's highest tower

1672/3 Charles Bernoiun flies with tensioned wings in Regensburg, Germany, assisted by rockets

c.1770 Canon Pierre Desforges fixes feathered wings to a French peasant, who declines to make the attempt

1783 Montgolfiers' balloon ascents. 19 Sept a rooster, duck and sheep are sent aloft at Versailles, France. 21 Nov first manned flight by Jean-François Pilâtre de Rozier and François Laurent, Marquis d'Arlandes, 16km across the Bois de Boulogne, Paris

1783 Frenchman Louis-Sébastien Lenormand descends from a tree with the aid of two parasols

5 June 1783 Joseph and Etienne Montgolfier demonstrate an 11m-diameter hot-air balloon at Annonay, France

27 Aug 1783 J. A. C. Charles, Anne-Jean Robert and Nicolas-Louis Robert replicate a Montgolfier balloon in the Champs de Mars, Paris. Instead of hot air their 4.6m-diameter 'Charlière' balloon is inflated with hydrogen gas

1783 General J.-B. Meusnier of the French Army makes designs for dirigible airships long before they become technically practical

1784–1809 Jean-Pierre Blanchard makes flights in most of the capital cities of Europe. On 7 Jan 1785 with John Jeffries he crosses the English Channel

7 Jan 1785 Jean-Pierre Blanchard and Dr John

The first balloon ascent in England, 1784

Jeffries fly across the English Channel in a hydrogen balloon

1791 Jean Blanchard drops animals by parachute from a balloon

1792–1815 French Revolutionary and Napoleonic Wars

1792 to 1857 pioneering activities of Sir George Cayley in England. He experiments with models and pioneers aerodynamic theory. He has been credited with the 'invention' of the aeroplane, contradicting the wing-flapping designs of the early theorists. Cayley experiments in three principal areas: lift and drag, general layout, and streamlining. He lays the foundations for aerodynamics and aircraft design

9 Jan 1793 Jean-Pierre Blanchard makes the first balloon ascent in America in the presence of George Washington. John Wise becomes the first American balloonist

1794 captive observation balloons are used at the siege of Mainz

2 April 1794 Aérostiers, French military tethered balloon organization. June 1794 first military reconnaissance from balloon at Maubeuge. Organization disbanded 1799

26 June 1794 French Army Captain Coutelle uses tethered hydrogen observation balloon at Battle of Fleurus

22 Oct 1797 André Garnerin makes first parachute jump, with a canvas canopy

Early experimenters with balloons include the Sadlers in Ireland, Lunardi and Zambeccari in Italy, Gay-Lussac and Biot in France, and Green and Coxwell in England

24 July 1808 R. Jordaki Kuparanto becomes the first man to bale out of a damaged aircraft when his Montgolfier balloon catches fire

1809 Cayley flies a pilotless full-scale glider

1809 Jakob Degen's ornithopter in Vienna actually depends upon a balloon for lift.

1 Oct 1812 James Sadler crosses the Irish Sea in a hydrogen balloon but is blown back offshore and he has to be rescued

In the half century following the Montgolfiers' balloons, more than 470 'aeronauts' take to the skies, including 49 women

1836 Charles Green's coal-gas-filled balloon Royal

The Royal Vauxhall, also known as the Nassau balloon

Vauxhall flies from London to Nassau in Germany, a distance of 480 miles

24 July 1837 Using a conical design, Robert Cocking attempts a parachute descent at Lee, in Kent, England, and perishes

Blanchard and Jefferies' aerostat (a word via French combining 'aero' and Greek 'statos' to mean a lighter-than-air craft

1842 W. H. Phillips builds steam-powered flying model helicopter

April 1843 William Henson's patent for an Aerial Steam Carriage is the first design for a 'fixed wing airscrew-propelled aeroplane of modern configuration'

Early balloons are non-dirigible – they cannot be steered. Developments necessary for directional navigation are the cigar shape of the envelope and a suitable power plant

1843 clockwork model airship demonstrated in London

1849 A tethered flight is made by a young boy in a glider built by Cayley

1850 Pierre Jullien builds Le Précurseur, a clockwork-powered, non-rigid airship model

24 Sept 1852 Henri Giffard flies a steam-driven, cigar-shaped airship 44m long from Paris to Elancourt, near Trappes. This marks the first true dirigible flight, but Giffard does not attempt to fly against the wind for a return voyage

1853 Cayley's coachman makes the first manned flight in a glider

1857 J. M. le Bris completes a flight in a glider

1857/8 Félix du Temple's steam-powered model. But in 1874 his full-size manned monoplane fails to leave the ground

1858 Nadar (Félix Tournachon) of France takes first aerial photographs from a tethered balloon. In 1863 he fits a complete photographic laboratory on a huge balloon, *Le Géant*, the two-storey gondola which can hold 14 people

29 March 1858 First ascent of a hydrogen balloon in Australia at Melbourne

2 July 1859 In the US 1,800 km is travelled in a

Inflating one of Lowe's balloons during the American Civil War

hydrogen balloon by Wise, Gager and La Mountain.

18 June 1861 First aerial telegraph message is transmittted from T. S. Lowe's hot air balloon *Enterprize*

1861–1865 American Civil War

1862–3 Union army's Aeronautics Corps deploys four balloons designed by Lowe of Connecticut

May 1863 balloon-borne observers detect first movements of Robert E. Lee's Confederate army en route to the Battle of Gettysburg

Confederates make only two unsuccessful attempts to launch observation balloons

First aviation exhibition at Crystal Palace, London, held by the Aeronautical Society of Great Britain in 1868

1870–1871 Franco-Prussian War

1870–71 66 balloon flights are made carrying people, letters etc. out of besieged Paris during Franco-Prussian War

1871 Alphonse Penand demonstrates a 20in-long rubber-band-powered model aeroplane in Paris, the Planophore

1873 John Wise attempts unsuccessfully to fly the Atlantic in a vast hydrogen balloon

1875 Gaston Tissandier attempts to reach a new altitude with the aid of oxygen. At 25,000ft he passes out, but survives; his two companions do not

1872 Paul Haenlein's semi-rigid airship powered by internal combustion engine lacks adequate power

8 Oct 1883 Gaston and Albert Tissandier attempt to fly an electric-motor-driven airship, but the power is inadequate and the batteries too heavy

1884 Aleksandr Mozhaysky's steam-driven monoplane flies for just a few seconds

1884 Horatio Phillips begins patents for thick wing sections with curved upper and lower surfaces. In 1893 he tests a multiplane model with wings that look like Venetian blinds

1884 M. A. Goupil designs a steam-powered monoplane with ailerons for lateral control. In 1917 Glenn Curtiss flies a reproduction (powered by a gasoline engine) to avoid infringing the Wright brothers' patents on lateral-control devices

9 Aug 1884 Charles Renard and A.-C. Krebs fly electric-powered airship La France in a 23-minute return flight. Controlled mechanical flight has arrived

1885 Establishment of Prussian Airship Arm

1886–1904 Samuel Pierrepont Langley's pioneering experiments: aerodynamic research at Pennsylvania University and at the Smithsonian; in the 1890s he builds model steam-powered aircraft he calls 'aerodromes' (from the Greek 'air runner'); in 1894–6 he experiments on the Potomac with catapult launches

12 Aug 1888 Dr Wölfert flies a balloon fitted with a Daimler petrol engine

9 Oct 1890 Clément Ader makes a 50m hop in Eole, a bat-like steam-driven monoplane

1893 Lawrence Hargrave in Australia invents the box kite

1893–6 Otto Lilienthal makes more than 2,000 gliding flights before being killed on 9 Aug 1896. His flights pioneer glider stability and control, necessary precursors to the success of the Wright brothers

July 1894 Sir Hiram Maxim (inventor of the machine-gun) aids aerial experimentation with a test-rig consisting of a huge steam-powered biplane with two propellers running on a circular rail

1896–7 Octave Chanute's group make over 1,000 glider flights at Lake Michigan, developing stability with bridge-truss biplane configurations

June 1897 Percy Pilcher in England glides to 750ft

14 June 1897 Wölfert and Knabe become the first people to be killed in a dirigible crash when the engine ignites Deutschland's envelope and explodes the gas

11 July 1897 August Andrée, Strindberg and Fraenkel attempt unsuccessfully to cross the North Pole by balloon. They crash, disappear and are only discovered with their notes and photographs in 1930

Nov 1897 Schwarz pioneers use of thin sheet aluminium as a covering material for his airship

Dec 1898 The US War Department grants Langley $50,000 to develop a man-carrying aircraft and he begins the search for a suitable power plant. His assistant, Charles Manley, develops a 50hp 85-kilo engine

By the end of the nineteenth century the means of attaining steerable powered flight are fast converging: the science of aeronautical stability and control plus a light-weight internal combustion engine

1898–1904 Alberto Santos-Dumont is the world's greatest builder of non-rigid airships

1899–1902 Anglo-Boer War: British Balloon Sections operate successfully in the war, spotting for artillery and as general intelligence observers. A balloon flies at besieged Ladysmith for a month before hydrogen runs out. At the Battles of Magersfontein and Paardeburg especially, balloons make significant contributions

Timeline of Aviation Events

1900–1937 Era of the Zeppelins

1900–10 the development of Zeppelins is plagued with difficulties and disasters. August 1908 LZ-4 is destroyed by fire, provoking much public distress in Germany and resulting in huge subscriptions to finance new Zeppelins

1900 Wright brothers build their Glider No.1. This biplane is successful but is considered to have had too little wing span

1900 A British Balloon Section is formed for service during the Boxer Rebellion and subsequently operates in India

2 July 1900 Zeppelin rigid airship (Luftschiff)

ZEPPELIN LZ first flight 2 July 1900

Powerplant: See notes
Primary role: Strategic bomber
Dimensions: Length 500–800ft (128–245m)
Payload: 2.8–60 tonnes
Speed: 30–130ft/sec (9–40m/sec)
Range: 10,000 miles (16,000km) max
Production total (all marks): c.120
Variants: a–i, k–z

Originally designed for civil transport, dirigibles served with both the German Army and Navy during World War I. Eighty-eight Zeppelins were built for the military during the war. They were potent weapons, flying at altitudes beyond the reach of anti-aircraft fire and fighter planes, and, carrying massive bomb loads and able to hover over their targets, they presented a real threat to Britain until improved interceptor aeroplanes and incendiary shells were developed. *LZ1*, built and commanded by Graf von Zeppelin, first flew on 2 July 1900, the Graf financing later models through a national lottery. Deutsche Luftschifffahrts AG was founded in 1909 to take over Zeppelin construction, producing craft for nearly thirty years. Early models were powered by two Daimler engines; *LZ9*, first flying on 2 October 1911, was the first to be equipped with three Maybachs. Powerplants

***Wright Flyer No.1**, 1900*

steadily increased in number and output, later models carrying up to seven MB IVs. Gas capacity grew from the *LZ1*'s 400,000 cubic feet (11,300m³) to 7,000,000 cubic feet (200,000m³) for the last two production models, the *Hindenburg* and the *Graf Zeppelin* (ii). After the war, some Zeppelins were handed over to other countries, serving in Britain, France, Italy and the United States. The Allies halted production of large-scale types after the war, but transatlantic airship crossings came into being with the *Graf Zeppelin* (LZ127), which first flew on 18 September 1928.

LZ-1, 420ft long (G). It makes only 3 flights owing to lack of funds

1901 Wright brothers build their Glider No. 2 with a new wing aerofoil and greater span; tests disappoint

1901 Wilhelm Kress (Austrian piano maker) attempts to take off from Lake Tullnerbach in a flying boat that uses a gasoline-powered engine and thin steel tubing construction

June 1901 Langley flies petrol-engined quarter-scale *Aerodrome*. This is the first aeroplane with a petrol engine to achieve level flight. It flies three times

13 July 1901 Germans A. Berson and A. J. Sürring make atmospheric survey flight in a balloon to 35,000ft, a record that remains theirs for 30 years

1902–4 progress towards powered heavier-than-air flight in Europe, in contrast to the USA, is minimal. France is the main centre of aviation activity after Santos-Dumont's flight in 1906 and Wilbur Wright's visit, when his flying skills create a sensation

Sept–Oct 02 Wright brothers successfully fly Glider No.3 many times, the design based not on previously published material but on their own research

Nov 1902 Henri Juillot's airship for the Lebaudys. In 1903 it sets a distance record of 61 miles and in 1905 an endurance record of 6.5 hours. The French Army purchases it in 1908

1902–8 Paul and Pierre Lebaudy create impressive semi-rigid airships La Jaune, La Patrie, La République (see overleaf) and La Liberté

7 Oct and 8 Dec 1903 Langley and Manley's

French dirigible La République

prototype aircraft fails to take off. Langley is ridiculed and retires, his funds cut off. But he has very nearly got it right and is recognized as one of the USA's great aviation pioneers, the first US aircraft carrier being named after him

17 Dec 03 Wright Flyer (US)

1905 SC-1 airship (Baldwin-Curtiss) is the first US military aircraft

9 Jan 06 Zeppelin LZ-3 (G). Makes 45 flights and is then taken over by the German Army

17 Jan 06 Zeppelin LZ-2 (G). Makes just one flight before being destroyed in a storm

30 Sept 06 The first international balloon race is held in Paris

Langley's aircraft fails. 1903

12 Nov 06 Santos-Dumont makes first recognized sustained flight by a piloted and powered aeroplane in Europe – World distance aeroplane record of 220m/722ft

1906-11 August von Parseval builds a series of semi-rigid airships in Germany

1907 Léob Lavavasseur's 8-cylinder 50hp Antoinette engine, which powers many of Europe's successful aircraft

1 Aug 07 Aeronautical Division, US Signal Corps, formed

10 Sept 07 Dirigible No. 1, *Nulli Secundus*, British Army's first dirigible. Soon followed by

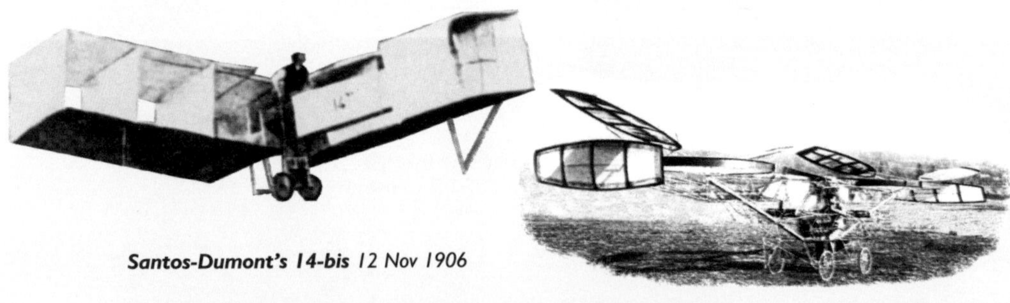

Santos-Dumont's 14-bis *12 Nov 1906*

Paul Cornu first free flight in a helicopter (F) 13 Nov 1907

Dirigible No. 2 *(GB)*, Beta *1908*

two more, *Beta* and *Gamma*

13 Nov 07 Paul Cornu makes the first free flight in a helicopter at Lisieux, France. Twin rotor machine is powered by an 18kw (24hp) Antoinette engine. The flight lasts 20 seconds, at a height of 0.3m (1ft)

30 Nov 07 Glenn Curtiss forms first aeroplane company in USA

1907 and 1909 American Walter Wellmann attempts unsuccessfully to fly semi-rigid airships over the North Pole

10 Feb 08 US Army signs contract for Wright Model A biplane as its first military aeroplane

5 Aug 08 Zeppelin LZ-4 (G). Burnt after becoming stranded

17 Sept 08 Lieutenant Thomas E. Selfridge becomes the first person to be killed in a powered aeroplane when a passenger in a Wright craft. Orville Wright, the pilot, is badly injured

16 Oct 08 S. F. Cody makes first aeroplane flight in Great Britain

31 Dec 1908 Wilbur Wright flies 77.5 miles in 2 hours 20 minutes to win the Michelin Prize

***Wright Flyer** (US) first flew 17 Dec 1903*

THE WRIGHT BROTHERS

1899–1900 Wright brothers test kites

1900 they experiment with tethered gliders 1901–2 they test gliders in free flight

1902 they make wind-tunnel tests

1902 their Glider No. 2 makes 1,000 flights

10.35 a.m. 17 Dec 1903 Orville Wright makes a 12-second flight achieving the world's first manned, powered, sustained and controlled flight by a heavier-than-air aircraft. Three more flights in *Flyer No. 1* follow that day, the fourth lasting 59 seconds and covering 852ft

1903–4 they build *Flyer No. 2*

20 Sept 1904 Wilbur describes a full-circle flight

9 Nov he is in the air over 5 minutes making almost 4 complete circular flights

23 June 1905 *Flyer No. 3* flies; by Oct it flies to 24.5 miles

Then, until 1908, they halt flying for security reasons and organize patents on their innovations

1907–8 they negotiate with the US War Department

1907 Orville continues development while Wilbur visits Europe

1908 In France, Farman, Blériot and Delagrange make sustained flights, but in other European countries achievements are little beyond tentative hops

1908 Alexander Graham Bell's Aerial Experiment Association in New York and Nova Scotia includes Glenn Curtiss, designer of lightweight engines. Flights include Silver Dart (23 Feb 1909), 1st heavier-than-air flight in Canada

1908-14 Glenn Curtiss becomes the Wrights' greatest competitor and bitter rival; their patents battle centres on lateral controls

1909 First flight of A. V. Roe's triplane

1909 Duralumin alloy created in Germany, an ultra-light yet very strong metal ideal for airship framework

A. V. Roe's (GB) triplane of 1909

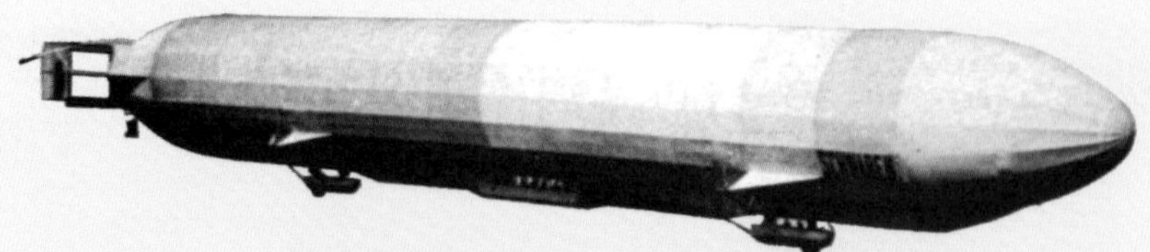

Zeppelin LZ-5 Schwaben *(G) first flew 26 June 1911*

26 May 09 First flight of Zeppelin *LZ-5* (G). 2nd Army ship; makes 16 flights before being stranded at Weiburg

17 July 1909 Curtiss flies his Gold Bug 24.7 miles at 35mph to win the second Scientific American prize in New York

25 July 09 Louis Blériot becomes the first man to fly successfully across the English Channel by aeroplane

30 July 1909 US Signal Corps accepts the Wrights' military aircraft, Model B, built to their specification

Aug 1909 Curtiss wins the Gordon Bennett Cup race at Rheims in his Golden Flyer

25 Aug 09 First flight of Zeppelin LZ-6 (G). Makes 73 flights including 34 with DELAG

16 Oct 09 Zeppelin forms world's first commercial airline DELAG (Deutsche-Luftschiffefahrts AG

1909–10 Curtiss designs seaplanes

1909–10 Igor Sikorsky experiments with helicopters, but with little success

1910 Curtiss' bombing and bomb sight experiments

13 June 10 C. Hamilton wins $10,000 for completing a return flight between New York and Philadelphia

19 June 10 First flight of Zeppelin LZ-7 *Deutschland* (G). Makes 7 flights with DELAG until stranded in the Teutoburger Forest after only six days in service

10 July 10 Walter Brookin is first to fly higher than a mile, Indianapolis, USA, in a Wright biplane, achieving 1,900m (6,234ft)

31 July 10 First flight of Bristol Boxkite (GB)

27 Aug 10 McCurdy (USA) transmits and receives radio messages between aircraft and ground

8 Sept 1910 First recorded air collision with two brothers flying separate aircraft in Austria

14 Nov 10 Ely makes first take-off from a ship, USS *Birmingham*

1910 First flight of German Taube monoplane, later manufactured by Rumpler

***Taube** (G) 1910*

***Blériot XI** (F) 23 Jan 1909*

18 Jan 11 Ely makes first landing on a ship, USS *Pennsylvania*

30 March 11 Zeppelin LZ-8 (G). Collides with its hangar after 24 flights

1 Apr 11 Air Battalion of the Royal Engineers formed in the UK

May 11 British Army receives a Bristol Boxkite for army co-operation duties

26 June 11 Zeppelin LZ-10 *Schwaben* (G). Makes 224 flights

22 Oct 11 First use of an aeroplane in war, Italian Capt Piazza flies Bleriot monoplane from Tripoli to Azizia on reconnaissance of Turkish forces

2 Oct 11 Zeppelin LZ-9 (G)

1 Nov 11 Italian Lt Gavotti drops grenades on Turkish forces; first dropping of bombs from an aeroplane in war

Certified Pilots in 1911 France 353, Britain 57, Germany 46, Italy 32, Belgium 27, USA 26

1912 Curtiss's Flying Fish is the prototype for all true flying boats

1912 Wilbur Wright dies of typhoid; his brother lives to 1948

14 Feb 12 Zeppelin LZ-11 *Viktoria Luise* (G). Carries over 22,000 passengers

25 April 12 First flight of Zeppelin LZ-12 (G). Army ship

1 Mar 12 Capt Albert Berry makes first parachute jump from an aeroplane in the USA

10 June 12 Airships are used to carry the first German airmail

July 1913 First flight of Avro 504

30 July 12 First flight of Zeppelin LZ-13 (G). Flies 44,000 miles for DELAG before being taken over by the Army

Aviation as entertainment 1910–12: great aerial circuses with big prizes for races and records attract large attendances; a show at Belmont Park, Long island, 22–31 Oct 1910, attracts 40 aircraft. Events include a race around the Statue of Liberty. In 1911–12 'circuit races', from town to town, become popular

21 Sept 13 A. Pegoud makes the first upside-down flight in a Blériot monoplane

1 Nov 13 Aerial combat takes place in Mexico, handgun shots exchanged between two aircraft

1910-1914 DELAG carries 34,228 passengers making 1,588 flights covering some 170,000 miles; but in 1913 LZ-14 and LZ-18 are destroyed on military duties, killing 50 people

By 1914 the German Army has 6 airships, the German Navy 1

1 Jan 1914 Jannus flies first scheduled air passenger flight, in Florida

1914 First flight of Voisin Type III

1914 Lawrence Sperry demonstrates a gyrostabilizer at the Paris air show

23 Feb 14 First flight of Bristol Scout (Baby Biplane)

Early 14 First flight of Tabloid float-plane

April 14 First flight of Fokker E1 Eindecker

May 14 First flight of Morane-Saulnier Type N

17 July 14 First flight of Vickers F.B.5 Gunbus

***Avro 504** (GB) first flew July 1913*

***Fokker E1 Eindecker** (G) first flew April 1914*

***Moraine-Saulnier** (F) first flew 1913*

***Vickers F.B.5 Gunbus** (GB) first flew 17 July 1914*

WORLD WAR I

6 Aug 1914 German airship LZ-21 bombs Liège, killing 9 civilians

30 Aug 14 Paris bombed by German Taube monoplanes, the first official bombing mission

2/3 Sept 14 1st airship raid: Zeppelin LZ-17 drops three bombs on Antwerp

22 Sept 14 British Tabloids make 1st raid on Germany: Cologne and Dusseldorf Zeppelin sheds

5 Oct 14 1st aircraft to be shot down by another: German Aviatik by French Sgt Franz over Reims

***Short 184 Bomber** (GB) first flew Early 1915*

***Royal Aircraft Factory F.E.2** (GB) first flew early 1915*

Late 14 First flight of Nieuport 10

21 Nov 14 3 British RNAS Avro 504s make long-range attack on Zeppelin sheds at Friedrichs-hafen

9 Dec 14 Germans bomb Warsaw

24 Dec 14 German aeroplane makes first air attack on Britain, bombing a garden in Dover

25 Dec 14 Cuxhaven raid by British floatplanes from *Engadine* and *Riviera* foiled by bad weather

Dates are those of first flights. Aircraft generally come into operational service several months later

1915 First flight of Albatros C-III

1915 First flight of C Types

1915 First flight of Albatros C-II Series

1915 First flight of AEG G-Series

1915 First flight of Breguet-Michelin Type BM series

Early 1915 First flight of Short 184 Bomber

Early 1915 First flight of Royal Aircraft Factory F.E.2

19 Jan 15 Zeppelins bomb England for the first time

1 April 15 Roland Garros, in a Morane monoplane fitted with deflector plates on its propeller blades, becomes first pilot using a fixed forward-firing machine-gun to shoot down an enemy aircraft

19 April 15 Garros's Morane 'L' falls into German hands; Fokker designs machine-gun interrupter-gear on E1 fighter

27 May 15 1st French bombing of Germany hits poison gas factory at Ludwigshaven

1 June 15 First flight of de Havilland D.H.2

ALBATROS D.III first flight 16 August 1916

***De Havilland D.H.2** (GB) first flew 1 June 1915*

***Sopwith 1½ Strutter** (GB) first flew Dec 1915*

6–7 June 15 Sub-Lt Warneford (GB) shoots down Zeppelin *LZ-37*

22 June 15 French bomb Karlsruhe: 266 civilian casualties

11 July 15 2 floatplanes spot for British monitors bombarding German cruiser *Königsberg* in Rufiji River, E. Africa

Aug 15 'Fokker Scourge' begins as Immelmann scores first victory with interruptor-gear-fitted E1 Eindekers

12 Aug 15 1st ship torpedoed from air: Turkish steamer hit by floatplane from HMS *Ben-My-Chree*

Sept 15 First flight of Fokker EIV Eindecker

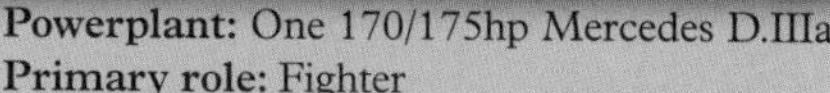

Powerplant: One 170/175hp Mercedes D.IIIa
Primary role: Fighter
Dimensions: Wingspan 29ft 8¼in (9.05m); length 24ft 0½in (7.33m)
Armament: Two Spandau machine-guns above fuselage
Weights: Empty 1,457lb (661kg); loaded 1,953lb (886kg)
Speed: 103mph (166kph) max
Endurance: 2 hrs
Crew: 1

The D.III was a variant of the D.I and D.II biplanes and, like them, was used in Jagdstaffeln 14-plane units. It was produced early in 1917 and featured V-strutter wings copied from captured Nieuports. Some 446 aircraft were on the front line in November 1917, but the type was from then superseded by the D.V. The D.III was a successful fighter despite its weakness of a lower wing that could twist and break in a dive.

1 Oct 15 Passenger airship LZ-11 is wrecked while docking

3 Oct 15 1st carrier deck take-off by wheeled aircraft, Bristol Scout from *Vindex*

Dec 15 First flight of Sopwith 1½ Strutter

5 Nov 15 1st steam catapult launch of aircraft from ship: Curtiss flying boat from USS *North Carolina*

12 Dec 15 First flight of Junkers J1 Blechsel (Tin Donkey)

15 Dec 15 First flight of Handley Page O/100

On the outbreak of war the Royal Navy converts three cross-Channel packets, *Engadine*, *Riviera* and *Empress*, to seaplane carriers

1916 First flight of Morane-Saulnier Type P

1916 First flight of Voisin Types 1 to X

1916 First flight of Gotha G Types

Early 16 First flight of Sopwith Pup

Jan 16 Scarff-Dibovski machine-gun synchronization adapted for use on Sopwith 1½ Strutter, Bristol Scout, etc

Early 16 First flight of Albatros D-1

Early 16 First flight of Halberstadt D-II

April 16 First flight of Spad S.VI

May 16 First flight of Armstrong Whitworth F.K.8

28 May 16 First flight of Sopwith Triplane

18 June 16 Immelmann, who developed fighter combat tactics, is killed in action while flying his Fokker E.III

19 June 16 French leaflet raid on Berlin

Summer 16 First flight of Hanriot HD-1

1 Jul 16 Battle of the Somme. Both sides fight for air superiority; eventually the Allies take control

14 July 16 First flight of Bristol M.1A

Aug 16 First flight of de Havilland D.H.4

Aug 16 First flight of Albatros D.III

23 Aug 16 Germans form 1st regular fighter squadron, Jasta 1

***Bristol F.2A/B** (GB) first flew 9 Sept 1916*

9 Sept 16 First flight of Bristol F.2A/B
15 Sept 16 1st submarine sunk by aircraft: 2 Austrian Lohner flying boats sink French submarine *Foucault* – and land to save the crew
Late 16 First flight of de Havilland D.H.5
Late 16 First flight of Nieuport 17
8 Oct 16 Luftstreitkrafte, German Air Force, formed
Nov 16 First flight of Breguet-Michelin Type 14
21 Nov 16 First flight of Bréguet 14
22 Nov 16 First flight of Royal Aircraft Factory S.E.5
22 Dec 16 First flight of Sopwith Camel

1917 *L-55* reaches 24,000ft, altitude record for airships subsequently unsurpassed

Feb 17 First flight of Nieuport 24
Feb 17 First flight of Junkers J.4
8 March 17 Count Ferdinand von Zeppelin dies
Apr 17 First flight of Spad S.XIII, Salmon 2
Apr 17 'Bloody April' Nearly 140 RFC aircraft lost in two weeks, mainly to German Albatros D.IIIs. German technical superiority and training overwhelms inexperienced Allied pilots: British airman's life expectancy is 23 days
24 Apr 17 1st Kampfstaffel, German special ground attack in support of infantry
26 Apr 17 Boeing Airplane Co founded
May 17 First flight of Sopwith 5F.1 Dolphin
May 17 First flight of Albatros D.V
25 May 17 German Gotha bombers begin raiding Britain

***Royal Aircraft Factory S.E.5** (GB) first flew 22 Nov 1916*

NIEUPORT 17 TO 28 first flight late 1916

Powerplant: One 160hp Gnome
Primary role: Fighter
Dimensions: Wingspan 26ft 9in (9.08m); length 21ft 0in (6.4m)
Armament: Two Vickers machine-guns firing forwards
Weights: Empty 825lb (374kg); loaded 1,543lb (701kg)
Speed: 128mph (206kph) max
Endurance: 2¼ hrs
Crew: 1

One of the great fighters of World War I, the Nieuport 17 first entered service early in 1916 and was used until summer 1917. A larger and more powerful replacement for the Nieuport Type 11 Bèbè, it was employed by French, British, Belgian, Italian and Russian squadrons and was matched only by the Albatros D.I. The later and much less sussessful Nieuport 28 was a fast and manoeuvrable machine, but its performance was compromized by serious structural weakness in the wings.

SOPWITH F.1 CAMEL first flight 22 December 1916

Powerplant: One 130hp Clerget or 150hp Bentley B.R.1
Primary role: Fighter
Dimensions: Wingspan 28ft (8.53m); length 18ft 9in (5.71m)
Armament: Two Vickers machinc-guns above front fuselage; optionally four 25lb (11kg) bombs under fuselage
Weights: Empty 929lb (421kg); loaded 1,453lb (659kg)
Speed: 115mph (185kph) max
Endurance: 2½ hrs
Crew: 1
Variants: F.1, 2F.1
A more powerful and manoeuvrable successor to the Pup, the Camel entered service in mid-1917 and became the greatest fighter of the war, with 1,294 kills claimed, including the German ace von Richthofen. The aircraft was employed in ground-attack and fighter roles in the Battles of Ypres and Cambrai, and it served on most fronts and at sea. Variants had differing engines and armament. Naval 2F.1 Camels had detachable rear fuselages for extra stowage.

25 May 17 1st mass daylight bombing raid on England by 21 German Gotha bombers
June 17 First flight of Pfalz D-III
June 17 First flight of Sopwith Cuckoo (GB)
13 June 17 First large-scale bombing of London by 14 Gotha bombers
July 17 First flight of de Havilland D.H.9
1 July 17 First flight of Fokker Dr.I **(see overleaf)**
2 July 17 Dunning makes first aircraft landing on a moving ship, HMS *Furious*
31 July 17 German Army Airship Service disbanded: 26 airships have been lost
Sept 17 First flight of Handley Page O/400
Autumn 17 First flight of Sopwith Snipe
1 Oct 17 London balloon barrage operational
Nov 1917 First intercontinental flight: Zeppelin L-59 takes 15 tons of supplies from Bulgaria to German East Africa, 4,200 miles in 95 hours
30 Nov 17 First flight of Vickers Vimy

***Vickers Vimy**(GB) first flew 30 Nov 1917*

FOKKER Dr.I first flight 1 July 1917

Powerplant: One 110hp Obersursel URII or Swedish-built Le Rhône
Primary role: Fighter
Dimensions: Wingspan 23ft 7in (7.19m); length 18ft 11in (5.77m)
Armament: Two Spandau machine guns above fuselage
Weights: Empty 893lb (405kg); loaded 1,289lb (585kg)
Speed: 115mph (185kph) max
Endurance: 1½ hrs
Crew: 1
Production total: 320

The favourite machine of ace von Richthofen. The revolutionary design of the prototype, with no interplane bracing struts, caused wing vibration. Single struts on each side were added, but several machines nevertheless broke up in mid-air. The type acquired a high reputation but its performance was only indifferent because of the engine's low power. The Dr.I saw service from August 1917 to mid-1918.

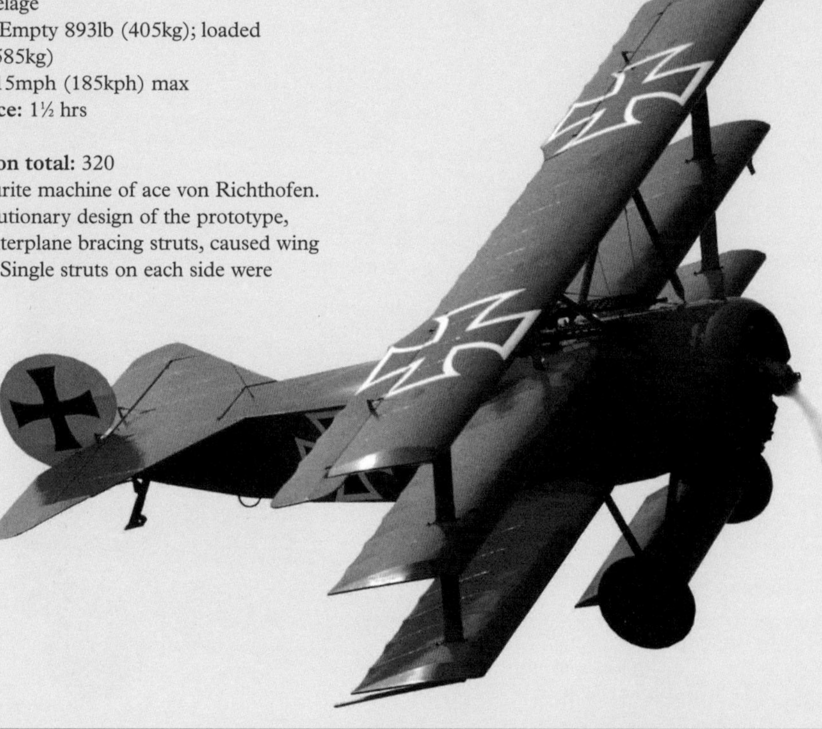

***Handley Page V/1500** (GB) first flew 18 May 1918*

Fokker D.VII (G) first flew Dec 1917

Dec 17 First flight of Fokker D.VII

Jan 18 First flight of Blackburn Kangaroo
30 Jan 18 Gothas begin bombing Paris
16/17 Feb 18 The giant Zeppelin Staaken R.VI bomber becomes the first to drop a 1,000kg bomb on England
4 March 18 First flight of de Havilland H.10
April 18 First flight of Junkers D-I (Junkers J.9)
12 April 18 Last Zeppelin raid on UK; total casualties in airship raids was 557 killed and 1,358 injured
21 April 18 Top German ace, von Richthofen is killed in action while flying his Fokker Dr.I
May 18 First flight of Handley Page V/1500
May 18 First flight of Pfalz D-XIII
19/20 May 18 Last German bomb of WW1 to land on UK soil
June 18 First flight of Nieuport 29
6 June 18 First flight of Fairey IIIA
27 June 18 Lt Steinbrecher 1st fighter pilot to escape successfully by parachute
7 Aug 18 First flight of Blériot-Spad S.XX
21 Aug 18 First flight of Nieuport-Delage NiD 29

More than 100 Zeppelins are deployed by Germany in World War I, dropping 196 tons of bombs. Raids in Britain kill 557 people and injure over 1,000; 500 Zeppelin aircrew are killed. After the war the Allies specifically confiscate Zeppelins and Fokker D.VIIs
World War I sees the military aircraft come of age, evolving from observation missions to air-to-air combat, ground attack, strategic bombing and resupply by air, specialist types being developed for these roles including naval torpedo bombers and floatplanes

1919 First flight of Savoia S.16 flying boat (IT)
1919 DELAG's airship *Bodensee* sets a speed record of 82mph
Feb 19 First flight of AEG J.II (G)
8 Feb 19 First flight of Farman Goliath series (F)
March 19 First flight of de Havilland D.H.16 (GB)
March 1919 USS *Texas* test fires her big guns using aerial spotting
22 March 19 First regular international passenger service opened between Paris and Brussels by Aériennes Farman flying Farman F60 Goliath
April 19 A single RAF Handley Page V/1500 bombs Kabul during the Afghan War
13 April 19 First flight of Vickers Vimy Commercial (GB)
May 1919 Read makes first solo crossing of the Arlantic, via Azores
10 May 19 First flight of Avro Baby (GB)
14/15 June 19 First non-stop crossing of the Atlantic is made by Alcock and Brown in a converted Vimy bomber
25 June 19 First flight of Junkers F.13 (G)
28 June 19 Versailles Peace Treaty forbids Germany from having an air force
2 July 1919 British airship R-34 makes the first airship crossing of the Atlantic, and is in the air more than 108 hours

***Above:* Fokker** *F.II (G) first flew 19 Oct 1919* ***Below:* Handley Page** *W.8 (GB) first flew 2 Dec 1919*

Oct 19 First flight of Fokker F.II (high wing) monoplane airliner (US/H)

Oct 19 First flight of Vickers Viking amphibious (GB)

7 Oct 19 KLM, Royal Dutch Airlines was formed

Nov 19 First flight of Blériot-Spad 27 (F)

16 Nov 19 Capt Wrigley and Lt Murphy are first aviators to fly across Australia, Melbourne to Darwin, taking 46 hrs in a B.E.2e

1 Dec 19 DELAG's airship service between Friedrichshafen and Berlin is suspended on orders of the Allied Control Commision

2 Dec 19 First flight of Handley Page W.8 bi-plane (purpose-built) airliner (GB)

5 Dec 19 Aerovias Nacionales de Colombia SA (Avianca). At the time of writing holding the record for the longest continuous service

27 Dec 19 First flight of Boeing B-1 seaplane (US)

After the massive boost to aviation caused by the demands of World War I, with great technical advances and a large pool of qualified pilots, the stage is set for the rapid development of civil aviation: pioneer fliers set distance records, passenger aircraft develop, and air routes are founded

1920 Chanak Crisis, Turkey. Small RAF force lends stability in a flashpoint situation

1920 Four RAF squadrons fly over 4,000 hours and drop some 98 tons of bombs in Mesopotamian tribal risings, for the loss of 16 aircrew and 11 aircraft

7 Feb 20 World speed record: 275.22 km/h/171.01 mph set by S. Lecointe (Nieuport-Delage 29)

29 March 20 The Farman F.60 Goliath is

Dornier Delphin (G) first flew 24 Nov 1920

introduced on the Le Bourget–Croydon service. This plane dominates European aviation for a decade.

4 Jun 20 US Army Air Service created

1 Aug 20 First flight of Fairey IIID (GB)

24 Nov 20 First flight of Dornier Delphin (G)

12 Dec 20 First flight of Blériot-Spad 33 (F)

14 Dec 20 The first fatal accident of a British scheduled commercial service takes place when a Handley Page O/400 crashes in fog at Cricklewood. Two crew members and two of the six passengers are killed.

1921 Founding of The Douglas Aircraft Co

19 April 21 First flight of Short N.3 Cromarty (GB)

June–July 1921 Billy Mitchell experiments with Martin MB-2 bombers, sinking the old German battleship *Ostfriesland* in 20 minutes

24 Aug 21 The British dirigible *R-38* breaks up during flight trials killing 44 people

1 Dec 21 First flight of US Navy dirigible *Goodyear Goodrich C7* (US)

Feb/March 22 The RAF becomes involved in the suppression of revolts in Iraq (GB)

26 March 22 First flight of de Havilland D.H.34 (GB)

7 April 22 First aerial collision of two civil airliners. A Daimler Airways DH.18A collides with a Farman Goliath of Cie des Grands Express Aériens over Thieuloy-Saint-Antoine, France, all seven onboard are killed

May 22 First flight of Bréguet 19 (F)

22 Aug 22 First flight of Vickers Victoria (GB)

27 Sept 22 Naval Aircraft Radio Lab at Anacostia makes first demonstration of radar signatures

***Vickers Victoria** (GB) first flew 22 Aug 1922*

13 Oct 22 First flight of Curtiss R.6 Racer (US)

23 Oct 22 A reversible pitch propeller is shown by the American Propeller Company

6 Nov 22 First flight of Dornier Do J Wal (G)

11 Nov 22 First flight of Etienne Oehmichen No 2 (F)

18 Nov 22 First flight of Dewoitine D 1 (F)

28 Nov 22 First flight of Fairey Flycatcher (GB)

***Fairey Flycatcher**(GB) first flew 28 Nov 1922*

24 Nov 22 First flight of Vickers Virginia (GB)
2 Dec 22 First flight of Handley Page W.8 (GB)

1923 First flight of Gloster Grebe (GB)
9 Jan 23 First flight of Cierva C 4 Autogiro (GB)

Cierva C 4 Autogiro *(GB) first flew 9 Jan 1923*

March 23 First flight of Fairey Fawn II (GB)
5 Mar 23 Russian born Igor Sikorsky forms the Sikorsky Aero Engineering Corporation in the USA
29 April 23 First flight of Boeing PW-9 (US)
2–3 May 23 Lt O.G. Kelly and Lt J.A. Macready, US Army Air Service make the first non-stop crossing of America by aeroplane
7 May 23 First flight of Armstrong Whitworth Siskin III (GB)

Armstrong Whitworth Siskin III *(GB) first flew 7 May 1923*

14 May 23 First flight of Curtiss PW-8 (US)
June 23 First flight of Fiat B.R.1 (IT)
June 23 First flight of Supermarine Sea Eagle flying boat (GB)
2 June 23 First flight of Boeing FB (US)
27/28 June 1923 In-flight refuelling demonstrated
30 July 23 First flight of de Havilland D.H.50 (GB)
22 Aug 23 First flight of Barling XLBN-1 (US)
23 Aug 23 First flight of Polikarpov I-1 (Il-400) (USSR)
4 Sept 23 First flight of US Navy *Shenandoah*

Shenandoah *(US) first flew 4 Sept 1923*

airship (US) (uses helium for lift)
9 Sept 23 First flight of Curtiss R2C-1 (US)
2 Oct 23 First flight of de Havilland D.H.53 (GB)
4 Nov 1923 World speed record: 429.96 km/h/267.16 mph by US Navy (Curtiss R2C-1)

1924 First flight of *Italia* and *Norge* (IT)
1924 First flight of Douglas O-2 series (US)
1924 First round the world flight using US Navy DT-2 torpedo bombers
31 Mar 24 Imperial Airways formed
May 24 First flight of Fokker CV (HO)
July 24 First flight of Gloster Gamecock (GB)
1 July 24 Daily mail flights San Francisco–New York begin
15 Oct 24 *Los Angeles* delivered to US Navy by the Zeppelin company (US)

1925 First flight of Savoia-Marchetti S.55 (IT)
1925 First flight of Supermarine Southampton (GB)
1925 First flight of Caproni Ca.73 (IT)
1925 The French Air Force involved in the suppression of rebels in Syria
1925 The French Air Force involved in the suppression of rebels in Morocco
3 Jan 25 First flight of Fairey Fox (GB)
Feb 25 First flight of Dornier Merkur (G)
13 Apr 25 Henry Ford starts the first regular US aeroplane freight service, Detroit–Michigan–Chicago
10 May 25 First flight of Armstrong Whitworth Atlas (GB)
June 25 First flight of Lioré et Olivier 20 (F)
6 July 25 First flight of Douglas DAM-1 (US)
7 July 25 First flight of Boeing Model 40 (US)
29 July 25 First flight of Blériot 155 (F)
3 Sept 25 US Navy airship *Shenandoah* crashes and 14 men are killed
4 Sept 25 First flight of Fokker VII (HO)
24 Nov 25 First flight of Tupolev TB-1 (ANT-4) (USSR)

1926 First flight of Handley Page Hyderabad (GB)
1926 First flight of Farman F.170 Jaribu (F)
1926 First flight of Vought O2U Corsair (US)

Farman F.170 Jaribu (F) *first flew 1926*

6 Jan 26 Deutsche Luft-Hansa formed
16 March 26 First flight of Armstrong Whitworth Argosy (GB)

Armstrong Whitworth Argosy (GB) *first flew 16 March 1926*

19 March 26 First flight of Fairey IIIF (GB)
9 May 26 First aeroplane flight over the North Pole
11-14 May 26 Norwegian Roald Amundsen expedition, first airship flight over the North Pole
11 June 26 First flight of Ford 4-AT Tri-motor (US)
19 June 26 First flight of Blackburn Iris (GB)
30 June–1 Oct 26 A. Cobbham completes the first return England to Australia flight
1 July 26 A Blackburn Dart makes the first night landing on an aircraft carrier, HMS *Furious*
30 Sept 26 First flight of de Havilland D.H.66 Hercules (GB)
30 Sept 26 First flight of Dornier DoR Super Wal (G)
Oct 26 First flight of Vought FU (US)
27 Oct 26 First flight of Blériot 165 (F)
3 Nov 26 First flight of Boeing F2B-1 (US)

1927 First flight of Curtiss A-3 Falcon (US)
1927 First flight of Keystone Bomber Series (US)
1927 First flight of Hawker Horsley (GB)
1927 First flight of Curtiss B-2 Condor (US)
28 Feb 27 First flight of Curtiss F7C Seahawk (US)
March 27 First flight of Westland Wapiti (GB)
2 March 27 First flight of Boeing F3B-1 (US)
5 March 27 First flight of Beardmore Inflexible (GB)

FORD 5-AT TRI-MOTOR first flight June 1926

Powerplant: Three 420hp Pratt & Whitney Wasp SC-1
Primary role: Short/medium range passenger transport
Dimensions: Wingspan 77ft 10in (23.72m); length 50ft 3in (15.32m)
Payload: 17 passengers/11,725lb (5,317kg) freight
Weights: Loaded 43,500lb (19,732kg)
Speed: 122mph (196kph) cruising
Range: 550 miles
Crew: 2
Variants: 2-AT through to 13-A

A classic 1920s airliner, the Tri-Motor evolved from the 2-AT Pullman, which had a high-wing cantilever metal layout with corrugated metal skinning, through the unsuccessful 3-AT, which had three uncowled radials instead of a single Liberty inline, to the improved 4-AT, which first flew in June 1926. Eighty-four 4-ATs were built, with 200hp Wright J-4 radials, for two crew and 8–12 passengers. The more powerful 5-ATs had longer wingspans and more seating; 117 were built. Nicknamed 'Tin Lizzie' or 'Tin Goose', many Tri-Motors flew for American Airways during the 1930s, and with Latin American, Mexican and Alaskan operators.

14 Mar 27 Pan American Airways formed
17 May 27 First flight of Bristol Bulldog (GB)
20 May 27 World long-distance record: 5,505km/3,420 miles by Flt Lts Carr and Gillman (Hawker Horsley)
20–21 May 27 Lindbergh makes first solo transatlantic flight (33 hrs 39 mins, 5,778km/3,590 miles)

'Spirit of St Louis' (a Ryan NYP) *(US) first solo transatlantic flight 20–21 May 1927*

17 July 27 USMC DH-4s dive-bomb hostile forces surrounding a Marine Corps garrison in Nicaragua
29 July 27 First flight of Cierva C.6D Autogiro (GB)
14–15 Oct 27 First non-stop aeroplane crossing of the South Atlantic

1928 First flight of Curtiss P-6 (US)
1928 First flight of Boeing Model 80 (US)
Feb 28 First flight of Boeing B3B (US)
15 Feb 28 First flight of Short Calcutta (GB)
26 Feb 28 First flight of Messerschmitt M.20 (G)
30 Mar 28 World speed record: 512.69 km/h/318.57 mph by Maj di Bernardi (Macchi 52*bis* floatplane)
April 28 First flight of Vickers Vildebeest (GB)
15 May 28 Australian Flying Doctor Service inaugurated
23 May 28 The Italian airship *Italia* attempts a flight over the North Pole, commanded by Gen Nobile but crashes on the return flight, during rescue mission Amundsen is killed, Nobile survives
June 28 First flight of Hawker Hart (GB)

Hawker Hart *(GB) first flew June 1928*

11 June 28 The sailplane *Ente* (Duck) becomes the first rocket-powered aeroplane
25 June 28 First flight of Boeing F4B (US)
25 June 28 First flight of Sikorsky S-38 (US)
18 Sept 28 First flight of Zeppelin LZ-127 *Graf Zeppelin* (G)
11 Oct 28 German airship L-27 *Graf Zeppelin* crosses the North Atlantic
14 Nov 28 First flight of Fairey Long Range Monoplane (GB)
Dec 28 First flight of Boeing Model 95 (US)
20 Dec 28 Australians Hubert Wilkins and Carl Ben Eielson fly over the Antarctic
20 Dec 28 First flight of PWS.5 (PO)
Dec 23 1928–Feb 25 1929 8 RAF Vickers Victoria transport aircraft and a Handley Page Hinaidi evacuate 586 people from Kabul, Afghanistan during tribal disturbances

1929 First flight of Tupolev Ant-9 (USSR)
1929 *R100* launched (GB)
1929 US carrier *Saratoga* makes successful 'strike' on the Panama Canal during naval exercizes
1 Jan 29 LOT, the Polish Airline, is founded
April 29 First flight of Boeing P-12 (US)
3 July 29 Lt A.W. Gordan US Navy successfullly hooks on to the airship *Los Angeles* in a modified Vought VO-1 observation biplane
25 July 29 First flight of Dornier Do X (G)
8–29 Aug 29 The LZ-127 *Graf Zeppelin* becomes the first airship to circumnavigate the world
25 Sept 29 First flight of PZL P-1 (PO)
27–29 Sept 29 World distance record; 7,905km/4,912 miles by Capt Costes and M. Bellonte (Bréguet 19 'Super Bidon')
28 Sept 29 First flight of Consolidated Commodore (US)
6 Nov 29 First flight of Junkers G.38 (G)
28–29 Nov 29 First flight over South Pole

Jan 30 First flight of Douglas Y1B-7 (US)
29 April 30 First flight of Polikarpov I-5 (USSR)
5–24 May 30 Amy Johnson becomes the first woman to fly solo from England to Australia
6 May 30 First flight of Boeing Model 200 Monomail (US)
15 May 30 Ellen Church the world's first airline stewardess, her first flight with Boeing Air Transport is between San Francisco and Cheyenne, USA
12 June 30 First flight of Handley Page Heyford (GB)

Boeing P-12 (US) first flew April 1929

DORNIER Do X first flight 25 July 1929

Powerplant: Twelve 600hp Curtiss Conqueror
Primary role: Passenger transport
Dimensions: Wingspan 157ft 5¾in (48.0m); length 131ft 4¾in (40.0m)
Payload: 100 passengers
Weights: Loaded 123,457lb (56,000kg)
Speed: 118mph (190kph) cruising
Range: 1,056 miles (1,700km)
Crew: 5
Production total (all marks): 3

The Do X was the largest aircraft in the world at the time of its first commercial flight on 21 October 1929, when it carried a crew of ten, 150 passengers and nine stowaways. Engine cooling problems with its twelve Siemens-Bristol Jupiters led to the substitution of Conquerors; the second and third models used Fiat engines. A Do X left Friedrichshafen for New York on 2 November 1930, taking nearly ten months to arrive via England, Portugal, the Canaries and Brazil and requiring two repairs on route. The boat never entered full service with Deutsche Lufthansa. All machines were destroyed by bombing in World War II.

R101 first flight 29 July 1930

Powerplant: Five Beardmore Tornado diesels
Primary role: Passenger transport
Dimensions: Length 777ft 2in (236.95m); height 139ft 1in (42.4m); width 131ft 9in (40.16m)
Payload: 100 passengers

First proposed in 1924 and built as a UK government competitor to the commercial *R100*, the *R101* was intended to be a long-distance, 100-passenger airship capable of linking the British Empire. Built at Cardington, near Bedford, for the Air Ministry, the *R101* had a doped fabric outer skin covering a skeleton of aluminium girders. It was more than three times as long as a Boeing 747 and twice as high. Its outer fabric covered five acres. The airship was completely redesigned in 1929 in order to solve a number of production problems: the engines proved to be weaker and heavier than planned, reducing payload and requiring an additional gas bag; the gas bags were abraded by the rigid metal framework, causing gas leaks; and the bags had to be more loosely tethered in order to increase capacity and lift. The *R101* was expected to make its maiden voyage to India in autumn 1930, but was given only one test flight, on 1 October 1930. Nose-heavy and with one engine failing, it still took off from Cardington for Karachi on 4 October. Near Beauvais, France, the nose fabric ripped in bad weather, tearing apart gas bags and bringing the nose down. To protect the damage to the nose, the engines were slowed, causing a lack of lift and bringing about a fatal nose-dive. The *R101* crashed at 2.09 a.m. on 5 October, telescoping on contact and bursting into flames on the ground. Forty-six of the 54 on board died in the crash, and two more died later in hospital. Parts of the aluminium frame were later used in the construction of the *Hindenburg*.

16 July 30 Transcontinental and Western Air (TWA)
29 July 30 The British *R100* begins its first passenger-carrying flight between England and Canada
24 Sept 30 First flight of Short Rangoon (GB)
5 Oct 30 The *R101* crashes flying from England to Egypt and India. 6 of the 54 people on board survive
13 Oct 30 First flight of Junkers Ju 52 (G)

***Short Rangoon** (GB) first flew 24 Sept 1930*

JUNKERS Ju 52/3m first flight April 1930

Powerplant: Three 830hp BMW 132T-2
Primary role: Medium transport
Dimensions: Wingspan 95ft 10in (29.2m); length 62ft (18.9m)
Armament/payload: One 7.9mm MG 15 (or 13mm MG 131) machine gun in dorsal position; one (optional) 7.9mm MG 15 machine gun each in forward upper and two beam positions; 18 troops or 12 litters
Weights: Empty 14,328lb (6,500kg); loaded 24,329lb (11,030kg)
Speed: 178mph (286kph) at 4,590ft (1,400m) max; 160 mph (257kph) cruising
Range: 930 miles (1,500km)
Crew: 3
Production total (all marks): 4,850

A development of the Ju 52/3m g3e and nicknamed 'Tante Ju' (Auntie Junkers), the g7e variant served in every campaign in every theatre during World War II. As a transport it suffered heavy losses in the invasions of the Low Countries, France, Norway and Crete. In the later stages of the war it was also used for supply and, at Stalingrad and in Tunisia, evacuation. It was employed by many satellite air arms, and the Soviet Union utilized 80 machines captured at Stalingrad in paramilitary Aeroflot service. The Ju 52 saw use post-war as both a military and a civilian transport; indeed, it was produced post-war as the AAC.1 Toucan in France and as the CASA 352 in Spain.

HANDLEY PAGE H.P.42W first flight 14 November 1930

Powerplant: Four 555hp Bristol Jupiter XBFM
Primary role: Short/medium range passenger transport
Dimensions: Wingspan 130ft (39.62m); length 89ft 9in (27.36m)
Payload: 38 passengers
Weights: Loaded 29,500lb (13,381kg)
Speed: 100mph (161kph) cruising
Range: 500 miles
Crew: 4
Production total (all marks): 8
Variant: H.P.42E

The H.P.42 was of metal construction with a fabric-covered rear fuselage and flying surfaces, the wings dispensing with wire bracing in favour of Warren trusses. The lower wing spars passed over rather than through the cabin, with the inner sections angled upwards. Designed for comfort and reliability with a small payload rather than speed with a heavy payload, the aircraft, which first flew in November 1930, was developed for Imperial Airways. Four H.P.42Es, with 490hp Jupiter XIFs, covered IA's eastern routes, carrying six (later twelve) passengers in the forward cabin and twelve aft, separated by 500 cubic feet of baggage/mail space; four H.P.42Ws served European routes, carrying eighteen passengers forward and twenty aft, separated by 250 cubic feet of baggage space.

14 Nov 30 First flight of Handley Page H.P.42 (GB)
25 Nov 30 First flight of Fairey Hendon (GB)

***Fairey Hendon** (GB) first flew 25 Nov 1930*

22 Dec 30 First flight of Tupolev TB-3 (ANT- 6) (USSR)

1931 First flight of Ar.65 (G)
1931 First flight of Beriev MBR-2 (USSR)
1931 First flight of Sikorsky S-40 (US)
1931 First flight of Curtiss F9F Sparrowhawk (US)

***Curtiss Sparrowhawk** (US) first flew 1931*

3 March 31 First flight of Fairey Gordon (GB)
20 March 31 *Graf Zeppelin* begins a regular service between Brazil and Germany
25 March 31 First flight of Hawker Fury I (GB)
13 April 31 First flight of Boeing 215 (US)
April 31 First flight of Junkers Ju 52/3m (G)
April 31 First flight of Boeing B-9 bomber (US)
26 May 31 First flight of Consolidated P2Y (US)
June 31 First flight of Curtiss Shrike (US)
1 July 31 United Airlines formed

Aug 31 First flight of PZL P.11 (PO)
Sept 31 First flight of Heinkel 59 (G)
18 Oct 31 First flight of Grumman F2F (US)
20 Sept 31 First flight of Hawker Nimrod (GB)
29 Sept 31 World speed record: 654.9 km/h/406.94 mph by Flt Lt Stainforth (Supermarine S.6B)
26 Oct 31 First flight of de Havilland Tiger Moth (GB)

Fiat C.R.32 *(It) first flew 1932*

1932 First flight of Fiat C.R.32 (IT)
1932 First flight of Caproni Ca 133 (IT)
24 Feb 32 25 Norden Mk XV bombsights are requested by US Army Air Corps from the US Navy
20 Mar 32 First flight of Boeing P-26 'Peashooter' (US)
26 Mar 32 First flight of Aeroflot
27 April 32 Imperial Airways begins regular service between Croydon, UK and Cape Town, South Africa
20–21 May 32 Amelia Earhart first woman to make a solo flight across the North Atlantic
26 May 32 First flight of Farman F.222 (F)
6 June 32 First flight of Armstrong Whitworth Atlanta (GB)
18 June 32 First flight of Dewoitine D 500 (F)
30 June 32 First flight of Short Sarafand (GB)
13 Aug 32 First flight of Grenville Brothers Gee Bee R1 (US)
18 Aug 32 Balloon altitude record: 16,201m/53,153ft by Picard and Cosyns, ascend over Switzerland
Sept 32 First flight of Focke-Wulf Fw 44 (G)
Nov 32 First flight of Heinkel He 51 (G)

Heinkel He 51 *(G) first flew Nov 1932*

Boeing P-26 'Peashooter' *(US) first flew 20 March 1932*

1932 US carriers *Lexington* and *Saratoga* launch 152 aircraft in a successful surprise 'strike' on Pearl Harbor in war game exercizes
4 Nov 32 First flight of Beech Model 17 Staggerwing (US)
14–18 Nov 32 Amy Johnson establishes a new solo record of 4 days, 6 hours and 54 mins between Lympne, UK and Cape Town, South Africa
1932–3 Conflict over the Leticia region between Peru and Colombia. Mixed bag of US and European aircraft used
1932–5 Chaco War between Bolivia and Paraguay makes great use of air power. Paraguay is equipped with mainly Italian aircraft, the Bolivians US and German types

By 1933 Sperry has built the first successful automatic pilot; the following year this begins to be fitted into airliners
Four powerful carriers emerge in the USA: Boeing-owned United Airlines runs the northern routes; TWA the central routes, American Airlines the south, and Eastern Airlines the New York to Florida run
8 Feb 33 First flight of Boeing Model 247 (US)
4 April 33 The US Navy dirigible USS *Akron* crashes into the sea off the New Jersey coast killing 73 people
14 May 33 First flight of Grumman JF and J2F Duck (US)
22 June 33 First flight of Tupolev ANT-25 (USSR)
23 June 33 First flight of the dirigable USS *Macon* (US)
July 33 First flight of Curtiss F-12C-1 (US)
1 July 33 First flight of Douglas DC-1 (US)
15 July 33 24 Italian seaplanes, commanded by Gen. Italo Balbo, land on Lake Michigan for the World's Fair. The Atlantic crossing takes 14 days in several stages
15–22 July 33 First round-the-world solo flight by Wiley Post, Lockheed Vega, 25,099km/ 15,596 miles
11 Sept 33 First flight of Bréguet 521 Bizerte (F)
28 Sept 33 World altitude record: 13,661m/ 44,820ft by G. Lemoine (Potez 50)
Oct 33 First flight of Polikarpov I-15/153 (USSR)
31 Oct 33 Air France is inaugurated. It is an

BOEING 247D first flight February 1933

Powerplant: Two 550hp Pratt & Whitney Wasp S1H-1G
Primary role: Medium-range passenger transport
Dimensions: Wingspan 74ft (22.56m); length 51ft 7in (15.72m)
Payload: 10 passengers
Weights: Loaded 13,650lb (6,190kg)
Speed: 189mph (304kph) cruising
Range: 745 miles (1,200km)
Crew: 3
Production total (all marks): 75

First flying in February 1933, the Model 247 revolutionized airliner design with its all-metal, low-wing cantilever monoplane layout, retractable landing gear and pneumatic de-icing boots on the wing leading edges. Boeing Air Transport (later part of United Air Lines) took 60, and fifteen went to individuals and other airlines. Earlier models were later refitted to match the Model 247D, with a rearward- instead of a forward-sloping windscreen, controllable-pitch propellers and low-drag NACA engine cowlings. The design lacked the trailing edge flaps that were to become standard, and the aircraft soon became too small for many airlines.

amalgamation of several smaller airlines and inherites 259 aircraft of 35 different types
Dec 33 First flight of Boeing Stearman (US)
30 Dec 33 First flight of Polikarpov I-16 (TsKB-12) (USSR)

Polikarpov I-16 *(USSR) first flew 30 Dec 1933*

1934 First flight of Savoia-Marchetti S.M.79 Sparviero (IT)
1934 First flight of Fokker C.X (HO)
1934 First flight of Sikorsky S-42 (US)
Feb 34 First flight of Gotha Go 145 (G)
1 Feb 34 Inaugural fight of South African Airways
7 Feb 34 First flight of CRDA Cant Z.501 (IT)
17 Feb 34 First airmail flight between New Zealand and Australia, the crossing taking 14 hours 10 mins
April 34 First flight of Amiot 143 (F)
April 34 First flight of Curtiss Seagull (US)
17 April 34 First flight of de Havilland D.H.89 Dragon Six (Dragon Rapide) (GB)

De Havilland Rapide *(GB) first flew 17 April 1934*

17 April 34 First flight of Fairey Swordfish (GB)
13 May 34 American Airlines formed
19 May 34 First flight of Tupolev ANT-20 Maxim Gorki (USSR)
4 July 34 First flight of Savoia-Marchetti S.73 (IT)

Savoia-Marchetti S.73 *(It) first flew 4 July 1934*

4 July 34 Inaugural fight of Delta Air lines
12 Sept 34 First flight of Gloster Gladiator (GB)

Gloster Gladiator *(GB) first flew 12 Sept 1934*

28 Sept 34 Luft-Hansa carries its millionth passenger
7 Oct 34 First flight of Tupolev SB-1/SB-2 (ANT-40) (USSR)
4 Nov 34 First flight of Junkers Ju 86 (G)
30 Dec 34 First flight of Martin M-130 seaplane (see overleaf) (US)

1935 First flight of Ilyushin Il-4 (USSR)
1935 First flight of Seversky P-35 (US)
1935 First flight of Yakovlev UT-2 (USSR)
1935 First flight of Savoia-Marchetti S.M.81 Pipistrello (IT)
Jan 35 First flight of Douglas TBD-1 Devastator (US)
7 Jan 35 First flight of Avro Anson (GB)
17 Jan 35 First flight of Latecoère 521, 522, 523 (F)
4 Feb 35 First flight of Mitsubishi A5M (Claude) (J)
12 Feb 35 The US Navy dirigible USS *Macon* crashes into the sea off the California coast. Two of the crew die
24 Feb 35 First flight of Heinkel He 111 (see overleaf) (G)
9 Mar 35 Germany announces the re-establishment of new national air force, the Luftwaffe

MARTIN M-130 first flight 30 December 1934

Powerplant: Four 800hp Pratt & Whitney R–1830 Twin Wasp
Primary role: Long-range passenger transport
Dimensions: Wingspan 130ft (39.62m); length 90ft 10½in (27.7m)
Payload: 43 passengers
Weights: Loaded 52,252lb (23,702kg)
Speed: 157mph (253kph) cruising
Range: 3,200 miles (5,150km)
Production total (all marks): 3

This was the first US-built flying boat to have aerofoil-shaped sea wings and sponsons to provide water stability, additional fuel tanks and lifting surfaces. Construction was all-metal. The type was designed for Pan American's trans-Pacific runs, and the first flight, by *China Clipper*, was made on 30 December 1934. This machine broke nineteen international records, making the first return airmail flight from America to the Philippines from 22 November to 6 December 1935, flying from San Francisco to Manila via Honolulu, Midway, Wake Island and Guam. *Philippine Clipper* entered PAA service on 9 December 1935, followed by *Hawaii Clipper* on 2 May 1936. This third boat operated the first passenger service in October 1936 but disappeared on 28 July 1938 between Guam and Manila. The two remaining M-130s served with PAA until 1942, when they were taken over by the US Navy. Both were destroyed during World War II.

***Consolidated PBY Catalina** (US) first flew 28 March 1935*

HEINKEL He111 first flight 24 February 1935

Powerplant: (111H-16) Two 1,350hp Junkers Jumo 211F-2
Primary role: (111H-16) Medium bomber
Dimensions: (111H-16) Wingspan 74ft 1¾in (22.6m); length 53ft 9½in (16.4m)
Armament: (111H-16) One 20mm MG FF cannon in nose, one 13mm MG 131 in dorsal hatch, one or two 7.9mm MG 81 in beam positions, two 7.9mm MG 81 in ventral gondola; up to 5,500lb (2,500kg) bomb load
Weights: (111H-16) Empty 19,136lb (8,690kg); loaded 30,870lb (14,000kg)
Speed: (111H-16) 270mph (435kph) max
Range: (111H-16) 1,200 miles (1,930km)
Crew: 4/5
Production total (all marks): 7,300
Variants: A–H, J, P, R, Z

The He 111 first appeared camouflaged as a civil transport in 1935. Early bomber versions entered service late 1936, and, 111B-1s first saw action with the Condor Legion in Spain in 1937. Early models with stepped cockpits had generally been withdrawn from first-line service by September 1939 but remained in service with the Spanish and Turkish Air Forces during the war. China employed ten He 111A-0s. The He 111P and its re-engined major variant the 111H served in all major offensives in the early part of the war, and subsequently in the Mediterranean and Eastern theatres, the P marks having a short production life as Daimler-Benz concentrated on fighter engines. Later 111Hs were also used as torpedo-bombers against Arctic convoys in 1942 and destroyed nearly 60 US fighters and bombers in ground attack missions at Poltava, USSR, on 21 and 22 June 1944. V-1 flying bombs were launched towards Britain from 111H-22s in 1944–45.

15 Mar 35 First flight of Dornier Do 18 (G)
16 Mar 35 Germany begins massive re-armament programme
20 Mar 35 First flight of Grumman F3F (US)
28 Mar 35 First flight of Consolidated PBY Catalina (US)
April 35 First flight of North American T-6 Texan (Harvard) (US)
12 April 35 First flight of Bristol Blenheim (GB)
May 35 First flight of Curtiss Hawk 75 (P-36 Mohawk) (US)
8 May 35 First flight of Henschel Hs 123 (G)

***Bristol Blenheim** (GB) first flew 12 April 1935*

18 May 35 The world's worst air disaster to date occurs when a Soviet ANT-20 Maxim Gorky is destroyed after collision with another aircraft killing 56 people

28 May 35 First flight of Messerschmitt Bf 109 (G)
6 June 35 First flight of Bréguet-Doraud Gyroplane Laboratoire (F)
19 June 35 First flight of Vickers Wellesley (GB)
July 35 First flight of Mitsubishi G3M (Nell) (J)
July 35 First flight of Douglas SBD/A-24 Dauntless (US)
23 July 1935 1st report on radio direction finding, later called radar, made to Britain's Air Defence Research Committee
28 July 35 First flight of Boeing Model 299 (US)
28 July 35 First flight of Boeing B-17 Fortress (US)
8 Aug 35 First flight of Morane-Saulnier M.S.406 (F)
Aug 35 First flight of Douglas B-18 Bolo (US)
17 Sept 35 First flight of Junkers Ju 87 Stuka (G)
3 Oct 35 Italy invades Abyssinia, using aircraft for close support

Junkers Ju 87 Stuka *(G) first flew 17 Sept 1935*

MESSERSCHMITT Bf 109 first flight 28 May 1935

Powerplant: (109E-1) One 1,100hp Daimler-Benz DB 601A
Primary role: Fighter
Dimensions: (109E-1) Wingspan 32ft 4½in (9.87m); length 28ft 4in (8.64m)
Armament: (109E-1) Two 20mm MG FF cannon and two 7.9mm MG 17 machine guns
Weights: (109E-1) Empty 4,421lb (2,005kg); loaded 5,523lb (2,505kg)
Speed: (109E-1) 354mph (570kph) max
Range: (109E-1) 412 miles (663km)
Crew: 1
Production total (all marks): 30,500
The Bf 109 saw service in the Spanish Civil War in 1937. It participated in the Polish, Norwegian, Low Countries and French campaigns, and was heavily involved in the Battle of Britain in 1940 (610 lost). Served in North Africa and in the invasion of Soviet Union, and later in volunteer and satellite air forces on the Eastern Front. The most numerous mark, the 109G, entered service in the summer of 1942 on the Channel Front, then served on all fronts in varying roles – interception, reconnaissance and fighter-bombing. The Bf 109 suffered heavy losses in the final months of the war but continued in service with the Finnish Air Force until the mid-1950s.

B-17 FLYING FORTRESS first flight 28 July 1935

Powerplant: (B-17G) Four 1,200hp Wright R-182-97.
Primary role: (B-17G) High-altitude heavy bomber.
Speed: (B-17G) 302mph (486kph) max at 25,000ft (7,620m), 160mph (257kph) cruising
Range: (B-17G) 3,400 miles (5,470km)
Weights: (B-17G) Empty 36,135lb (16,391kg); max 72,000lb (32,660kg)
Dimensions: (B-17G) Wing span 103ft 9in (31.62m); length 74ft 9in (22.78m)
Armament: (B-17G) Thirteen 0.5in Browning machine guns in chin, cheek, ventral, dorsal, waist and tail positions; max bomb load theoretically 17,417 lb (7,900 kg), but rarely flew combat missions with more than 5,071 lb (2,300 kg)
Crew: 10

The B-17 was America's most famous bomber of World War II. B-17Ds served in the Philippines at the start of the Pacific War, although more than half their number were lost to Japanese ground attacks; the remainder fought rearguard actions from the Philippines to Australia. RAF Fortress Is (one squadron) made their operational début in July 1941, but suffered severe losses to German fighters; four machines served subsequently as night bombers in the Middle East, others being transferred to Coastal Command for maritime reconnaissance duties. Early B-17Es replaced Ds in the Pacific, but the majority equipped the newly constituted Eighth Air Force in the UK; their operational début came on 17 August 1942 with an attack on the marshalling yards at Rouen. The improved F model soon replaced earlier marks and made the first attacks against Germany proper in January 1943, as well as equipping the Fifteenth Air Force in Italy. Late in 1943 the B-17G appeared, with an additional two-gun turret under-nose. Some Es and Fs were stripped and converted to BQ-17 radio-controlled bombs, used in summer 1944. B-17Gs entered service late in 1943 and became the mainstay of the Allies' daylight bombing offensive in Europe. August 1944 saw a peak strength of 4,574 B-17s in USAAF service. The G model was used mainly in UK-based groups and in Italy, although it also had a photo-reconnaissance role. RAF Fortress IIIs were employed by Coastal Command for maritime reconnaissance and by Bomber Command also on radio countermeasures, clandestine and decoy duties. In early post-war years the B-17 was employed by the USN and USCG as an early-warning aircraft, and the type also saw widespread foreign use.

HAWKER HURRICANE first flight 6 November 1935

Powerplant: (Mk I) One 1,030hp Rolls-Royce Merlin III
Primary role: Fighter
Dimensions: (Mk I) Wingspan 40ft 0in (12.19m); length 31ft 11in (9.73m)
Armament: (Mk I) Eight 0.303in Browning machine guns
Weights: (Mk I) Empty 4,670lb (2,118kg); loaded 6,600lb (2,993kg)
Speed: (Mk I) 324mph (522kph) max
Range: (Mk I) 425 miles (685km)
Crew: 1
Production total (all marks): 14,232
Variants: Mks I–IV, Sea Hurricane

The Hurricane Mk I entered service late 1937 and equipped nineteen squadrons by the beginning of World War II. It claimed the first RAF kill, on 30 October 1939, and fired the first rounds in the Battle of Britain on 8 August 1940. It was the mainstay of the RAF during the Battle of Britain, accounting for the majority of the RAF's air victories. It also saw action in Middle East (autumn 1940), in the Greek and Syrian campaigns and in the Far East. The air forces of Finland (1939–40), Belgium (May 1940) and Yugoslavia (April 1941) also employed Mk Is. The improved Mk II first saw action in September 1940; it was used as a night-fighter during the Blitz and in cross-Channel sweeps in 1941. Two squadrons were sent to northern Russia in August 1941 and the aircraft were later handed over to the Soviet Union. The Mk IIC was mainly UK-based, 1942–44, and the Mk IID was used in North Africa and Burma in the tank-busting and ground-attack roles. The Mk IV saw action in Sicily and Italy in 1943–44. A total of 98 RAF fighter squadrons were equipped with the Hurricane.

6 Nov 35 First flight of Hawker Hurricane (GB)

11 Nov 35 Balloon altitude record: 22,066m/72,395ft by Stevens and Anderson

17 Dec 35 First flight of Douglas DC-3 (C-47) Dakota (US)

Jan 36 First flight of Vought SB2U Vindicator (US)

10 Feb 36 First flight of Fiat B.R.20 Cicogna (IT)

17 Feb 36 Australian domestic airline, Ansett, begins first regular service

March 36 First flight of Curtiss SB2C Helldiver (US)

4 March 36 First flight of Zeppelin LZ-129 *Hindenburg* (G)

5 March 36 First flight of Supermarine Spitfire (GB)

DOUGLAS C-47 DAKOTA first flight 17 December 1935

Powerplant: Two 11,200hp Pratt & Whitney R-1830-92
Primary role: Troop/cargo transport
Dimensions: Wingspan 95ft 0in (28.9m); length 64ft 5 1/4in (19.63m)
Payload: 10,000lb (4,536kg)/28 troops or 18 litters
Weights: Empty 16,970lb (7,705kg); loaded 26,000lb (11,805kg)
Speed: 229mph (368kph) max; 185mph (296kph) cruising
Range: 1,500 miles (2,400km)
Crew: 3
Production total (all marks): 10,349 (plus Japanese and Russian production)
Variants: Skytrain (USAAF, C-47; US Navy, RD-4; RAF, Dakota), Skytrooper (USAAF, C-53; US Navy, R4D-3; RAF, Dakota II) and Skymaster (USAAF, C-54; US Navy, R5-D)

This series of aircraft started life as the DC-3 civil airliner and in many guises served in every war theatre as the Allies' most important transport and troop-carrier. The type equipped over 50 RAF and Commonwealth squadrons and 34 USAAF groups. Japan and the Soviet Union also used licence-produced machines. The C-47/DC-3 set a record for service longevity post-war (Berlin Airlift, Korea, Vietnam), and civil variants are still employed today.

ZEPPELIN LZ129 HINDENBURG first flight 4 March 1936

Powerplant: Four 1,300hp (894kW) Daimler-Benz LOF 6
Primary role: Passenger transport
Dimensions: Length 804ft (245m)
Payload: 50 passengers, later 72
Speed: 30.6 m/sec
Range: 10,000 km approx

Developed to maintain Germany's supremacy in transatlantic crossings, the *Hindenburg* was originally designed for the less flammable helium, but after German rearmament in the 1930s the United States, the world's main supplier of the gas, refused to sell it, so the *Hindenburg* was redesigned to utilize hydrogen. In 1936 the *Hindenburg* had traveled over 186,000 miles (300,000km) and had made seventeen return commercial Atlantic crossings, ten to the United States and seven to Rio de Janeiro, carrying a total of 2,800 passengers and 170 tonnes of mail and freight.

SUPERMARINE SPITFIRE MK IX first flight 5 March 1936

Power Plant: One 1,565hp Rolls-Royce Merlin 61 or one 1,650hp Merlin 63
Primary role: Fighter/fighter-bomber
Weights: Empty 5,610lb (2,545kg); maximum 9,500lb (4,309kg)
Dimensions: Wing span 36ft 10in (11.22m); length 31ft 0in (9.46m); height 12ft 7¾in (3.85m); wing area 242sq ft (22.48sq m)
Armament: Two 20mm Hispano cannon and four .303 machine guns; some modified to carry max bomb load of 1,000lb (454kg)
Performance: maximum speed at 25,000ft 408mph (655km/hr); cruising speed 324mph (521km/hr); maximum range 980 miles (1,576km); initial rate of climb 3,950ft/min (1,204m/min); service ceiling 43,000ft (12,106m)
Crew: 1
In Service: Australia, Canada, Great Britain (RAF/FAA), New Zealand, South Africa. USA (16 Mk IX, 8 P.R.Mk XI), USSR (1,186 L.F.Mk IX, 2 H.F.Mk IX).
Variants: Mk IX, F.IX, L.F.IX, H.F.IX, Mk.IXE, F.IXE, L.F.IXE, H.F.IXE, Mk IX Trainer, P.R.Mk IX, P.R.Mk XI
Total Spitfire production: 20,351 (of 26 different marks)
At the start of WWII 10 squadrons of Spitfire Mk Is were in service with the RAF. By the summer of 1940 19 squadrons were in service to play their vital part in the Battle of Britain. The Spitfire Mk IX entered service in June 1942, initially an interim answer to the Luftwaffe's Focke-Wulf Fw 190. Eventually equipped nearly 100 RAF and Commonwealth fighter squadrons. At the war's end (May 1945) and still flown by eight UK home-defence squadrons, five 2nd TAF squadrons in Europe (destroyed several Me 262 jets) and 22 squadrons of the Desert and Balkan AFs. Supplied in large numbers to USSR, also to USAAF; extensive post-war Commonwealth and foreign use.

10 March 36 First flight of Fairey Battle (GB)
17 March 36 First flight of Armstrong Whitworth Whitley (GB)
27 March 36 First flight of Fokker D.XXI (HO)
10 April 36 Trans Canada Air Lines founded (becomes Air Canada 1 Jan 1965)
4 April 36 First flight of Fieseler Fi 156 Storch (G)
25 April 36 First flight of Potez 63 (F)
6–14 May 36 The *Hindenburg* LZ-129 crosses the Atlantic for the first time
12 May 36 First flight of Messerschmitt Bf 110 (G)
27 May 36 Aer Lingus opens an air service from Baldonnel to Bristol
June 36 First flight of Mitsubishi F1M (Pete) (J)
15 June 36 First flight of Westland Lysander (GB)
15 June 36 First flight of Vickers Wellington (GB)

MESSERSCHMITT Bf 110 first flight 12 May 1936

Powerplant: (110C-4) Two 1,100hp Daimler-Benz DB 601A
Primary role: (110C-4) Long-range day and escort fighter
Dimensions: (110C-4) Wingspan 53ft 5in (16.28m); length 39ft 8in (12.1m)
Armament: (110C-4) Two 20mm MG FF cannon, four 7.9mm MG 17 machine guns and one flexibly mounted 7.9mm MG 15 machine gun
Weights: (110C-4) Loaded 15,300lb (6,939kg)
Speed: (110C-4) 349mph (562kph) max; 301mph (485kph) cruising
Range: (110C-4) 528 miles (850km)
Crew: 2
Production total (all marks): 6,000
Variants: A–F, G, H

The Bf 110C first flew in May 1936 and at the start of World War II equipped three squadrons. The type served in the Polish, Norwegian, Low Countries and French campaigns, as well as the Battle of Britain, when 200 were lost in August–September 1940. It served as a night fighter for the rest of the war, initially without radar. The Bf 110D was developed as a long-range heavy-fighter variant, took part in the Battle of Britain and served in the Balkans and Mediterranean; with surviving 110Cs, it was employed as a fighter-bomber on the Eastern Front. In 1942 the radar-equipped three-seat F-4 night fighter entered service. Bf 110s were due to be replaced by the Me 210, which proved a less successful machine; 110 production was restarted, and in late 1942 the 110G/H night fighters, with more powerful engines, followed. Bomber-destroyer models were able to deploy air-to-air rockets. The type served in the defence of Germany and on the Eastern Front, accounting for 60 per cent of Luftwaffe night-fighters in spring 1944.

21 June 36 First flight of Handley Page Hampden (GB)
26 June 36 First flight of Focke-Wulf Fw 61 helicopter (G)
1 July 36 Continental Airlines founded
3 July 36 First flight of Short S.23 C Class Flying Boat (see overleaf) (GB)
14 July 36 First flight of Kawanishi H6K (Mavis) (J)

SPANISH CIVIL WAR
20 July 36 Ju 52s transport Nationalist troops from Morocco in Spanish Civil War; world's first large-scale airlift
7 Aug 36 Germans supply Heinkel He 51 fighters to Spanish Nationalists
19 Aug 36 First flight of Cant Z.506B Airone (IT)
13 Oct 36 Soviet assistance to Spanish Republicans in the form of I-15 and I-16 fighters

SHORT S.23 'C' CLASS first flight 3 July 1936

Name: Short S.23 'C' Class
Powerplant: Four 920hp Bristol Pegasus XC
Primary role: Passenger transport
Dimensions: Wingspan 114ft (34.75m); length 88ft (26.82m)
Payload: 24 passengers/7,840lb (3,556kg) freight
Weights: Loaded 43,500lb (19,732kg)
Speed: 165mph (266kph) cruising
Range: 760 miles (1,220km)
Production total (all marks): 31
Variants: S30, S33

This design adopted technical advances such as an all-metal monocoque structure, a tapered cantilever wing with electrically actuated flaps, and variable-pitch propellers. Other design innovations were a sleeping cabin, a promenade lounge and a steward's pantry. The first flight, by the flagship *Canopus*, took place on 3 July 1936, and 28 machines entered service with Imperial Airways on the Alexandria–Brindisi route. Operating from Hythe, 'C' class boats took over Imperial's routes from Croydon to Australia, East Africa, Egypt, Malaya and South Africa. Six machines were employed by Qantas Empire Airways by 1938. Following war service, the 'C' class were retired in 1947.

15 Oct 36 First flight of Nakajima Ki-27 (Nate) (J)
Nov 36 First flight of Mitsubishi Ki-21 (Sally) (J)
6 Nov 36 Nationalist Forces bomb Madrid
7 Nov 36 First flight of Dornier Do 17 (G)
15 Nov 36 German Condor Legion begins operations in Spain
21 Dec 36 First flight of Junkers Ju 88 (G)
27 Dec 36 First flight of Petlyakov Pe-8 (ANT-42) (USSR)

Jan 37 First flight of Nakajima B5N (Kate) (J)
Feb 37 First flight of Mitsubishi Ki-30 (Ann) (J)
9 Feb 37 First flight of Blackburn Skua (GB)
26 Feb 37 First flight of Fiat C.R.50 Freccia (IT)
16 March 37 First flight of Fokker G.1 (HO)
30 March 37 The crew of a Pan American Sikorsky S-42B flying boat completes an 11,265km (7,000 mile) survey flight from Pago Pago, American Samoa to Auckland, New Zealand
26 April 37 Guernica bombed by Luftwaffe causing heavy loss of life
30 April 37 Spanish Nationalist battleship *España* is sunk by Republican air attack
6 May 37 The LZ-129 *Hindenburg* is destroyed by fire at Lakehurst, New Jersey
11 May 37 First flight of Cant Z.1007 Alcione (IT)
18–20 June 37 Soviet ANT-25 flies non-stop via North Pole to USA

***Blackburn Skua** (GB) first flew 9 February 1937*

FOCKE-WULF Fw 200A CONDOR first flight 27 July 1937

Powerplant: Four 537 kW (720hp) BMW 132G-1
Primary role: Medium-range passenger transport
Dimensions: Wingspan 107ft 9in (32.84m); length 78ft 3in (23.85m)
Payload: 26 passengers
Weights: Loaded 32,187lb (14,600kg)
Speed: 208mph (335kph) cruising
Range: 901 miles (1,450km)
Crew: 4

Hoping to develop a landplane airliner for the North Atlantic route, in 1936 Focke-Wulf planned the Condor as a low-wing, all-metal monoplane. The prototype Fw 200 V1 first flew in July 1937, powered by Pratt & Whitney 875hp (652kW) radials. The next craft was supplied to Hitler as a personal aeroplane. Fw 200As powered by the BMW 132G-1 radial served with Lufthansa (four machines), Danish Air Lines (two) and the Brazilian Syndicato Condor (four). The long-range Fw 200S-1 followed, making a 25-hour Berlin to New York crossing without refuelling. Variants included the Fw 200B-1, with 850hp (634kW) 132Dc radials, and the Fw 200B-02, with the 830hp (619kW) 132H.

19 June 37 First flight of Airspeed Oxford (GB)
22 June 37 First flight of de Havilland D.H.94 Moth Minor (GB)
2 July 37 In an attempt to circuit the world Amelia Earhart disappears over the S. Pacific
27 July 37 First flight of Focke-Wulf Fw 200 Condor (G)
29 July 37 First flight of Lockheed Model 14 Super Electra (US)
Aug 37 First flight of Sukhoi Su-2 (USSR)
11 Aug 37 First flight of Boulton Paul Defiant (GB)
23 Aug 37 First fully-automatic landing made at Wright Field, Ohio
2 Sept 37 First flight of Grumman F4F-3 Wildcat (US)
1 Oct 37 First flight of Bloch 152C-1 (F)
15 Oct 37 First flight of Boeing XB-15 (US)
17 Dec 37 First flight of Consolidated Vultee PB2Y Coronado (US)
24 Dec 37 First flight of Macchi C.200 Saetta (Lightning) (IT)
1938 First flight of Reggiane Re 2000 (IT)
Jan 38 First flight of Aichi D3A (Val) (J)

***Grumman F4F-3 Wildcat** (US) first flew 2 Sept 1937*

***Macchi C.200 Saetta (Lightning)** (It) first flew 24 Dec 1937*

Jan 38 First flight of Arado Ar 96 (G)
20 Jan 38 Imperial Airways carries out the first in-flight refuelling test of a C class flying-boat
6 Feb 38 First flight of Short Mayo Composite (GB)
15 Feb 38 First flight of Bloch 174/175 (F)
23 March 38 First flight of Bréguet 690 (F)
6 Apr 38 First flight of Bell P-39 Airacobra (US)
May 38 First flight of Arado Ar 196 (G)
June 38 Heinkel HeS 3B turbojet test flown on an He118, the first 'flying test bed' for a jet engine
7 June 38 First flight of Boeing 314 (US)
21 June 38 First flight of Douglas DC-4 (US)
July 38 First flight of Vought OS2U Kingfisher (US)
10 July–11 Aug 38 Soviet Air Force used during combat against Japanese in the Lake Khasan incident
21–22 July 38 First commercial crossing of North Atlantic
Aug 38 First flight of Dornier Do 217 (G)
Aug 38 First flight of Supermarine Sea Otter (GB)
Aug 38 Soviet Air Group in Spain begins withdrawal, leaving their aircraft with Spanish Republicans
14 Sept 38 First flight in Germany of the sister ship of the ill fated *Hindenberg*, the Zeppelin LZ-130 *Graf Zeppelin II*
2 Oct 38 First flight of Dewoitine D.520 (F)
11 Oct 38 First flight of Westland Whirlwind (GB)

***Bell P-39 Airacobra** (US) first flew 6 April 1938*

BOEING 314 first flight 7 June 1938

Powerplant: Four 1,600hp Wright R-2600 Double Cyclone
Primary role: Long-range passenger transport
Dimensions: Wingspan 152ft (46.33m); length 106ft 1in (32.31m)
Payload: 77 passengers/8,745lb (3,967kg) freight
Weights: Loaded 82,500lb (37,422kg)
Speed: 175mph (282kph) cruising
Range: 3,000 miles (4,800km)
Crew: 10
Production total (all marks): 12

Contracted for in July 1936, six of these machines were developed for Pan American Airways for non-stop Atlantic crossings. The first flight took place on 7 June 1938. The type entered service with PAA on 28 June 1938. On 26 March 1939, Pan American made its first trial transatlantic flight from Baltimore, Maryland to Foynes, Ireland using a Boeing 314 (*Yankee Clipper*). Six improved 314As were developed for PAA and this variant first flew on 20 March 1941. Three were transferred to BOAC, and Churchill used one for wartime transatlantic crossings. Two machines were lost during World War II and one in 1947. After post-war use by independent operators, the survivors were scrapped in 1950–51.

Dewoitine D.520 *(F) first flew 2 Oct 1938*

Curtiss P-40 Tomahawk/Kittyhawk *(US) first flew 14 Oct 1938*

14 Oct 38 First flight of Curtiss P-40 Tomahawk/ Kittyhawk (US)

15 Oct 38 First flight of Bristol Beaufort (GB)

26 Oct 38 First flight of Douglas A-20 Boston/Havoc (US)

Late 38 First flight of Aichi E13A (Jake) (J)

Dec 38 First flight of Brewster F2A Buffalo (US)

10 Dec 38 First flight of Lockheed Hudson (US)

12 Dec 38 First flight of Fairey Albacore (GB)

23 Dec 38 First flight of Blackburn Roc (GB)

By 1939 the Douglas has practically driven the competition from the skies in the USA: 75% passengers are flown in DC-3s; 90% in the DC-3 or DC-2. The DC-3 is durable and in military service becomes the C-47 transport

1939 Henschel Hs 129 (G)

1939 First flight of Sud-Est S.E.161 Languedoc (F)

1939 First flight of Junkers Ju 290 (G)

1939 First flight of Fairchild PT-19 Cornell (US)

1939 First flight of Savoia-Marchetti S.M.82 Canguru (IT)

The Spanish Civil War 18 July 1936 – 1 April 1939 clearly demonstrates the success of close-support aircraft. German propagandists quickly point out the devastating power of the Stuka dive-bomber, soon to terrorize half of Europe

1939 First flight of Fiat C.R.42 Falco (IT)

Lockheed P-38 Lightning *(US) first flew 27 Jan 1939*

North American B-25 Mitchell *(US) first flew 10 Feb 1939*

Jan 39 First flight of Nakajima Ki-43 Hayabusa (Oscar) (J)

Jan 39 First flight of Kawasaki Ki-45 Toryu (Nick) (J)

17 Jan 39 The UK Air Ministry announces the fomation of the Auxiliary Air Force Reserve

27 Jan 39 First flight of Lockheed P-38 Lightning (US)

10 Feb 39 First flight of North American B-25 Mitchell (US)

18 Feb 39 First flight of Martin PBM Mariner (US)

14 March 39 First flight of Martin Maryland (US)

1 April 39 First flight of Mitsubishi A6M1 (Zero/Zeke) (J)

26 April 39 World speed record: 755.138 km/h/469.22 mph by Flugkäpitan Wendel (Me 209V1)

7 May 39 First flight of Petlyakov Pe-2/Pe-3 (USSR)

14 May 39 First flight of Short Stirling (GB)

20 May 39 The first regular trans-Atlantic airmail service. A Pan American Boeing 314 flying-boat *Yankee Clipper* flies from New York to Southampton, via the Azores, Lisbon and Marseille

20 May to 16 Sept 39 Nomonhan Incident. Aerial and ground battles between Soviet and

MITSUBISHI A6M2 'ZEKE' (ZERO) first flight 1 April 1939

Type: Carrier-borne fighter/fighter-bomber.
Power Plant: One 950hp Nakajima NK1C Sakae 12.
Maximum speed: at 14,930ft (4,550m) 332mph (534km/hr).
Cruising speed: 207mph (333km/hr).
Maximum range: 1,930 miles (3,105km).
Climb rate: time to 19,685ft (6,000m) 7min 27sec.
Service ceiling: 32,810ft (10,000m).
Empty: 3,704lb (1,680kg).
Maximum: 6,164lb (2,796kg).
Wing span: 39ft 4in (12.0m).
Length: 29ft 8in (9.06m).
Height: 10ft 0in (3.05m).
Armament: Two 20mm Type 99 cannon in wings; two 7.7mm Type 97 machine-guns in upper fuselage decking; bomb load 264lb (120kg).
Crew: 1.
Total Production: approx 11,283 (all Marks).

Synonymous with Japanese wartime air-power, the 'Zero' remains to this day the best-known of all Japanese aircraft. Early models made their operational debut in the Sino-Japanese conflict, autumn 1940, in which the Zero demonstrated an excellent performance/kill-ratio largely unnoticed by Western Allies. By the outbreak of the Pacific War A6M2s comprized over 60 per cent of the IJNAF's carrier-fighter force. The Zero burst upon unsuspecting US-Allied forces, sweeping the length and breadth of the Pacific and Indian Ocean war zones, participatin in the Pearl Harbor and Wake Island attacks, escorting bombing raids on Australia and Ceylon, and supporting land campaigns in the Philippines and Netherlands East Indies. The Zero suffered its first severe reverse at Midway, June 1942, and subsequently relinquished the initiative to newer US designs

FOCKE-WULFE 190 first flight 1 June 1939

Powerplant: (190A-8) One 1,700hp BMW 801D–2
Primary role: (190A-8) Fighter
Dimensions: (190A-8) Wingspan 34ft 5½in (10.5m); length 29ft 0in (8.84m)
Armament: (190A-8) Four 20mm MG 151 cannon and two 13mm MG 131 machine guns
Weights: (190A-8) Empty 7,000lb (3,175kg); loaded 9,750lb (4,422kg)
Speed: (190A-8) 408mph (657kph) max; 298mph (480kph) cruising
Range: (190A-8) 500 miles (805km)
Crew: 1
Production total (all marks): 19,500
Variants: A–G; Ta 152

Hailed as Germany's greatest wartime fighter, the Fw 190 first saw action on the Channel Front in early 1941, and by 1942–43 it was involved on all major theatres. In Europe it defended Germany against bombers and carried out fighter-bomber raids on southern England. Its roles in the later war years were those of a home defence fighter against US daylight raids and a limited night fighter. The Fw 190F was a day and night ground-attack variant that entered service in the winter of 1942/43 on the Eastern Front, covering the retreat from Russia to the Oder from 1943 to 1945. A long-range fighter-bomber variant, the 190G, made its début at the end of the Tunisian campaign and also served on the Eastern Front, taking part in the Battle of Kursk in July 1943. The 190D, nicknamed *Langnase* (Long-Nose) or 'Dora', entered service in autumn 1944, at first defending airfields where experimental jet fighters were operating. On 1 January 1945 Fw 190s took part in the last-ditch German attack on Allied airfields in the Low Countries, Operation *Bodenplatte* (Baseplate).

Focke-Wulfe Fw 190A first entered service in March 1941

Focke-Wulfe Fw 190D-9 (Dora), first flew July 1943

Japanese aircraft in Outer Mongolia. Japan's initial aerial superiority does not last

1 June 39 First flight of Focke-Wulf Fw 190/Ta 152 (G)

20 June 39 First flight of Heinkel He 176 (G)

20 June 39 At Peenemunde, first flight of a manned rocket-powered aircraft specifically designed for that purpose. The He 176 research aircraft is powered by one Walter HWK R I-203 rocket motor

July 39 First flight of Kawasaki Ki-48 (Lily) (J)

1 July 39 Operational use by Soviet fighters of rockets against Japanese targets in Outer Mongolia

17 July 39 First flight of Bristol Beaufighter (GB)

25 July 39 First flight of Avro 679 Manchester (GB)

***Bristol Beaufighter** (GB) first flew 17 July 1939*

***Avro Manchester** (GB) first flew 25 July 1939*

27 July 39 First flight of Douglas B-23 Dragon (US)

Aug 39 First flight of Nakajima Ki-49 Donryu (Helen) (J)

13 Aug 39 First flight of Vickers Warwick (GB)

27 Aug 39 First flight of Heinkel He 178 (G)

27 Aug 1939 First flight of a turbojet-powered aircraft, German Heinkel He 178, designed by Dr Pabst von Ohain

WORLD WAR II

1 Sept 39 Germany invades Poland after heavy pre-dawn air bombardment. Over 1,500 German first-line aircraft committed to the campaign. Ju 87s spearhead the blitzkrieg as 'flying artillery' with great accuracy. Poland has approximately 300 combat-capable aircraft

2 Sept 39 First flight of Messerschmitt Me 210/Me 410 Hornisse (G)

3/4 Sept 39 RAF Whitley IIIs drop propaganda leaflets over Germany

4 Sept 39 First RAF raids of the war. Three separate attacks on shipping in the Schilling Roads. Seven out of 30 bombers are lost and only one ship is slightly damaged

14 Sept 39 First flight of Vought-Sikorsky VS-300 (US)

THE INITIAL BOMBER LINE-UP

Germany has three main bombers, early versions having been tested in the Spanish Civil War: Heinkel He 111, Dornier Do 17, Junkers Ju 87 dive-bomber. Junkers Ju 88 enters service as the war begins, modified for dive-bombing. German aircraft are first to be equipped with self-sealing fuel tanks

Poland's P.Z.L. P38 Los can carry a good bomb weight but is not available in sufficient numbers to make an impact

France's bombers are obsolescent, the new types such as the Lioré et Olivier LeO 451 coming too late

Britain has three main heavy bombers: Armstrong Whitworth Whitley, Handley Page Hampden, Vickers-Armstrong Wellington, which has strong geodetic framework structure and can carry a good load long distances. The Bristol Blenheim twin-engine bomber bears the initial brunt of RAF daylight operations. The single-engine Fairey Battle is inadequate, slow and vulnerable.

Italy's principal bombers are the Savoia-Marchetti SM79 and Cant Z1007, both trimotors, the former becoming a capable torpedo-plane, and the Fiat BR20

Soviet Petlyakov Pe 2 is fast and good for shallow dive-bombing; the single-engine Ilyushin Il2 Shturmovik ground-attack aircraft has an armoured shell to protect crew and engine from ground fire

MITSUBISHI G4M (BETTY) first flight Oct 1939

Powerplant: Two 1,539hp Mitsubishi MK4A Kasei 11
Primary role: Medium bomber
Dimensions: Wingspan 82ft 0½in (25.0m); length 65ft 7½in (20.0m)
Armament: (G4M2) Two 7.7mm machine guns in nose, two 7.7mm machine guns in beam hatches, one 20mm cannon in dorsal turret, one 20mm cannon in tail turret
Weights: (G4M2) Empty 17,990lb (8,160kg); loaded 27,558lb (12,500kg)
Speed: (G4M2) 272mph (438kph) max; 196mph (316kph) cruising
Range: (G4M2) 3,765 miles (6,060km)
Crew: 7
Production total (all marks): 2,446
Variants: G4M1, G4M2, G4M3, G6M1

Japan's most famous and numerous wartime bomber, the G4M equipped over twenty *Kokutais*. The G4M1 made its operational début in the summer of 1941 over China, and served throughout South-East Asia for the duration of the Pacific War. It was widely employed in the New Guinea, Netherlands East Indies and Solomons campaigns. However, the design had major flaws – for example a lack of crew and fuel tank armour and a tendency to catch fire – and G4M1s were replaced by later models and relegated to transport, maritime reconnaissance and training duties. The G4M2, with a heavier armament but shorter range, entered service in mid-1943 but suffered heavy losses defending the Philippines, Marianas and Okinawa. The G4M2e began launching Ohka suicide missiles on 21 March 1945. The improved G4M3 appeared too late in the war to affect the outcome.

***Curtiss C-46 Commando** (US) first flew 26 March 1940*

Consolidated B-24 Liberator *(US) first flew 29 Dec 1939*

25 Sept 39 Luftwaffe launch massive 400-bomber raid on Warsaw

6 Oct 39 First flight of Curtiss Seamew (US)

16 Oct 39 First enemy aircraft destroyed over Britain in WW II, a Ju 88 shot down by Spitfires

23 Oct 39 First flight of Mitsubishi G4M (Betty) (J)

25 Oct 39 First flight of Handley Page Halifax (GB)

Nov 39 First flight of Mitsubishi Ki-46 (Dinah) (J)

Handley Page Halifax *(GB) first flew 25 Oct 1939*

18 Nov 39 German aircraft drop first anti-shipping magnetic mines in British coastal waters

19 Nov 39 First flight of Heinkel He 177V-1 (G)

21 Nov 39 First flight of Piaggio P108B (IT)

24 Nov 39 British Airways and Imperial Airways merge as BOAC

30 Nov 39 Soviet Union invades Finland, initially supported by nearly 700 aircraft. Finland has only 145 aircraft

18 Dec 39 12 of 24 RAF Wellington bombers lost in daylight attack on German shipping in Schilling Roads. These and other losses result in RAF switch to night operations with consequent loss of accuracy

29 Dec 39 Consolidated B-24 Liberator (US) is long range and helps close the air gap in long-distance ocean patrols across the Atlantic; it becomes the most numerous US type of the war, over 18,000 built

30 Dec 39 First flight of Ilyushin Il-2 TsKB-35 Shturmovik (USSR)

Ilyushin Il-2 Shturmovik *(USSR) first flew 30 Dec 1939*

1940 First flight of Junkers Ju 188 (G)

1 Jan 40 First flight of Yakovlev I-26 (Yak-1) (USSR)

4 Jan 40 First flight of Fairey Fulmar (GB)

22 Feb 40 Sqn Ldr Faraquhar of No 602 Squadron, Royal Auxiliary Air Force, takes the first British gun-camera film of the war while attacking and destroying a Heinkel He 111 over Coldingham, Berwickshire

24 Feb 40 First flight of Hawker Typhoon (GB)

13 Mar 40 Ceasefire in Finland. Soviets lose 750 aircraft, Finns 61

26 March 40 First flight of Curtiss C-46 Commando (US)

Hawker Typhoon *(GB) first flew 24 Feb 1940*

NORTH AMERICAN P-51 MUSTANG first flight 26 October 1940

Power Plant: One 1,400hp Packard Merlin V-165-3.
Maximum speed: at 30,000ft (9,144m) 440mph (708km/hr).
Cruising speed: 362mph (582km/hr).
Maximum range: 2,200 miles (3,540km).
Climb rate: Time to 10,000ft (3,068m) 1min 48sec.
Service ceiling: 42,000ft (12,800m).
Empty weight: 6,8401b (3,103kg).
Maximum weight: 11,200lb (5,080kg).
wing span 37ft 1in (11.89m).
Length: 32ft 3in (9.83m).
Height: 8ft 8in (2.64m).
Wing area: 233sq ft (21.65sq m).
Armament: Four .5in Browning machine-guns; max bomb load 2.000lb (907kg).
Crew: 1.
Total Production: 15,469 (all Marks).
First of Packard Merlin variants; served primarily with UK-based US 8th AF as long-range escort fighter; first operation, to Kiel, 13 Dec 1943; first Allied fighters over Berlin, March 1944: flew 'shuttle' missions to USSR: also operated by 9th AF in both fighter and reconnaissance (F–6C) roles; served Mediterranean and CBI theatres: equipped British and Commonwealth sqns in UK, NW Europe (2nd TAF), and Italy (DAF). Numerically the most important Mustang variant was the P-51D/Ks operated in both European and Pacific theatres; outstanding long-range high-altitude escort/interceptor performance; participated many UK-USSR and UK–North Africa shuttle raids; also employed Italy and SE Europe; closing stages Pacific War, based Iwo Jima escorted B-29s against Japan; first land-based US fighter over Tokyo; equipped thirteen RAF sqns plus Commonwealth Afs; continued late-and post-war development for USAAF, inc P-82B Twin Mustang; also world-wide post-war foreign service, inc Communist China; participated Korean war and 1956 Arab–Israeli conflict.

Aug 40 First flight of Sud-Ouest S.O.30P Bretagne (F)

Aug 40 First flight of Nakajima Ki-44 Shoki (Tojo) (J)

Aug 40 First flight of DFS 194 (G)

25/26 Aug 40 First RAF attack on Berlin, by 43 bombers

28 Aug 40 First flight of Camproni-Campini N-1 (IT)

28 Aug 40 First flight of Focke-Achgelis Fa 223 Drache (G)

7 Sept 40 First flight of Blohm/Voss Bv 222 Wiking (G)

Oct 40 First flight of Tupolev Tu-2 (ANT-58) (USSR)

26 Oct 40 First flight of North American P-51 Mustang (US)

Tupolev Tu-2 *(USSR) first flew Oct 1940*

Nov 40 First flight of Yokosuka D4Y Suisei (Judy) (J)

11 Nov 40 Taranto Raid. Carrier-based British Swordfish torpedo-bombers attack Italian fleet and torpedo three battleships and one heavy cruiser

25 Nov 40 First flight of Martin B-26 Marauder (US)

25 Nov 40 First flight of de Havilland Mosquito (GB)

7 Dec 40 First flight of Fairey Barracuda (GB)

De Havilland Mosquito *(GB) first flew 25 Nov 1940*

18 Dec 40 First flight of Henschel Hs 293A (G)

18 Dec 40 First successful flight of Henschel Hs 293 radio-controlled bomb

18 Dec 40 First flight of Curtiss SNC Helldiver (US)

Battle of Britain 10 July – 1 Nov 40 fighter control based on radar takes the Luftwaffe by surprise

24 Aug to 6 Sept Goering sends 1,000 aircraft a day against Britain

The change to attacking cities gives RAF Fighter Command time to recover

10 July – 12 Aug Convoy attacks, initial skirmishes

13 Aug – 6 Sept Assault on the Airfields

7 Sept – 1 Oct The Attacks on London

1 Oct – 1 Nov Hit-and-Run Raids, start of Night Blitz

Martin B-26 Marauder *(US) first flew 25 Nov 1940*

AVRO LANCASTER first flight 9 January 1941

Powerplant: Four 1,640hp Rolls-Royce Merlin 24
Primary role: Heavy bomber
Dimensions: Wing span 102ft 0in (31.09m); length 69ft 6in (21.18m)
Armament: Two 0.303in Browning machine guns each in nose and dorsal turrets; four 0.303in Browning machine guns in tail turret; max bomb load 18,000lb (8,165kg)
Weights: Empty 37,000lb (16,780kg); loaded 65,000lb (29,480kg)
Speed: 245mph (394kph) max
Range: 2,530 miles (4,070km)
Crew: 7
Production total: 7,378.

A redesign of the twin-engine Manchester, the Lancaster first saw action in March 1942 and soon became the backbone of offensive operations against Germany. It equipped over 40 squadrons by summer 1944. The daylight attack on Augsburg, the destruction of the Mohne and Eder dams (dam-busting) and the sinking of the battleship *Tirpitz* were amongst its many successes. It flew 156,000 sorties and it was the only bomber able to carry the 22,000lb (9,979kg) 'Grand Slam' bomb. The type was employed by Coastal Command on maritime reconnaissance duties after the war, and post-war recipients included Egypt, France and Sweden.

Luftwaffe loses some 1,880 aircraft and 2,660 aircrew, the RAF 1,020 aircraft and 537 aircrew

THE BLITZ 7 Sept 1940 – 11 May 1941
24/25 Aug 40 First German bombing of central London
7 Sept to 12 Nov 40 Germans fly 58 major raids on London
14/15 Nov 40 Coventry raid by 449 bombers destroys much of the city's heart and almost a third of the houses. Heavy raids follow: 19 Nov Birmingham, 23 Nov Southampton, 24 Nov Bristol, 12 Dec Sheffield, 20 Dec Liverpool
29 Dec 40 heavy incendiary raid on London
13 Jan 40 Heavy raid on Plymouth
13, 14 March 40 Heavy raids on Clydebank
8 April 40 Another raid on Coventry
17 and 19 April 40 renewed attacks on London. Five more raids almost destroy Plymouth
1 May 40 8-day 'Blitz' against Liverpool, heavy damage to city and 33 ships sunk in the port
3 May 40 Major raid against Belfast
7 May 40 Major raid against Hull
10/11 May 40 Last and heaviest raid on London renders a third of the streets in Greater London impassable

Jan 41 First flight of Kawanishi H8K1 (Emily) (J)

Jan – Apr 41 Luftwaffe join air attacks on Malta, greatly increasing their intensity

9 Jan 41 First flight of Avro Lancaster (GB)

9 Jan 41 'Circus' operations: British begin fighter and light-bomber sweeps over occupied Europe

Kawanishi H8K1 (Emily) *(J) first flew Jan 1941*

10 Jan 41 First of many Luftwaffe attacks on British shipping in the Mediterranean: aircraft carrier *Illustrious* seriously damaged

1941 First flight of Gotha Go 242/Go 244 (G)

20 Feb 41 First flight of Spitfire Mk V (GB)

25 Feb 41 First flight of Messerschmitt Me 321 Gigant (glider) (G)

March 41 First flight of Arado Ar 231 (G)

Spring 1941 Siege of Malta begins. Almost incessant air attacks by Italians and Germans, Malta being resupplied by convoys, themselves subject to air attack, from each end of Mediterranean

1 April 41 First use of 4,000lb 'Block Buster' bomb by RAF

2 April 41 First flight of Heinkel He 280V-1 (G)

6 April 41 Germany invades Yugoslavia and Greece supported by over 800 aircraft. Belgrade bombed by some 500 aircraft killing as many as 20,000

18 April 41 First flight of Messerschmitt Me 262 (G)

20 April 41 Bf 109Es in North Africa outclass

MESSERSCHMITT Me 262 first flight 18 April 1941

Powerplant: Two 1,984lb (900kg) s.t. Junkers Jumo 109-0048
Primary role: Fighter/fighter-bomber
Dimensions: Wingspan 40ft 11½in (12.48m); length 34ft 9½in (10.6m)
Armament: Four 30mm cannon
Weights: Empty 14,108lb (6,400kg)
Speed: 540mph (869kph) at 19,685ft (6,000m) max
Range: 525 miles (845km)
Crew: 1
Production total (all marks): over 1,100

Nicknamed Schwalbe (Swallow) and equipping squadrons from summer 1944, the Me 262 was the world's first turbojet-powered aeroplane to enter operational service. The design originated as early as 1938, when Messerschmitt was asked to create a fighter using two BMW or Junkers turbojets. The first prototype flew in April 1941 with a piston engine, and the first jet flight was in July 1942 with Junkers 109-004s. Pre-production Me 262A-0s followed, but full production began only in November 1943, when Hitler gave the go-ahead, demanding that the type be used as the Sturmvogel (Stormbird) high-speed bomber. In-service variants were the Me 262A-1 with different armament for fighter/fighter-bomber roles, and the Me 262B two-seaters for training and night-fighting. Other projects were the rocket-boosted Me 262C, and the rocket-armed Me 262D/E bomber interceptors.

***Republic P-47 Thunderbolt** (US) first flew 6 May 1941*

Hurricanes and Kittyhawks of British Desert Air Force

During the Blitz, over 33,000 Luftwaffe sorties are flown against Britain's cities, with over 500 German aircraft lost during the campaign. It ends as Luftwaffe forces move east for the coming offensive against the USSR

May 41 First Soviet RUS-I and RUS-2 air defence radar sets put into service

6 May 41 First flight of Republic P-47 Thunderbolt (US)

10/11 May 41 Rudolf Hess, Deputy Führer of Germany, flies to Britain and lands by parachute in Scotland

15 May 41 First flight of Gloster E.28/39 (GB)

May 41 Nakajima J1N1 Gekko (Irving) (J)

20 May – 1 June Battle for Crete

20 May 41 Operation 'Mercury', largest airborne assault by Luftwaffe in WW II, seizes Crete but suffers loss of some 5,600 men and 150 transport aircraft. Royal Navy loses three cruisers and six destroyers to air attack, plus 17 other ships damaged

1941 First flight of Waco CG-4A Haig/Hadrian (US)

Spring 41 First flight of Yakovlev Yak-3 (USSR)

26 May 41 German battleship *Bismarck* sunk in Atlantic by British capital ships after steering gear damaged by Swordfish torpedo-bombers from aircraft carrier *Ark Royal*

June 41 *Audacity*, Royal Navy's first escort carrier (CVE) commissioned: converted merchantmen with flight deck and hangar, these ships escort convoys, transport aircraft and supplement fleet carriers in battle

14 June 41 First flight of Martin Baltimore (US)

22 June 41 Operation 'Barbarossa': German invasion of Soviet Union supported by 2,000 aircraft begins with massive surprise air attack. Day one sees Luftwaffe destroy nearly 1,500 Soviet aircraft on the ground and over 300 in the air

***Martin Baltimore** (US) first flew 14 June 1941*

27 June 41 First flight of Douglas B-19 (US)

July 41 First flight of Vultee A-31/A-35 Vengeance (US)

31 July 41 First flight of Lockheed PV-1/B-34 Ventura/Harpoon (US)

1 Aug 41 First flight of Grumman TBF-1 Avenger (US)

RAF tactical air support comes initially from Hurricanes, later from Typhoons, P-47

Grumman Evenger *(US) first flew 1 Aug 1941*

Thunderbolts and P-51 Mustangs of the USAAF. Tactical bombing by 'cab rank' system of radio-directed fighter bombers, usually with rockets, first deployed in the Western Desert campaign

6 Aug 41 Germany announces destruction or capture of over 9,000 Soviet warplanes

13 Aug 41 First flight of Messerschmitt Me 163 Komet (see overleaf). 300 built; shoot down only 9 enemy aircraft (G)

12 Sept 41 First flight of Airspeed AS.51 Horsa glider (GB)

12 Oct 41 BOAC begins a UK–Cairo service using C-class flying-boat

Oct 41 First flight of Heinkel He 111Z-1 (G)

7/8 Nov 41 Multiple raids on German targets result in heavy RAF losses. Temporary programme of conservation introduced

4 Oct 41 USA and UK to provide monthly shipments of aircraft to Soviet Union. USA alone provides 3,600 planes between middle of 1942 and 1943

22 Dec 41 First flight of Fairey Firefly (GB)

Dec 41 First flight of Kawasaki Ki-61 Hien (Tony) (J)

1942 First flight of Yakovlev Yak-9 (USSR)

Jan 42 First flight of Lavochkin La-5/La-7 (USSR)

14 Jan 42 First flight of Sikorsky XR-4 (US)

Dec 41 Luftwaffe renew air attacks on Malta, with even greater intensity than before

Dec 41 to Feb 42 RAF bomb German warships *Scharnhorst*, *Gneisenau* and *Prinz Eugen* in Brest

December 1941: beginning of World War II in the Pacific

Japanese raid Pearl Parbor, 7 Dec

7 Dec 41 Japan uses carrier-based aircraft to attack Pearl Harbor, Hawaii, causing major losses to US Fleet

10 Dec 41 Sinking of Force Z. British capital ships *Prince of Wales* and *Repulse* sunk by Japanese G3M 'Nell' bombers

Main Japanese Landings on Philippines, 22 Dec

Philippines: US B-17s caught undispersed on the ground by the Japanese and destroyed

1942 Britain introduces Short Stirling and Handley Page Halifax four-engine bombers; and in March the Avro Lancaster, the best heavy night bomber of the period. These bombers carry twice the load of foreign designs

1942 First flight of Yakovlev Yak-9 (USSR)

Jan 42 First flight of Lavochkin La-5/La-7 (USSR)

14 Jan 42 First flight of Sikorsky XR-4 (US)

Feb 42 First flight of Blackburn Firebrand (UK)

Blackburn Firebrand *(GB) first flew Feb 1942*

14 Feb 42 First flight of Douglas C-54 Skymaster (see overleaf) (US)

15 Feb 42 Surrender of Singapore to Japanese

19 Feb 42 Japanese air attack on shipping at Port Darwin, Australia

Feb 42 'Bomber' Harris takes over RAF Bomber Command. His raiders drops a 50:50 mix of high-explosive and incendiary bombs

3/4 March 42 Renault plant in Paris successfully bombed

8/9 March 42 First use of GEE target-marking navigation aid by RAF

20 March 42 First flight of Mitsubishi J2M1 Raiden (Jack) (J)

Mitsubishi J2M1 'Jack' *(J) first flew 20 March 1942*

MESSERSCHMITT Me 163 KOMET first flight 13 August 1941

Powerplant: One 3,748lb (1,700kg) s.t. Walter HWK 509A-2
Primary role: Interceptor
Dimensions: Wingspan 30ft 7¼in (9.33m); length 19ft 2⅓in (5.85m)
Armament: Two 30mm Rheinmetall-Borsig MK cannon
Weights: Loaded 9,480lb (4,300kg)
Speed: 596mph (960kph) max at 9,845ft (3,000m)
Range: 50 miles (80km)
Crew: 1
Production total (all marks): c.380
Variants: 163A, 163B, 163S, 163D

Prototypes of this aircraft first flew in August 1941, but the Komet (Comet) was so radical that the Luftwaffe did not form a test squadron for it until 1944. Planned around the new liquid-fuelled rocket motor, the Komet was small and tailless, took off from a detachable wheeled trolley, had no undercarriage and landed as a glider, skidding on its underbelly, when fuel ran out. On 2 October 1941 test pilot Heini Dittmar became the first man to approach the speed of sound, achieving Mach 0.84 (over 620mph, 1,000kph), having had his Me 163A towed to 13,000ft (3,960m) by a Messerschmitt Bf 110 before being released from the tow and igniting the motor. Komets could reach 30,000ft in less than three minutes, and were about 300mph faster than their prey – heavy daylight bombers. Komet pilots developed unique tactics: a rocket-assisted near-vertical take-off propelling them to unprecedented heights, a glide down to the vicinity of their targets, using the motor for final attack, and a glide in to land. However, Komets were ultimately unsuccessful as fighters. With the aircraft's high attack speed, pilots had only 3 or 4 seconds of firing time, and their cannon often jammed. The experimental motors gave them only about six minutes of powered flight, and they were easy targets when gliding to land. The aircraft were unstable and dangerous to take off and land, and their fuel mixture of hydrogen peroxide (T-Stoff) and hydrazine hydrate in methanol (C-Stoff) was highly explosive and some machines blew up on landing. Even worse, the acidic mixture actually dissolved the pilots if it escaped from the motor; hence pilots wore rubber suits for 'protection'. Me 163As and two-seat 163Ss were used as training gliders, the 163B being the operational aircraft, and improved variants were planned as the 163C/D and 263. The Komet saw service from August 1944 but claimed only nine enemy bombers.

DOUGLAS C-54 SKYMASTER first flight 14 February 1942

Powerplant: Four 1,290hp Pratt & Whitney R-2000-7
Primary role: Long-range transport
Dimensions: Wingspan 117ft 6in (35.81m); length 93ft 10in (28.6m)
Payload: 30–50 passengers
Weights: Empty 37,000lb (16,783kg); loaded 62,000lb (28,123kg)
Speed: 275mph (442kph) max
Range: 3,900 miles (6,275km)
Crew: 6
Production total (all marks): 1,122

Launched into service late in 1942, the C-54 made nearly 80,000 wartime ocean crossings with the loss of only three machines. Regular routes included transatlantic; USA to Australia over the Pacific; Australia to Ceylon over Indian Ocean; and India to China. The type also served in North Africa and in Alaska to the Aleutians. One C-54A was converted to a VIP transport for Presidential use with state/conference rooms and an elevator, while Churchill used a Lend-Lease C-54B as a personal transport. The type was employed extensively post-war, serving in Korea and in the Berlin Airlift.

27 March 42 First flight of General Aircraft Hamilcar glider (GB)
March 42 First flight of Focke-Achgelis Fa 330 (G)
March 42 First flight of Nakajima B6N Tenzan (Jill) (J)
March 42 First flight of Messerschmitt Me 323 Gigant (powered variant) (G)
April 42 First flight of Spitfire Mk IX (GB)
April 42 First flight of Boeing B-17F (US)
2–9 Apr 42 Japanese carriers enter Indian Ocean and strike Ceylon. Numerous British ships sunk, including aircraft carrier *Hermes* and two cruisers
18 Apr 42 Doolittle Raid. 16 B-25s led by Lt Col Doolittle fly off US carrier *Hornet* to make first bombing raid on Japan
19 April 42 First flight of Macchi C.205 (IT)

Macchi C.205 *(It) first flew 19 April 1942*

24 April 42 First flight of Miles Martinet (GB)
24 April 42 German raid on British city of Exeter, first of so-called 'Baedeker' raids, named after famous guidebook. Bath and Norwich raided on the two following nights
May 42 First flight of Aichi Ryusei B7A (Grace) (J)
7–8 May 42 Battle of the Coral Sea, between carrier-based aircraft of Japan and USA. First naval battle to occur without any surface ship sighting enemy fleet
20 May 42 Singleton Report advocates use of new H2S navigation aid
26 May 42 First flight of Northrop P-61 Black Widow (US)
29 May 42 First flight of Commonwealth CA-12 Boomerang (AU)
30/31 May 42 RAF mounts first 1,000-bomber raid on Germany; 1,046 aircraft deployed against Cologne. The bomber stream, first used in 1,000-bomber raid on Cologne, is designed to overwhelm the German defences
3–4 June 42 Battle of Midway, although a US victory, brings stalemate. Japanese begin the war with 8 aircraft carriers, but new ships replace losses by end 1942. USA begins war with 6 full-size carriers but has not begun the building programme in time. After Guadalcanal only 2 carriers are left, being repaired. Thus heavy reliance on Henderson Field, Guadalcanal, as 'unsinkable aircraft carrier'. Feb to Nov 1943 therefore relative stalemate in the Pacific: US cannot advance without more carriers
25/26 June 42 RAF raid on Bremen ends 1,000-bomber raids for two years
26 June 42 First flight of Grumman F6F-3 Hellcat (US)
July 42 RAF 'Circus' operations: series of sweeps of up to 200 fighters, strafing targets of opportunity through northern France
5 July 42 First flight of Avro York (GB)

Avro York *(GB) first flew 5 July 1942*

3 July 42 First flight of Martin PB2M-1 Mars (US)
4 July 42 six American Bostons join raid on Dutch airfields, marking entry of USAAF into European theatre
30 July 42 First flight of Grumman Hellcat (US)
7 Aug US landings on Guadalcanal
11 Aug 42 RAF Pathfinder Force established to lead and mark bombing attacks
17 Aug 42 USAAF first heavy bomber attack on western European targets – Rouen-Scotteville marshalling yards in France
19 Aug 42 Dieppe raid. RAF losses are 106 aircraft, Luftwaffe 46
24 Aug 42 Battle of the Solomon Is. US carrier planes sink Japanese carrier and destroy 90 aircraft, only losing 20 planes and a carrier damaged
2 Sept 42 First flight of Hawker Tempest (GB)
7 Sept 42 First flight of Consolidated Vultee B-32 Dominator (US)
Sept 42 First flight of Douglas A-26 Invader (US)

Douglas A-26 Invader *(US) first flew Sept 1942*

GRUMMAN F6F HELLCAT first flight 30 July 1942

Powerplant: One 2,000hp Pratt & Whitney R-2800-10W
Primary role: Carrier- and land-based naval fighter
Dimensions: Wingspan 42 ft 10in (13.05m); length 33ft 7 in (10.23m)
Armament: Six fixed forward-firing 0.5in Browning machine guns or two 20mm cannon plus four 0.5in guns in the night fighter version; max bomb load 2,000lb (907kg) or six rocket projectiles underwing
Weights: Empty 9,238lb (4,190kg); loaded 15,413lb (6,991kg)
Speed: 380mph (611kph) max; 168mph (270kph) cruising
Range: 945 miles (1,520km)
Crew: 1
Production total (all marks): 12,275
Variants: XF6F-1, XF6F-2, XF6F-3, F6F-3, F6F-3N, F6F-3E, F6F-5, F6F-5N, F6F-5P, XF6F-6; Hellcat I, Hellcat II, Hellcat NF.II (RAF equivalents of F6F-3, F6F-5 and F6F-5N respectively).

The F6F was employed by the US and Royal Navies. Launched into action in August 1943, it quickly gained air supremacy in the Pacific for the US Navy. It also operated as a night fighter (F5F-3N and -5N). Hellcats were credited with over 5,000 enemy aircraft, including 75 per cent of all those downed by USN carrier pilots during the last two years of the war. Hellcats equipped fourteen Fleet Air Arm squadrons, 1,182 examples being supplied via Lend-Lease.

Boeing B-29 Superfortress *(US) first flew 21 Sept 1942*

21 Sept 42 First flight of Boeing B-29 Superfortress (US)
1 Oct 42 First flight of Bell P-59 Airacomet (US)
3 Oct 42 First successful launch of German A4 (V2) ballistic rocket at Peenemunde
26/27 Oct 42 Battle of Santa Cruz. Japanese carrier planes sink US carrier and destroy 70 aircraft, losing 100 planes and a carrier damaged
Nov 42 First flight of Kyushu K11W Shiragiku (J)
13 Nov 42 RAF ends 'Circus' sweeps over occupied Europe: over 600 aircraft have been lost to Luftwaffe's less than 200
15 Nov 42 First flight of Heinkel He 219 (G)
25 Nov 42 Start of Luftwaffe supply flights to German forces at Stalingrad
30 Nov 42 First flight of Mustang P-51B (US)
Dec 42 First flight of Messerschmitt Me 264 (G)
7 Dec 42 First flight of Bell P-63 Kingcobra (US)
22 Dec 1942 First flight of Fairey Firefly (GB)
27 Dec 42 First flight of Kawanishi N1K1-J Shiden (George) (J)

1943 First flight of Mitsubishi Ki-67 Hiryu (Peggy) (J)
1943 First flight of Yokosuka P1Y1 Ginga (Frances) (J)
Early 43 First flight of Junkers Ju 290/390 (G)
Spring 1943 Boeing B-17G (US). Backbone of

Fairey Firefly *(GB) first flew 22 Dec 1942*

Kawanishi N1K1-J Shiden *(George) (J) first flew 27 Dec 1942*

LOCKHEED SUPER CONSTELLATION first flight 9 January 1943

Powerplant: Four 2,200hp Wright R3350 Duplex Cyclone
Primary role: Passenger transport
Dimensions: Wingspan 123ft (37.49m); length 116ft 2in (35.5m)
Payload: 69–92 passengers
Weights: Loaded 137,500lb (62,368kg)
Speed: 370mph (596kph) max; 305mph (491kph) cruising
Range: 4,610 miles (7,420km)
Production total (all marks): Model 049/749 – 233; Model 1049 – 579; Model 1649 – 44

Originally the C-69 military transport, first flown on 9 January 1943, the 43–60-seat Lockheed L-049 Constellation entered commercial service with Pan American World Airways and Trans World Airways in early 1946 and also served with Air France, BOAC, KLM and Panair do Brash. The L-649 and L-74g Constellations gave increased passenger accommodation, engine power and range, and the L-1049 Super Constellation, with an 18ft 4in (5.59m) fuselage stretch, was developed from these models. This version, which entered service with Eastern Airlines on 17 Dec 1951, went through several variants and ended in the tip-tanked 3,400hp 83350-powered L-1049G 'Super G' and 109-seat passenger/cargo L-1049H marks. The L-1649A Starliner, first flown in 1956, featured an entirely new high-aspect ratio wing with increased fuel capacity, making non-stop transatlantic flights possible in either direction.

the US bomber offensive against Germany

Jan 43 Casablanca Conference approves Combined Bombing Offensive, USAAF striking by day, RAF by night

9 Jan 43 First flight of Lockheed Constellation (US). The Constellation has a pressurised cabin, cruises at 20,000ft at 280mph, with a top speed of 340mph. It can fly US coast-to-coast non-stop. In military service becomes C-69.

27 Jan 43 First USAAF heavy-bombers raid Germany. 8th Air Force aircraft attack Emden and Wilhelmshaven

30 Jan 43 Canadian Pacific Airlines founded

30/31 Jan 43 First operational use by the RAF of the radar navigational aid H2S during a bombing raid on Hamburg

31 Jan/2 Feb 43 Surrender of German forces at Stalingrad

2 Feb 43 Battle of Stalingrad ends in major German defeat. During the airlift the Luftwaffe lose approximately 475 transport planes and 200 fighters. The attempt to supply the trapped German army by air is a total failure

9 Feb 43 US forces secure Guadalcanal

March 43 First flight of Nakajima Ki-84 Hayate (Frank) (J)

May 43 Turning-point in Battle of the Atlantic

5/6 March 43 to 9/10 June 43 Battle of the Ruhr. Over 18,506 RAF sorties flown against the industrial towns and cities in the Ruhr valley, with 872 aircraft lost during 38-raid campaign. German nightfighters become increasingly effective

GLOSTER METEOR F.8 first flight 5 March 1943

Powerplant: Two 3,000lb (1,360kg) s.t. Rolls-Royce Derwent 8
Primary role: Day fighter
Dimensions: Wingspan 37ft 2in (11.32m); length 44ft 7in (13.58m)
Armament: Four 20mm cannon in nose, rockets or fuel tanks underwing
Weights: Empty 10,626lb (4,819kg); loaded 19,100lb (8.662kg)
Speed: 590mph (950kph) max at sea level
Range: 980 miles (1,578km)
Crew: 1
Variants: Day fighter, night fighter and reconnaissance variants

First flying on 5 March 1943, the Meteor Mk I entered service with No 816 Squadron in July 1944, becoming the RAF's first operational jet. The Mk I, with Welland engines, was soon followed into service by the Derwent-powered Meteor III and both saw wartime service, particularly against V-1s. The F.4, with uprated engines, was the mainstay of Fighter Command during the late 1940s, and from 1950 was replaced by the much improved F.8, which had uprated engines and a lengthened fuselage, giving greater fuel capacity and improved high-speed handling. F Mk 8s also had a new tail unit and an ejection seat as standard. The last front-line squadron disbanded in April 1957, but Meteors continued to serve as hacks and target tugs until 1982.

5 March 43 First flight of Gloster Meteor (GB)

11 March 43 US Fourteenth AF activated in China

7 April 43 Heavy Japanese air attacks against US bases in Solomons, made in attempt to forestall US threat to Rabaul

18 April 43 Admiral Yamamoto, Japan's protagonist of naval air power, killed when Mitsubishi GM4 'Betty' carrying him and his staff is ambushed by USAAF P-38 Lightnings over Bougainville. Decrypts reveal his route and timetable

May 43 First flight of Spitfire Mk XIV (GB)

May 43 MAC ships enter convoy service: merchant ships with flight deck fitted above the hold. CAM ships are merchant ships equipped with a catapult for a single aircraft

7 May 44 Allies take Tunis

11 May 43 BOAC begins service between UK and Lisbon

15 May 43 First flight of Nakajima C6N Saiun (Myrt) (J)

16/17 May 43 Dambusters Raid breaches Mohne and Eder dams in Ruhr using Wallis's bouncing bombs

23/24 May 43 826 RAF aircraft strike Düsseldorf

17 June 43 26 of 60 B-17 bombers lost on raid against Kiel, highlighting the problem of attacking targets beyond the range of contemporary fighters

July 43 Sicily invaded after a month of airstrikes on the island and southern Italy

July 43 First flight of Focke-Wulfe Fw 190D (G)

4-13 July Battle of Kursk

5 July 43 2,830 Axis warplanes are opposed by some 2,500 Soviet while supporting their respective armies during the great tank battle of Kursk

10 July–25 Aug Allied conquest of Sicily

18 July 43 Only US airship destroyed by enemy in WWII, US Navy airship *K-74* is shot down by a German submarine off the Florida coast

19 July 43 First flight of Curtiss XP-55 Ascender (US)

***Arado Ar 234 Blitz (Lightning)** (G) first flew 30 July 1943*

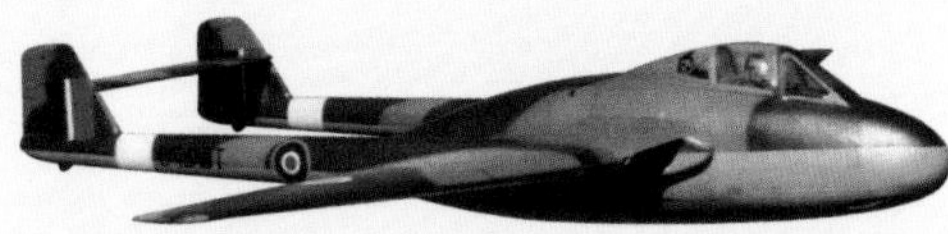

***De Havilland Vampire** (GB) first flew 20 Sept 1943*

21 July 43 First flight of Curtiss XP-62 (US)

30 July 43 First flight of Arado Ar 234 Blitz (Lightning) (G)

25 July–3 Aug 43 Used for the first time, the Allied anti-radar device 'Window' reduces RAF aircraft losses during the Hamburg raids from about 6 per cent to about 2.6 per cent

1 Aug 43 USAAF B-24 Liberators make low-level attack on Ploesti oil refineries in Romania; first USAAF low-level attack by heavy bombers against well-defended target, and its longest-range bombing mission to date. 54 out of 163 B-24 Liberators lost, but 40% of the refining capacity destroyed

17 Aug 43 USAAF raids on Schweinfurt and Regensburg. Germans take advantage of the limited escort range of the P-47s. 60 of 376 bombers are lost, 60 more damaged and scrapped.

17/18 Aug 43 First operational use by Luftwaffe of Henschel HS 293A-1 rocket-powered, remote-controlled, glide bomb, sinking British corvette *Egret*

17/18 Aug 43 RAF bombers attack German Peenemunde missile development base in the Baltic to destroy or delay development of advanced weapons

23/24 Aug 43 57 out of 719 RAF bombers lost while attacking Berlin. High casualty rate of 127 bombers on 2,262 sorties in four raids cause the RAF to call off its campaign against the German capital

24 July to 3 Aug 43 Hamburg bombed. Firestorm kills 40,000.

Sept 43 First flight of Kyushu Q1W Tokai (Lorna) (J)

Sept 43 First flight of Kawasaki Ki-96 (J)

3 Sept 43 Italy surrenders

9 Sept 43 Allies invade Italy

9 Sept 43 The 43,000-ton Italian Battleship *Roma* is sunk by a German Fritz X radio-controlled air-launched bomb

15/16 Sep 43 An RAF Lancaster makes first operational use of 'Tallboy' 12,000lb (5,443 kg) bomb on the Dortmund–Ems Canal

20 Sept 43 First flight of de Havilland Vampire (GB)

20 Sept 43 First flight of Consolidated Vultee PB4Y-2 Privateer (US)

22/23 Sept 43 RAF first uses spoof raid decoy system

9 Oct 43 USAAF successful strikes on Focke-Wulf plants in Anklam and Marienburg

14 Oct 43 'Black Tuesday' Schweinfurt raid. 60 US bombers lost of 290 sent

26 Oct 43 First flight of Dornier Do 335 Pfeil (Arrow) (G)

***Dornier Do 335 Pfeil (Arrow)** (G) first flew 26 Oct 1943*

31 Oct 43 US Navy gains first aerial victory by use of airborne interception radar, destroying a Japanese aircraft

5 Nov 43 US carrier aircraft strike a newly arrived Japanese naval task force at Rabaul, badly damaging seven cruisers and two destroyers, forcing the Japanese force to withdraw

17 Nov 43 First flight of Mustang P-51D (see page 88) (US)

18/19 Nov 43 to 25 March: Battle of Berlin Over 9,000 RAF sorties flown against Berlin, with more than 500 aircraft lost during the 16-raid campaign. The Luftwaffe is severely weakened in both aircraft and experienced pilots and Berlin ruined. After 8 March the Luftwaffe cannot defend Berlin adequately: 9 March 300 B-17s raid Berlin without fighter opposition. Germany's experienced pilots are being lost. Berlin is meanwhile pulverised from both west and east as the Russians advance

Dec 43 First flight of Kawasaki Ki-64 (J)

Dec 43 The TR-1 (VDR), first Soviet turbojet engine, reportedly completes its offical bench running tests

Dec 43 P-51 Mustang long-range fighter air cover is available for daylight operations over the whole of Germany

2 Dec 43 First flight of Grumman F7F-3N Tigercat (US)

***Grumman F7F-3N Tigercat** (US) first flew 2 Dec 1943*

16/17 Dec 43 RAF begin attacking V-1 sites in France

Winter 43 First flight of Messerschmitt Bf 109K (G)

1944 General fighter type deployments, based upon range: Spitfires cover the English Channel and North Sea; P-47s reach into Germany; P-38s fly beyond the Ruhr; P-51s with drop-tanks reach Berlin

1944 Raids do not stop German production but draw fighters and artillery away from the battle fronts to defend the homeland. And by Aug 1944 Germany's petroleum production has been devastated, placing constraints on both ground and air operations. Germany's transport network is being shut down and the Ruhr area, maintaining high output despite the bombing, is becoming isolated from the rest of Germany

LOCKHEED P-80 SHOOTING STAR first flight 9 January 1944

Powerplant: One 3,850lb (1,746kg) s.t. General Electric J33-GE-9 or I-16
Primary role: Fighter/fighter-bomber
Dimensions: Wingspan 38ft 10½in (11.85m); length 34 ft 6in (10.52m)
Armament: Six 0.5in machine guns, plus provision for ten 5in (127mm) rockets or two 1,000lb (454kg) or 500lb (227kg) bombs underwing
Weights: Loaded 14,000lb (6,350kg)
Speed: 550mph (885kph) max at sea level
Range: 625 miles (1,000km)
Crew: 1

The P-80 originated with Bell's P-59B plans for a single I-16 turbojet aspirated by wing-root inlets, but this project was handed over to Lockheed when Bell ran out of time. Lockheed produced the XCP-80 prototype, a clean low-wing monoplane with a de Havilland Goblin turbojet, in 143 days, and the aircraft had its first flight in January 1944. To avoid lengthy licence-production of the Goblin, the engine was replaced with the I-40 (J33), producing the XP-80A, which first flew in June 1944. Orders were placed for thirteen YP-80As and 5,000 P-80As, but only two arrived in a combat theatre and orders were cut back to 917 after World War II. By the late 1940s Shooting Stars equipped twelve fighter squadrons in the United States, and they were deployed to the war in Korea. The first jet-versus-jet aircraft battle took place on 8 November 1950 in which an F/P-80 shot down a MiG-15. The P-80 was the first turbojet-powered aircraft accepted for USAAF combat units.

Jan 44 First flight of Junkers 388 V2 (G)
22 Jan 44 Anzio landing in Italy
4 Jan 44 First high-altitude mine-dropping operation, by an RAF Halifax bomber off Brest, France
6 Jan 44 First flight of McDonnell XP-67 Bat (US)
9 Jan 44 First flight of Lockheed P-80 Shooting Star (US)
2 Feb 44 First flight of Replublic XP-72 (US)
15 Feb 44 The Allies heavily bomb the historic monastery of Monte Cassino, turning it into a ruin

***Curtiss SC-1 Seahawk** (US) first flew 16 Feb 1944*

16 Feb 44 First flight of Curtiss SC-1 Seahawk (US)
21 Feb 44 Start of 'Big Week' Allied bombing offensive: 20,000 tons of bombs are dropped on Brunswick, Schweinfurt, Augsburg, Regensburg, etc. But nearly 400 bombers are lost for some 500 German fighters shot down
26 Feb 44 600 Soviet aircraft attack Helsinki, Finland
March 44 First flight of Kawasaki Ki-102 (Randy) (J)
1 May 44 Allied aircraft initiate a major air offensive against the rail/transport system of occupied Europe
5 March 44 Brig Gen Orde Wingate's special force lands at 'Broadway' North Burma, in a night glider operation
6 March 44 In first major USAAF attack on Berlin a force of 660 bombers lose 69 of their number and eleven escorting fighters
10 March 44 First flight of Blohm/Voss Bv 238 (G)
30/31 March 44 RAF suffers its worst raid loss of the war in a raid on Nuremberg losing 96 of 795 aircraft involved, losses of 12%, 545 men (greater than Fighter Command's losses in Battle of Britain)
1 April 44 First flight of Bell P-77 (US)
23 April 44 First flight of Northrop XP-56 Black Bullet (US)

***Blohm/Voss Bv 238** (G) first flew 10 March 1944*

***Kawasaki Ki-108** (J) first flew June 1944*

June 44 First flight of Kawasaki Ki-108 (J)
June 44 Arado AR 234, world's first jet bomber, enters service
6 June 44 First flight of Lockheed XP-58 Chain Lightning (GB)
6 June 44 D-Day landings in Normandy by the Allies, preceded by airdrops and supported by massive Allied air force operations
7 June 44 The first Allied airstrip to be completed in Normandy following the D-Day landings becomes operational at Asnelles northeast of Bayeux

***Avro Lincoln** (GB) first flew 9 June 1944*

9 June 44 First flight of Avro Lincoln (GB)
V-1 'Flying Bombs': 6,725 V-1s reach the coast of England, and over half are then destroyed by the air defenses. 2,340 reach London and kill over 5,000 people. The Germans then launch some 750 V-1s by air, but only 1 in 10 hits London area

13 June 44 First German V-l 'flying bombs' launched from France against British targets

15 June 44 USAAF B-29 Superfortresses make first attack on Japan flying from bases in China. 18 bombers out of 70 lost

15 Jun 44 US carriers provide massive air support for forces landing on Saipan, Mariana Is

19/20 June 44 Battle of the Philippine Sea – the 'Great Marianas Turkey Shoot'. 219 Japanese aircraft lost against 29 US. This breaks the back of Japanese naval air power

15 July 44 First flight of Vough XF5U-1 Skimmer(US)

17 July 44 US FORCES LAND ON GUAM

17 July 44 First operational use of napalm incendiary material, by USAAF on a fuel depot at Coutances, France

20 July 44 Deployment completed of barrage of anti-aircraft guns around England's south coast for defence against German V-l flying bombs

De Havilland Hornet *(GB) first flew 28 July 1944*

28 July 44 First flight of de Havilland Hornet (GB)

Aug 44 First flight of Junkers Ju 388 (G)

4 Aug 44 A Gloster Meteor flies alongside a V-l and destroys it by using the aircraft's wing tip and forcing it into the ground

4 Aug 44 Radio-controlled B-17s, each with 20,000lb (9,072kg) of TNT, are launched against German V2 sites under construction in France

16 Aug 44 Messerschmitt Me 163B-1 Komet rocket-powered interceptor fighters used operationally for the first time

24 August 44 First flight of Focke-Wulfe Ta 152 H D (G)

28 Aug 44 First jet-powered aircraft to be shot down in air combat, an Me 262

Grumman F8F-1 Bearcat *(US) first flew 31 Aug 1944*

31 Aug 44 First flight of Grumman F8F-1 Bearcat (US)

4 Sept 44 End of German V-1 attacks on Britain

8 Sept 44 German V-2 ballistic rockets land on Paris and London

10 Sept 44 First flight of Fairchild C-82 (C-119 Packet) (US)

Fairchild C-82 (C-119 Packet) *(US) first flew 10 Sept 1944*

BOEING STRATOCRUISER first flight 8 July 1947

Powerplant: Four 3,500hp Pratt & Whitney 8-4360-83 Wasp Major
Primary role: Passenger transport
Dimensions: Wingspan 141 ft 3in (43.05m); length 110ft 4in (33.62m)
Payload: 61 passengers/23,640lb (10,722kg)
Weights: Empty 83,500lb (37,874kg); loaded 148,000lb (67,131kg)
Speed: 375mph (604kph) max; 340mph (377kph) cruising
Range: 4,200 miles (6,762km)
Production total (all marks): 56 (civilian models)

A development of the C-97 military transport, the Boeing 377 Stratocruiser first flew on 8 July 1947. In 1949 it entered service with Pan American World Airways on North Atlantic 'Presidential' routes, and also served with American Overseas Airlines, Northwest Orient Airlines, United Airlines and the British Overseas Airways Corporation on long-haul routes. The Stratocruiser offered new standards of comfort, with single- and double-berth sleeping accommodation in two-deck pressurised cabins. It was the inspiration for Aero Spacelines Corporation's Guppy and Super Guppy oversize cargo aircraft.

17-26 Sept 44 Operation 'Market Garden', Arnhem airborne assault: Three Allied airborne divisions are dropped to capture three bridges as a precursor to the crossing of the Rhine. 10,000 men of 1st Airborne Division land; only 2,000 escape

Oct 44 First flight of Yokosuka MXY-7 Baka (J)

1 Oct 44 First flight of Lavochkin La-7 (USSR)

23 Oct 44 Start of Battle of Leyte Gulf during which Japanese begin the use of Kamikaze attacks by suicide planes. US navy carriers sink four Japanese aircraft carriers

3 Nov 44 Start of Japanese 'Fu-Go Weapon' (balloon bomb) campaign against USA; balloons carrying incendiary material released in Japan and carried by jet streams across the Pacific

12 Nov 44 The German battleship *Tirpitz* is sunk by RAF using 12,000lb 'Tallboy' bombs

15 Nov 44 First flight of Boeing C-97 Stratofreighter (Stratocruiser) (US)

24 Nov 44 The first B-29 raid mounted on Japan from bases in the Marianas

25 Nov 44 The carriers USS *Hancock*, *Intrepid*, *Cabot* and *Essex* and the battleships USS *Colorado* and *Maryland* are struck by kamikaze aircraft off Leyte

27 Nov 44 First flight of Boeing XP8 B-1 (US)

4 Dec 44 First flight of Bristol Brigand (GB)

6 Dec 44 First flight of Heinkel He 162 Salamander (G)

***Heinkel He 162** (G) first flew 6 Dec 1944*

8 Dec 44 US bombers carry out a continous 72-day air bombardment of Iwo Jima in preparation for the Marine landings

14 Dec 44 First flight of Short Shetland (GB)

16 Dec 44 Carrier aircraft from the British Pacific Fleet attack Japanese oil facilities on Sumatra

16 Dec–28 Jan 44 German Ardennes offensive: 'Battle of the Bulge'

1945 First flight of Pilatus P-2 (SWI)
In Pacific, initial B-29 daylight raids disappoint.

Jan 1945 LeMay mounts area bombing with incendiaries, from low-flying aircraft with all but the tail armament removed to increase speed and bomb load

1 Jan 45 Luftwaffe's last major attack, Operation 'Bodenplatte', to cause as much destruction as possible of Allied aircraft in a surprise attack on Allied airfields: 900 German aircraft destroy 300 Allied, most on the ground

4–9 Jan 45 The American Seventh Fleet, off Formosa and Luzon, is subject to heavy Kamikaze attacks. One escort carrier is sunk, three battleships among the other ships badly damaged

26 Jan 45 First flight of McDonnell FD-1/FH-1 Phantom (US)

1 Feb 45 First flight of Kawasaki Ki-100 (J)

7 Feb 45 First flight of Consolidated-Vultee P-81 (US)

11 Feb 45 First flight of Convair XP-81 (US)

12 Feb 45 First flight of Morane Saulnier M.S.472 Vanneau (F)

13–15 Feb 45 RAF and USAAF night and day attacks on Dresden, Germany, create a devastating fire storm and huge loss of life

21 Feb 44 Kamikazes sink an escort carrier and badly damage a fleet carrier off Iwo Jima

***Hawker Sea Fury** (GB) first flew 21 Feb 1945*

21 Feb 45 First flight of Hawker Sea Fury (GB)

25 Feb 45 First flight of Bell P-83 (US)

27 Feb 45 First flight of Curtiss XF15C-1 (US)

28 Feb 45 First flight of Bachem Ba 349 Natter (Viper) (G). The German test pilot is killed after the first manned flight test of the vertical take-off Bachem Ba 349 Natter (Viper) rocket-powered target-defence interceptor

March 45 First flight of Nakajima Ki-115 Tsurugi (J)

9/10 March 45 First major US incendiary raid on Japan, a low-level, night-time attack by 333 Marianas-based B-29s. The attack devastates 16 square miles of Tokyo, killing 84,000 people in the ensuing firestorm.

11–19 Mar 45 Three separate nights of US incendiary raids on Nagoya, Osaka and Kobe

14 Mar 45 First operational use of 22,000lb (9,979 kg) 'Grand Slam' bomb, by a Lancaster on the Bielefeld Viaduct, Germany

***Douglas BT2D-1 Skyraider** (US) first flew 18 March 1945*

18 Mar 45 First flight of Douglas BT2D-1 Skyraider (US)

18 Mar 45 heavy raid on Berlin by 1,221 bombers, 632 fighters attacked by 37 German jets with new air-to-air rockets

20 Mar 45 The last attack on the United Kingdom by the Luftwaffe, sortie made by night

21 Mar 45 First sortie by Japanese Yokosuka Ohka purpose-built suicide aircraft

6–7 April 45 During US invasion of Okinawa, massive Kamikaze attacks on invasion fleet hit 28 ships sinking three. Further attacks follow over the next weeks

7 April 45 Giant Japanese battleship, *Yamato*, sunk by US Navy carrier-based aircraft

7 April 45 The first P-51 Mustang escort operation, from Iwo Jima, for B-29 attacks on Japan

15 April 45 First flight of North American P-82 Twin Mustang (US)

North American P-82 Twin Mustang *(US) first flew 15 April 1945*

29 April 45 RAF Bomber Command airdrops 6,000 tons of food and clothing to the Dutch people

May 45 First flight of Auster A.O.P.6 (GB)

Auster A.O.P.6 *(GB) first flew May 1945*

4–8 May 45 Official surrenders of German forces

17 May 45 First flight of Lockheed P2V-5 Neptune (US)

14 June 45 First flight of Avro Tudor (GB)

22 June 45 First flight of Vickers Viking (GB)

Lockheed P2V-5 Neptune *(US) first flew 17 May 1945*

Vickers Viking *(GB) first flew 22 June 1945*

5 July 45 PanAm and TWA authorised to operate over North Atlantic

21 July 45 Mustangs and Spitfires decimate Japanese forces as they attempt to cross Sittang River in Burma

3 Aug 45 First flight of Kyushu J7W Shinden (J)

5 Aug 45 627 B-29 Superfortress bombers attack Hachioji, Nagaoki, Mito and Toyama, the last named being totally destroyed

6 Aug 45 B-29 Superfortress *Enola Gay* drops world's first operational atomic bomb, 'Little Boy' over Hiroshima. 42 square miles of the city are devastated, killing 90,000 Japanese outright and seriously injuring 37,000

7 Aug 45 First flight of Nakajima J8N1 Kikka (J)

9 Aug 45 B-29 Superfortress *Bock's Car* drops the second operational atomic bomb, 'Fat Man' over Nagasaki, killing 40,000 Japanese outright and seriously injuring 60,000

15 Aug 45 The last, but abortive, Kamikaze mission is flown by seven Japanese aircraft against allied forces at Okinawa

2 Sept 45 Formal Japanese surrender aboard US battleship *Missouri* in Tokyo Bay. Japanese forces on the mainland of South-East Asia surrender formally in Singapore on 12 Sept

12 Sept 45 First flight of Northrop XP-79B Flying Ram (US)

25 Sept 45 First flight of de Havilland D.H.104 Dove (Devon) (GB)

29 Sept 45 Swissair resume flights to London, the first post-war flights

22 Oct 45 Air France re-opens Paris to London route

22 Oct 45 SABENA resumes commercial flights from Brussels to London
20 Nov 45 First flight of Saab-91B Safir (SK50) (SW)
1 Dec 45 First flight of Grumman AF-2 Guardian (US)
2 Dec 45 First flight of Bristol 170 Freighter (Wayfarer) (GB)

***Bristol 170 Freighter** (GB) first flew 2 Dec 1945*

4 Dec 45 TWA Constellation sets commercial record for Atlantic crossing Washington–Paris
7 Nov 45 World speed record: 975.67 km/h/606.25 mph by Gp Capt Wilson (Gloster Meteor)
8 Dec 45 First flight of Bell Model 47 (US)

1946 First flight of Yakovlev Yak-18 (USSR)
1 Jan 46 Heathrow handed over to Ministry of Civil Aviation
19 Jan 46 First unpowered flight of Bell X-1 (US)

***Bell X-1** (US) first flew 19 Jan 1946*

15 Feb 46 First flight of Douglas DC-6 (US)
28 Feb 46 First flight of Republic P-84 Thunderjet (US)
March 46 French aircraft strafe and bomb Viet Minh forces
8 March 46 Bell Model 47 receives Type Approval Certificate for a commercial helicopter
31 March 46 First flight of Percival Prentice (GB)
9 April 46 First flight of Handley Page Hastings (GB)
24 April 46 First flight of Yakovlev Yak-15 (USSR)

***Mikoyan MiG-9** (USSR) first flew 24 April 1946*

24 April 46 First flight of Mikoyan MiG-9 (USSR)
17 May 46 First flight of Douglas XB-43 (US)
19 May 46 First flight of Handley Page Marathon (GB)
22 May 46 First flight of de Havilland Canada Chipmunk (CA)
June 46 First flight of Martin B-48 (US)
6 June 46 First flight of Aerocentre NC.3020 Belphegor (F)
7 June 46 First flight of Short Sturgeon (GB)
25 June 46 First flight of Northrop XB-35 (US)
1 July 46 'Operation Crossroads', a US B-29 bomber drops an atom bomb experimentally on 73 naval vessels at Bikini Atoll
21 July 46 First flight of McDonnell FH-1 Phantom (US)
24 July 46 First manned ejection from an aircraft by a Martin Baker ejection seat
27 July 46 First flight of Supermarine Attacker (GB)
1 Aug 46 Birth of BEA (British European Airways)
8 Aug 46 First flight of Convair B-36 (US)
2 Oct 46 First flight of Vought F6U Pirate (US)
1 Nov 46 The US Navy non-rigid airship *XM-1* makes a flight of 170hr 3 min, which is a world record for flight unsustained by any form of refueling
7 Nov 46 First flight of Lockheed Constitution (US)
16 Nov 46 First flight of Saab 90-A-2 Scandia (SW)
22 Nov 46 First flight of Martin 2-0-2 (US)
25 Nov 46 400 French paratroops are dropped north of Haiphong to recapture the airfield at Cat Minh, heavy fighting breaks out
12 Dec 46 First flight of Westland Wyvern (GB)

***Westland Wyvern** (GB) first flew 12 Dec 1946*

1947 First flight of Fokker S.11 Instructor (HO)
1947 VOR (Very high-frequency Omnidirectional Range) transmitting stations aid navigation
Jan 47 First flight of Martin P4M-1 Mercator (US)
Jan 47 First flight of Scottish Aviation Pioneer (GB)
6 Jan 47 First flight of Ilyushin Il-12 (Coach) (USSR)
11 Jan 47 First flight of McDonnell F2H-2 Banshee (US)
Feb 47 Aden. British aircraft are used to help subdue rebels in the Protectorate. The Army, RAF and Royal Navy aircraft give support to ground forces during the protracted guerrilla war which continues until independance is gained, Nov 1967
10 Feb 47 First flight of Dassault M.D.315 Flamant (F)
10 March 47 First flight of Saab 21R (J 21R) (SW)
16 Mar 47 French Naval Dauntless SBD-5 aircraft carried by the French carrier *Dixmude* strafe and bomb Viet Minh forces
17 March 47 First flight of North American B-45 Tornado (US)
3 April 47 First flight of Convair B-46 (US)
5 May 47 Alitalia begins service (Catania to Rome)
28 May 47 First flight of Douglas Skystreak (US)
17 June 47 First flight of Yakolev Yak-23 (USSR)
19 June 47 World speed record: 1,003.60 km/h/623.61 mph by Col Boyd (F-80 Shooting Star)
30 June 47 First flight of Vickers Valetta (GB)
2 July 47 First flight of Mikoyan MiG-15 (USSR)
10 July 47 Airspeed Ambassador (Elizabethan) (GB)

***Saunders-Roe SR.A/1** (GB) first flew 16 July 1947*

16 July 47 First flight of Saunders-Roe SR.A/1 (GB)
24 July 47 First flight of Ilyushin Il-22 (USSR)
24 July 47 First flight of Bristol Sycamore (GB)
27 July 47 First flight of Tupolev Tu-12 (USSR)
15 Aug 47–31 Dec 49 On gaining independence, and following the partition of India and Pakistan, fighting immediately breaks out. The Royal Indian Air Force is divided between the two countries and combat and support missions are flown

***Bristol Sycamore** (GB) first flew 24 July 1947*

***Mikoyan MiG-15** (USSR) first flew 2 July 1947*

16 Aug 47 First flight of de Havilland Canada DHC-2 Beaver (CA)

25 Aug 47 World speed record: 1,047.33 km/h/650.78 mph by Maj Carl, USMC (Douglas Skystreak)

31 Aug 47 First flight of Antonov An-2 (USSR)

2 Sept 47 First flight of Hawker Sea Hawk (GB)

18 Sep 47 United States Air Force (USAF) founded; it becomes an independent service within US armed services

Oct 47 French Operation 'Lea', a 15,000 troop deployment, is supported by Naval Dauntless SBD-5 aircraft carried by the French carrier *Dixmude*, attacking Viet Minh forces

Oct 1947 First flight of Grumman SA-16A Albatross (US)

1 Oct 47 First flight of North American F-86 Sabre (US)

14 Oct 47 First flight of Bell X-1A (US)

14 Oct 47 Capt Charles Yeager in the Bell X-1 rocket-powered research aircraft becomes the first in the world to exceed the speed of sound in level flight 1,078km/h (670mph) at 12,800m (42,000ft)

21 Oct 47 First flight of Northrop B-49 (US)

Nov 47 First flight of Cessna Model 170 series (US)

2 Nov 47 First flight of Hughes H-4 Hercules (US)

2 Nov 47 Howard Hughes lifts off in his 180-ton flying boat, the Hercules (Spruce Goose), flying just one mile. It is intended to carry 700 passengers

24 Nov 47 First flight of Grumman F9F-5 Panther (US)

Dec 47–summer 48 Pakistani Tempest II fighters are in action in the Khyber Pass area in support of ground forces suppressing a revolt

17 Dec 47 First flight of Boeing B-47 Stratojet (US)

22 Jan 48 First flight of Short Sealand (GB)

15 Feb 48 First flight of Curtiss F-87 Blackhawk (US)

9 Mar 48 First flight of Gloster E.1/44 (GB)

23 Mar 48 First flight of Douglas F3D Skyknight (US)

***Douglas F3D Skynight** (US) first flew 23 March 1948*

3 May 49 Newly formed Air-India makes its inaugural London to Bombay service

4 May 48 First flight of Martin P5M-2 Marlin (US)

ISRAELI WAR OF INDEPENDENCE

15 May 1948–20 July 1949

20 May 48 First action between Israeli Air Force against Arab Air forces.

1 June 48 The first post-war pressurised airliner enters service in US with American Airlines, the Convair 240

2 July 48 First flight of North American AJ-2 Savage (US)

***Grumman F9F-5 Panther** (US) first flew 24 Nov 1947*

NORTH AMERICAN F-86 SABRE first flight 1 October 1947

Powerplant: (F-86F) One 5,970lb (1,255kg) s.t. J47-GE-27
Primary role: Fighter and fighter-bomber
Dimensions: (F-86F) Wingspan 37ft 1in (11.3m); length 37ft 6in (11.43m)
Armament: (F-86F) Six 0.5in Colt-Browning M-3, plus two 1,000lb (454kg) bombs or sixteen 5in (126.5mm) rockets
Weights: (F-86F) Empty 10,950lb (4,966kg), loaded 17,000lb (7,710kg)
Speed: (F-86F) 690mph (1,110kph) max
Range: (F-86F) 1,270 miles (2,045km)
Crew: 1
Production total (all marks): 9,502 (including 300 Mitsubishi-built)
Variants: F-86A–L, CL-13 and Orenda Sabre (Canadian), and CA-26 and Avon Sabre (Australian)

Developed as Army and Navy fighters, with versions as all-weather interceptors. The land-based prototypes adopted swept-back wings and tail in 1945, but Navy prototypes were ordered on 1 January 1945 as conventional straight-wing aircraft. The first flight of the XJF-1 was made on 27 November 1946 and that of the XP-86 on 1 October 1947; service delivery (F-86A) took place in December 1948. The first flight of the all-weather YF-86D was made on 22 December 1949. In 1949 the XP-86 with the 5,000lb TG-190 (J47) engine broke the world speed record at 671mph (1,080kph). Despite inferior climb and altitude performance, the F-86E, with slatted wing and powered 'flying tail', and the F-86F, with extended leading edges and small fences, outmatched the MiG-15 in the Korean War. Innovations such as an autopilot and radar-directed collision-course interception appeared in the complex F-86D interceptor, whereas the simpler K, a stern-chase interceptor with guns, was mass-produced by a consortium in Italy and Germany. USAF Sabres were completed by the powerful H model, but Navy counterparts soon appeared – the FJ-2 (resembling a cannon-armed F) and the more powerful FJ-3 and -4 (F-1C and E). Boasting a toss-bombing system, FR probe, new avionics and increased fuel capacity, the AF-1E was the peak of Sabre development. More Sabres have been produced than any other Western military aircraft since 1945 except the Huey helicopter. As well as Australian variants and Canadair's Cl-13 series (originally licensed E and F models, of which 430 were given by Mutual Aid funds to the RAF), the aircraft was also used by Argentina, Bangladesh, Bolivia, Burma, Ethiopia, Indonesia, Japan, South Korea, Malaysia, Pakistan, Peru, the Philippines, Portugal, Saudi Arabia, South Africa, Taiwan, Thailand, Tunisia, Venezuela and Yugoslavia.

VICKERS VISCOUNT first flight 16 July 1948

Powerplant: Four 1,990shp Rolls-Royce Dart 525
Primary role: Passenger transport
Dimensions: Wingspan 93ft 8½in (28.57m); length 85ft 5in (26.03m)
Payload: 65–71 passengers/14,500lb (6,577kg) freight
Weights: Empty 41,565lb (18,853kg); loaded 72,500lb (32,885kg)
Speed: 350mph (563kph) cruising
Range: 1,760 miles (2834km)
Production total (all marks): 444

The original V630, designed as a 32-passenger airliner for British European Airways, first flew on 16 July 1948. In 1950 the prototype Viscount was launched as the world's first passenger-carrying turboprop, serving the London, Paris and Edinburgh routes. The production Viscount 700 carried 40–53 passengers and was powered by four 1,540shp Rolls-Royce RDa3 Dart 505 turboprops. The Viscount 802, developed for BEA and first flying on 27 July 1956, carried 65–71 passengers in a longer cabin and was powered by 1,742shp Dart 510 engines. The more powerful 800-series Viscounts followed, ending in the Viscount 810. The type also served with Capital Airlines, Trans Canada Airlines, British Air Ferries, Guernsey Airways and Virgin Airways.

6 July 48 First attacks by RAF Spitfires against communist insurgents during the Malayan Emergency, which continues until 31 July 1960. Brigands and then Hornets are flown with some success. Resupply from the air is often a necessity, Dakotas, Valettas and later Hastings being extensively used

10 July 48 First flight of Boulton Paul Balliol (GB)

16 July 48 First flight of Vickers Viscount (GB)

Aug 48 First flight of Lavochkin LA-15 (USSR)

8 Aug 48 First flight of Ilyushin Il-28 (Beagle) (USSR)

16 Aug 48 First flight of Northrop F-89 Scorpion (US)

23 Aug 48 First flight of McDonnell F-85 Goblin (US)

1 Sept 48 First flight of Saab J-29 (SW)

15 Sept 1948 World speed record: 1,079.61 km/h/670.84 mph by Maj Johnson (F86A Sabre)

18 Sept 48 First flight of Consolidated-Vultee F-92A (US)

29 Sept 48 First flight of Chance Vought F7U-3 Cutlass (US)

Oct 48 First flight of Saunders-Roe Skeeter (GB)

20 Oct 48 First flight of McDonnell F-88 Voodoo (US)

2 Dec 48 First flight of Beech Model 45 Mentor (US)

3 Dec 48 First flight of Handley Page Hermes IV (GB)

7 Dec 48 First flight of Cierva Air Horse (GB)

***Beech Model 45 Mentor** (US) first flew 2 Dec 1948*

1949 First flight of Cessna L-19A Bird Dog (US)

7 Jan 49 While on patrol the RAF lose five fighters, four to Israeli fighters and one to ground fire in unprovoked attack by Israeli forces

12 Jan 49 First flight of S.E. Armagnac (F)

15 Feb 49 First flight of Bréguet 763 Deux-Ponts (F)

26 Feb-2 Mar 49 A B-50 makes first non-stop flight around the world with the aid of inflight refuelling

28 Feb 49 First flight of Dassault M.D.450 Ouragan (F)

5 Mar 49 First flight of Curtiss XF-87 (Model 29A) Blackjet (US)

9 March 49 First flight of Avro Shackleton (GB)

16 April 49 Peak day of Berlin Airlift; 12,940 tons of supplies in 1,398 sorties

21 April 49 First flight of Leduc O.10 (F)

***Avro Shackleton** (GB) first flew 9 Mar 1949*

3 May 49 Aerolineas Argentinas founded
13 May 49 First flight of English Electric Canberra (GB)
4 June 49 First flight of Lockheed F-90 (US)
10 June 49 First flight of Nord 2501 Noratlas (F)
July 49 First flight of Vickers Varsity (GB)
July 49 US supplies P-63C Kingcobras and later F6F-5 Hellcats to French Airforces fighting in Indo-China
27 July 49 First flight of de Havilland Comet (GB)
Aug 49 First flight of Auster Autocar (GB)
10 Aug 49 First flight of Avro Canada C-102 Jetliner (CA)
2 Sept 49 First flight of de Havilland Venom (GB)
4 Sept 49 First flight of Bristol Brabazon (GB)
4 Sept 49 First flight of Avro 707A/707B/707C (GB)
26 Sept 49 First flight of North American T-28 Trojan (US)
29 Sept 49 First flight of Fairey Gannet (GB)
30 Sept 49 Berlin Airlift ends Over 2.3 million tons of food, fuel and equipment carried into the city by aircraft
Oct 49 First flight of Martin B-51 (US)
14 Oct 49 First flight of Chase/Fairchild C-123 Provider (Avitruc) (US)
Nov 49 First flight of Beech L-23A Twin Bonanza (US)

Sikorsky S-55 *(US) first flew 7 Nov 1949*

7 Nov 49 *First flight of* Sikorsky S-55 (US)
18 Nov 49 A Douglas Globemaster flies non-stop from the USA to the UK with 102 passengers and crew, the largest number to date
27 Nov 49 First flight of Douglas C-74 (C-124A) Globemaster (US)
29 Dec 49 First flight of Supermarine 510 (GB)

1950 First flight of Martin 4-0-4 (US)
1950 First flight of Piasecki HUP-1 Retriever (US), twin rotor helicopter
1950 First flight of SIPA S.12 (F)
1950 Helicopters begin to be increasingly used during Malayan Emergency for assault and casualty evacuation

English Electric B-57 Canberra *(GB) first flew 13 May 1949*

DE HAVILLAND COMET first flight 27 July 1949

Wingspan: 35.05m (115ft 0in)
Overall Length: 28.35m (93ft 0in)
Powerplant: 4 x de Havilland Ghost 50 Mk 2, 2268 kg (5,000 lb) st each
Payload: 44 passengers
Max weight: 52164 kg (115,000 lb)
Cruising speed: 490 mph at 40,000 ft
Endurance: about 2,000 miles with maximum payload

World's first jetliner, originally designed in 1943. Initial tailless plan discarded for design of conventional but advanced 32-passenger aeroplane, capable of high-altitude North Atlantic crossing. First flight in July 1949. The Comet 1(9 built) entered service with BOAC in May 1952, followed by the Comet 1A with greater power and weight (15), the 44-seat Comet 2 with Rolls-Royce Avons (15) and the proposed 78-seat Comet 3 with more fuel and uprated Avon RA.16 engines. Comet wasgrounded after two metal fatigue crashes, resulting in order-cancellations, and the UK's loss of four-year jetliner lead. Revized 81-seat Comet 4 with Avon Mk 524 engines (28 built) arrived in 1958, then the 99-seat Comet 4B (18) and finally the long-range Comet 4C (28).

MIKOYAN MiG-17 (FRESCO) first flight 14 January 1950

Powerplant: (-17, -17P) One 5,952lb (2,700kg) thrust Klimov VK-1 single-shaft centrifugal turbojet
Primary role: Fighter
Dimensions: Wingspan 31ft 0in (9.45m); length 36ft 3in (11.0m)
Armament: (-17) One 37mm and two 23mm NS-23 cannon
Weights: Empty 9,040lb (4,100kg); loaded 14,770lb (6,700kg)
Speed: 711mph (1,145kph) max at 9,850ft (3,000m)
Range: 913 miles (1,470km) with drop tanks
Crew: 1
Production total (all marks): 5,000+ (including 1,000+ produced in China)
Variants: MiG-17, -17P, -17F, -17PF, -17PFU, Lim-5P, Lim-5M, S-104, F-4

Design began in 1949 as a new fighter, to overcome the MiG-15's poor performance at high speeds. With new, thinner wings, a different section and planform, three fences, no taper and an inboard sweep of 47 degrees, MiG-17s showed vastly improved high-Mach behaviour, and may have been able to produce a sonic bang on diving. The rear fuselage was longer than the -15's, and systems and equipment were also new, although the VK-1 engine was originally unchanged. Variants included the -17P, a limited all-weather version with longer nose housing the same Izumrud ('Scan Odd') AI radar and ranging avionics as in the MiG-19, production beginning in 1958; the -17F, the most important sub-type with enlarged rectangular airbrakes returned to the tail instead of aft of the wing as in some earlier versions (in Poland this was manufactured as the Lim-5P – the SM being a rough-field close-support version with larger tyres and drag chute – in Czechoslovakia it was made as the S-104 and in China it appeared as the F-4); the -17PF, the afterburning all-weather interceptor; and the -17PFU, the final model, with guns removed and wing pylons for four beam-riding 'Alkali' air-to-air missiles. Many -17Fs remained in use to the mid-1970s. Mig-17s were used by Afghanistan, Albania, Algeria, Angola, Bulgaria, China, Cuba, Czechoslovakia, Egypt, East Germany, Guinea, Hungary, Indonesia, Iraq, Kampuchea, North Korea, Mali, Morocco, Nigeria, Poland, Romania, Somalia, South Yemen, the Soviet Union, Sri Lanka, Sudan, Syria, Tanzania, Uganda, Vietnam and Yemen.

***Lockheed F-94C Starfire** (US) first flew 18 Jan 1950*

14 Jan 50 First flight of Mikoyan MiG-17 (USSR)

18 Jan 50 First flight of Lockheed F-94C Starfire (US)

19 Jan 50 First flight of Avro Canada CF-100 Canuck (CA)

23 Feb 50 First flight of Percival Provost T.1 (GB)

Mar 50 RAF and RAAF Lincoln bombers begin area bombing to assist ground forces in the subjugation of communist insurgents during Malayan Emergency

13 Mar 50 QANTAS makes its first (survey) flight across the S. Pacific from Sydney to Valparaiso, Chile

8 April 50 A US Navy Privateer is shot down by Soviet fighters while on reconnaissance over the Baltic

30 April 50 First flight of SNCASE S.E.2410 Gronnard I (F)

10 May 50 First flight of de Havilland D.H.114 Heron (GB)

***De Havilland Heron** (GB) first flew 10 May 1950*

19 June 50 First flight of Hawker P.1052 (UK)

20 June 50 First flight of Blackburn Beverley (GB)

***Blackburn Beverley** (GB) first flew 20 June 1950*

25 June 1950 KOREAN WAR begins

27 June 50 First flight of FMA I.A.e.33 Pulquí II (Arrow II) (Arg)

27 June 50 First North Korean aircraft shot down by a F-82G twin Mustang

27 June 50 First B-29 bombing missions over Korea

3 July 50 US Navy aircraft from USS *Valley Forge* and British carrier HMS *Triumph* carry out the Korean War's first strikes by carrier-based aircraft. Grumman F9F-2 Panther of US Navy is the first jet to see action during the Korean War

HAWKER HUNTER first flight 21 July 1951

Powerplant: (F.6) One 10,000lb (4,535kg) s.t. Rolls-Royce Avon 203
Primary role: (F.6) Day interceptor fighter
Dimensions: Wingspan 33ft 8in (10.26m); length 45ft 10½in (13.98m)
Armament: (F.6) Four 30mm Aden cannon; underwing pylons for two 1,000lb (454kg) bombs and twenty-four 3in rockets (later or refurbished aircraft also two 230 Imp gal drop tanks)
Weights: (F.6) Empty 14,400lb (6,530kg); loaded 17,750lb (8,050kg)
Speed: (F.6) 715mph (1,150kph) max at sea level
Range: (F.6, with drop tanks) 1,840 miles (2,965km)
Crew: 1
Production total (all marks): 1,985 including 445 licence-built in Belgium and Netherlands
Variants: F.1–6, T.7, T.8, FGA.9, FR.10, GA.11

An all-round combat aircraft, the Hunter was Britain's most successful post-war fighter. The prototype P.1067 first flew on 20 June 1951 and the production Hunter F.1 on 16 May 1953; final deliveries from new took place in 1966. The prototype, with a 6,500lb thrust Avon 100, was built to Specification F.3/48. It reached supersonic speeds in a shallow dive and packed the devastating four Aden cannon in a quick-release pack winched up as a unit. After being fitted with bulged cartridge boxes and an external airbrake under the rear fuselage, it became the standard fighter. Armstrong Whitworth built the F.2 with an 8,000lb Sapphire 101, which, unlike the early Avon, stayed lit when the guns were fired. The one-off Mk 3 gained a world speed record of 727.6mph. The F.4 had fuel capacity raised from 334 to 414 gal and carried underwing stores, and the F.5 was a Sapphire-engine Mk 4. The F.6 introduced the 10,000lb Avon 203 and extended-chord, dogtooth wings. The T.7 had the 8,000lb Avon 122 and side-by-side dual controls, the T.8 was a naval trainer, and the most important mark was the FGA.9, with a 10,150lb Avon 207 and a heavier underwing load. The FR.10 was a camera-equipped fighter and the GA.11 was a ground-attack naval trainer. Exports totalled 429 new machines and over 700 refurbished or completely remanufactured craft. The Hunter saw service with Abu Dhabi, Britain (RAF and Royal Navy), Chile, India, Iraq, Kenya, Kuwait, Lebanon, Oman, Peru, Qatar, Rhodesia, Singapore and Switzerland.

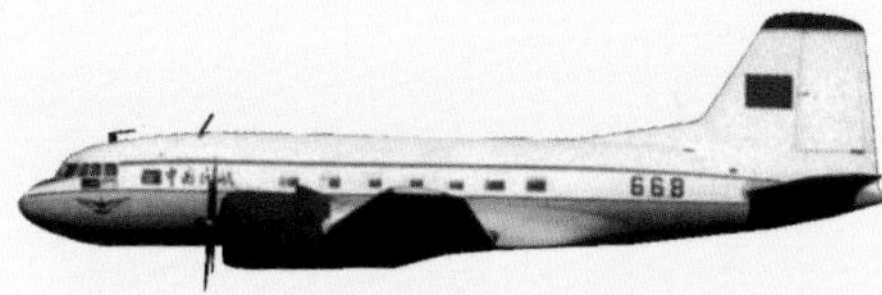

Ilyushin Il-14 (Crate) *(USSR) first flew 15 July 1950*

Dassault Mystère II *(F) first flew 23 Feb 1951*

15 July 50 First flight of Ilyushin Il-14 (Crate) (USSR)

22 Sept 50 First non-stop trans-Atlantic flight by a jet aircraft, a F-84 Thunderjet, is achieved with the aid of in-flight refueling. Pilot is forced to bail-out over Labrador

1 Oct 50 First TWA service to New York from Frankfurt via London using a Lockheed Constellation

10 Oct 50 First flight of Boulton Paul P.111 (GB)

13 Oct 50 First flight of Lockheed Super Constellation (US)

1 Nov 50 Chinese MiG-15s appear over North Korea for the first time

8 Nov 50 First victory to be scored in the first all-jet combat is by Lt Brown USAF 51st Fighter Interceptor Wing flying a Lockeed F-80C destroying Chinese MiG-15

9 Nov 50 First US B-29 bomber shot down by a MiG-15

9 Nov 50 In the first encounter between US Navy jets and MiG-15s, Lt Cdr Amen in a Grumman F9F-2 Panther is the first USN pilot to destroy another jet fighter in combat

11 Nov 50 F-86As directed to Korea to counter the MiG-15

17 Dec 50 First action between 4 F-86A Sabres and 4 MiG-15s ten miles south of the Yalu River, one MiG-15 is shot down

22 Dec 50 First F-86A is brought down

13 Jan – 12 April 51 Korea, B-29 bombers use TARZON 12,000lb guided bombs to destroy bridges. They launch 30 bombs, destroying six bridges and damage one, 19 bombs miss and two fail to detonate

23 Jan 51 First flight of Douglas F4D-1 Skyray (US)

Feb 51 French begin to operate US supplied B-26 bombers and F8 Bearcats against Viet Minh in Indo-China

6 Feb 51 Valmet Vihuri (FIN)

12 Feb 51 First flight of Piaggio P.148 (IT)

23 Feb 51 First flight of Dassault Mystère II (F)

12 March 51 First flight of Fairey FD.1 (GB)

15 Mar 51 First flight of Sud-Ouest SO.30R (F) France's first jet transport

22 April 51 A gunner of a B-29 bomber shoots down two MiG-15s, the first time jets have been downed by bomber defending fire

1 May 51 Eight Skyraiders attack with torpedoes and breach the North Korean Hwachon Dam

1 May 51 A US Navy Neptune reconnaissance aircraft is shot down by Soviet fighters off Siberia

18 May 51 Bridgeman flys more than a thousand miles per hour in a Douglas D-558-II – Mach 1.72/1130 mph

18 May 51 First flight of Vickers Valiant (GB)

20 May 51 First flight of Fokker S.14 Mach-Trainer (HO)

Mid-June 51 First dogfights involving Soviet instructors flying MiG-15s. By the month's end F-86s bring down 42 for the loss of only 3 Sabres

20 June 51 First flight of Bell X-5 (US) The first jet aircraft to be flown with variable-sweepback wings

8 July 51 First flight of Mil Mi-2 Hare (USSR)

21 July 51 First flight of Hawker Hunter (GB)

1 Aug 51 Japan Air Lines is formed making use of aircraft and crew loaned by Northwest Airlines

5 Aug 51 First flight of Supermarine Swift (GB)

7 Aug 51 First flight of McDonnell F3H-1 Demon (US)

10 Aug 51 First flight of Short S.A.4 Sperrin (GB)

McDonnell F3H-1 Demon *(US) first flew 7 Aug 1951*

Gloster Javelin *(GB) first flew 26 Nov 1951*

13 Aug 51 First flight of Hindustan HT-2 (IN)
25 Aug 51 First flight of Aero Commander 500B (US)
21 Sept 51 Korea. First main move of troops to the battlefront by helicopter – 228 US Marines are delivered in 12 Sikorsky S-55s
26 Sept 51 First flight of de Havilland Sea Vixen (GB)
23 Oct 51 The biggest air battle of the Korean War when 8 B-29s escorted by 55 F-84Es and 35 F-86Es are attacked by some 150 MiG-15s. In five minutes six MiG-15s are brought down for three B-29s downed and damaged beyond repair and one F-84 lost. The B-29 is then confined to night bombing
26 Nov 51 First flight of Gloster Javelin (GB)
5 Dec 51 Tourist Class introduced on North Atlantic routes by 11 airlines
12 Dec 51 First flight of de Havilland Canada DHC-3 Otter (CA)
31 Dec 51 For the first time, air passenger miles flown exceed passenger miles travelled by rail in the USA (10.6 air miles to 10.2 rail miles)

April 52 First flight of Convair B-60 (US)
3 Jan 52 First flight of Bristol Belvedere (GB)
1 April 52 Colonel Gabreski scores his fifth 'kill' of the Korean War, thereby becoming an 'Ace' in WW II and the Korean War
11 April 52 First flight of Piasecki (Vertol) H-21C (US)
12 April 52 First flight of Grumman S2F-1 Tracker (US)

Grumman S2F-1 Tracker *(US) first flew 12 April 1952*

TUPOLEV Tu-16 (BADGER) first flight 27 April 1952

Powerplant: Two 20,950lb (9,500kg) s.t. Mikulin AM-3M turbojets
Primary role: Medium bomber and reconnaissance aircraft
Dimensions: Wingspan 110ft 0in (33.5m); length 120ft 11in (36.87m)
Armament: ('Badger-A') Seven 23 mm cannon and max 19,800lb (9,000kg) weapon load; ('Badger-B') two 'Kennel' or 'Kelt' ASMs underwing; ('Badger-C') one 'Kipper' stand-off bomb mounted beneath the fuselage; ('Badger-G') two 'Kelt' or 'Kingfish' ASMs underwing
Weights: Empty 88,185lb (40,000kg); loaded 169,757lb (77,000kg)
Speed: 587mph (945kph, Mach 0.87) max at 35,000ft (10,700m); 490mph (790kph) cruising at 32,800ft (10,000m)
Range: 3,000 miles (4,800km)
Crew: 7
Production total (all marks): over 2,000
Variants: 'Badger-B' and -C (with ASMs); -D, -E, -F, -K, with additional electronic equipment, mounted partly in underwing pods; -H and -J, ECM aircraft; Xian B-6, Chinese copy

The Tupolev Tu-16 'Badger' was ordered into production in 1950 as a jet bomber to match the British Valiant and American B-47. The prototype first flew in 1952 and the type entered Soviet service in 1955; it also equipped the Chinese, Egyptian, Indonesian and Iraqi air arms. The Tu-16 saw action in various Middle East wars. Although the 'Badger' was conceived as a heavy bomber, mid-life conversions gave it several different roles, and its operational life has spanned almost fifty years.

15 April 52 First flight of Boeing B-52 Stratofortress (see overleaf) (US)
27 April 52 First flight of Tupolev Tu-16 (Badger) (USSR)
29 April 52 First operational use of in-flight refueling for a combat sortie
29 May 52 First use of air refueling in support of a combat mission – 12 F84 Thunderjets refuelled by KB-29 tankers in Korea
17 June 52 US Navy takes delivery of world's largest non-rigid airship, *2PN-1* (324 ft long)
23 July 52 First flight of Fouga Magister (F)

***Fouga Magister** (F) first flew 23 July 52*

BOEING B-52 STRATOFORTRESS first flight 15 April 1952

Powerplant: (B-52H) Eight 17,018lb (7,718kg) Pratt & Whitney TF 33-P-3 turbofans
Primary role: Strategic heavy bomber
Dimensions: Wingspan 185ft (56.39m); length 157ft (47.85m)
Armament: (B-52H) One 20mm ASG-21 tail cannon, plus weapon load of up to fifty-one 750lb (340kg) bombs (27 in fuselage bay, 24 underwing) or up to twenty AGM-69A SRAM ASMs
(8 in fuselage bay, 12 on two underwing hard-points)
Weights: Empty 245,535lb (111,350kg); loaded 505,090lb (229,066kg)
Speed: 665mph (1,070kph, Mach 0.95) max at 40,000ft (12,200m)
Range: 10,130 miles (16,303km)
Crew: 6
Production total (all marks): 480
Variants: B-52B, RB-52B, B-52C, D, E, F, G, H

The prototype, YB-52, first flew on 15 April 1952 piloted by Tex Johnson, and the B-52H on 6 March 1961. Although there were two prototypes and three pre-production models,

the only in-service marks were the B-52D, G and H. Production continued from 1954 to 1962. With conventional and nuclear bombing roles the Boeing B-52 has been the epitome of US air power since the 1950s. It has seen action in Vietnam, in the Gulf Wars of 1991 and 2003, over Kosovo in 1999 and Afghanistan from 2001. In South-East Asia, the most important mark was the B-52D, which was given the 'Big Belly' conversion allowing it to carry a vastly increased load of 500lb (226kg) or 750lb (340kg) bombs. Even more could be carried on new wing pylons, making a total of 108 500lb weapons. The B-52G could theoretically carry a maximum bomb load of 50,000lb, but the unmodified weapons bay of the aircraft allowed only the carriage of 27 500lb or 750lb bombs, well below the aircraft's capabilities. From 1973 96 Gs and Hs and 80 Ds were modernized. With the introduction of the AGM-86 air-launched cruise missile, the B-52G and H picked up a new role and some 269 were converted in 1981–82. The G-model carries 12 on two wing pylons while the H-model adds another eight in an internal rotary launcher.

22 Aug 52 First flight of Saunders-Roe S.R.45 Princess (GB)
16 Aug 52 First flight of Bristol Britannia (GB)
23 Aug 52 First flight of Boulton Paul P.120 (GB). (Crashes 3 weeks later)
30 Aug 52 First flight of Avro Vulcan (GB)
6 Sept 52 28 killed, 60 injured as prototype de Havilland 110 Sea Vixen disintegrates in flight at Farnborough Air Show, UK
10 Sept 52 US BOMARC surface-to-air missile first successful launch
20 Sept 52 First flight of Douglas X-3 (US)
28 Sept 52 First flight of Dassault Mystère IVA (F)
7 Oct 52 USAF RB-29 Superfortress reconnaissance aircraft shot down by Soviet fighters over the Kurile Islands

BRISTOL BRITANNIA first flight 16 August 1952

Powerplant: Four 2,800–5,500shp Bristol Proteus 625/705
Primary role: Passenger transport
Dimensions: Wingspan 142ft 3in (43.35m); length 124ft 3in (37.87m)
Payload: 99 passengers/28,000lb (12,700kg) freight
Weights: Empty 88,000lb (39,915kg); loaded 185,000lb (83,914kg)
Speed: 397mph (639kph) max; 357mph (575kph) cruising
Range: 5,780 miles (9,300km)
Production total (all marks): 85

Originally intended as a medium-range 32–36 passenger piston-engined airliner for the British Overseas Airways Corporation, the design was drastically changed to produce the turboprop-powered prototype. With 90 seats, this first flew on 23 December 1953. On 1 February 1957 the production Britannia 102, known as the 'Whispering Giant', entered service on the London–Johannesburg route with BOAC. The Britannia 300 series, carrying 99–133 passengers, were the long-range models, and began non-stop London–New York flights with BOAC on 19 December 1957. Britannia 312s were the first turbine-powered airliners to cover transatlantic routes. Britannias saw service with Aeronaves de Mexico, Canadian Pacific, Cubana, El Al, Ghana Airways and RAF Transport Command.

AVRO VULCAN first flight 30 August 1952

Powerplant: Four 20,000lb (9,072kg) s.t. Bristol Siddeley (RR) Olympus 301 turbojets
Primary role: Heavy bomber
Dimensions: Wingspan 111ft 0in (33.83m); length 99ft 11in (30.45m)
Armament: One Blue Steel Mk 1 stand-off weapon or twenty-one 1,000lb (454kg) bombs
Weights: Loaded 200,180lb (90,800kg)
Speed: 645mph (1,038kph, Mach 0.96) max at 39,375ft (12,000m); 627mph (1,009kph, Mach 0.95) cruising at 55,100ft (16,800m)
Range: (Ferry) 4,750miles (7,650km)
Crew: 5
Production total (all marks): 132
Variants: B.1, B.lA, B.2

The second of the V-Bombers (after the Valiant) to enter service, the Avro Vulcan equipped the RAF for nearly thirty years. The first prototype, with a promising delta wing offering good manoeuvability at high altitude, had its maiden flight on 30 August 1952, followed by the B.1 on 4 February 1955 and the B.2 on 19 August 1958. On 11 July 1957 No 83 Squadron, the first Vulcan front-line unit, was formed, and aircraft numbers built up rapidly by the end of 1958. Vulcans could launch Blue Steel 'stand-off' weapons, which had to be carried semi-recessed in the bomb bay, as well as free-fall nuclear bombs. In 1968 the strategic nuclear deterrent was taken over the by RN Polaris-carrying submarines and Vulcans reverted to a tactical role using conventional bombs. Production ended in 1964, and although the Vulcan force was being run down, the 1982 Falklands War saw five aircraft conducting bombing and missile attacks from Ascension Island, 3,880 miles (6,250km) from the target. The last remaining bomber units were disbanded after the Falklands War. Some Vulcans were also converted to tanker aircraft, in which capacity they served until March 1984.

Douglas A3D-1 Skywarrior *(US) first flew 28 Oct 1952*

16 Oct 52 First flight of Sud-Ouest Vautour (F)
23 Oct 52 First flight of Hughes XH-17 (US)
28 Oct 52 First flight of Douglas A3D-1 Skywarrior (US)
2 Nov 52 Korea. First jet-to-jet nightfighter combat, US Navy Douglas F3D Skyknight shoots down Yak-15
3 Nov 52 First flight of Saab 32 Lansen (SW)
12 Nov 52 First flight of Tupolev Tu-95 (Bear) (USSR)
20 Nov 52 First flight of Percival (Hunting) Pembroke (GB)
Dec 52 The French aicraft-carrier *Arromanches* and French airforce units support ground forces during intense fighting around Hoa Binh in Indo-China
24 Dec 52 First flight of Handley Page Victor (GB)

1953 Lufthansa re-established after World War II
1953 First flight of Ryan Navion 205 (US)
1953 First flight of Yakovlev Yak-25 (USSR)
1953 During Malayan Emergency increasing use of helicopters. 12,000 British troops are transported into operational areas during the year
Jan 53 First flight of Hurel-Dubois H.D.321 (F)
3 Jan 53 First flight of Cessna 310C (US)

Tupolev Tu-95 (Bear) *(USSR) first flew 12 Nov 1952*

Handley Page Victor *(GB) first flew 24 Dec 52*

29 Jan 53 First flight of Morane Saulnier M.S.755 Fleuret (F)

21 Feb 53 First flight of Brantly B-2 (US)

3 March 53 Comet I crashes on take-off at Karachi, Pakistan, killing all on board

10 March 53 USAF F-84G Thunderjet shot down near Czech frontier by two Czech MiG-15s

12 March 53 RAF Avro Lincoln shot down by MiG fighters in Berlin Corridor

9 April 53 First flight of Convair F2Y-1 Sea Dart (US)

18 April 53 World's first scheduled passenger service with a turboprop airliner, a BEA Viscount

1 May 53 Delta Air Lines Merges with Chigaco and Southern Airlines Inc.

2 May 53 Another Comet I crashes near Calcutta with loss of 43 lives

12 May 53 First Bell X-2 explodes while preparing to be dropped from belly of EB-50A mother ship. The test pilot, Jean Ziegler, is killed

18 May 53 First flight of Douglas DC-7 (US)

21 May 53 First flight of C.A.S.A. 202B Halcon (SP)

25 May 53 First flight of North American F-100 Super Sabre (US)

18 June 53 A USAF C-124 Globemaster II

North American F-100 Super Sabre *(US) first flew 25 May 1953*

LOCKHEED U-2 first flight 1 August 1953

Powerplant: One 17,000lb (7,711kg) Pratt & Whitney J75-P-138
Primary role: High-altitude strategic reconnaissance
Dimensions: Wingspan 80ft 2in (24.43m); length 50ft (15.24m)
Armament: None
Weights: Loaded 22,452lb (10,225kg)
Speed: 465mph (749kph) cruising at 85,000ft (25,900m)
Range: 2,880 miles (4,635km)
Crew: 1
Production total (all marks): 50
Variants: A/B/C/D/R/S
First proposed in 1954, the U-2 entered service in 1956, designed for high-altitude reconnaissance over the USSR. Basically powered sailplanes, early versions were difficult to fly

crashes on take off from Tachikawa AFB, Tokyo, killing 129 people. The world's first air disaster involving the deaths of more 100 people

3 July 53 First flight of North American FJ-3 Fury (US)

27 July 53 Korean War ends

Official US statistics for Korea War:

USAF fighters destroy 954 enemy aircraft in air combat. 810 by F-86 Sabres, including 792 MiG-15s The war produces 39 F-86 Sabre aces, who claim a total of 305 enemy aircraft Capt Joseph McConnel with 16 kills, the most successful ace. 605 USAF fighter aircraft are lost to enemy action, including 78 Sabres in air combat

28 July 53 USAF RB-50 shot down by MiG-15s off Vadivostock in international air space

1 Aug 53 International Air India established (the International dropped 1962)

1 Aug 53 First flight of Sud-Est S.E.5000 Baroudeur (F)

1 Aug 53 First flight of Lockheed U-2 (US)

20 Aug 53 First official supersonic world speed

and land. Variants included 48 U-2As with the 11,200lb (5,080kg) J57-P-37A, the more powerful J75-P-13-engined U-2Bs, the U-2C elint platforms converted from U-2Bs, and the larger, heavier, redesigned U-2R (wingspan 103ft/31.4m and weighing over 140,000lb/63,490kg) with wing pods for extra sigint and/or optical reconnaissance equipment.

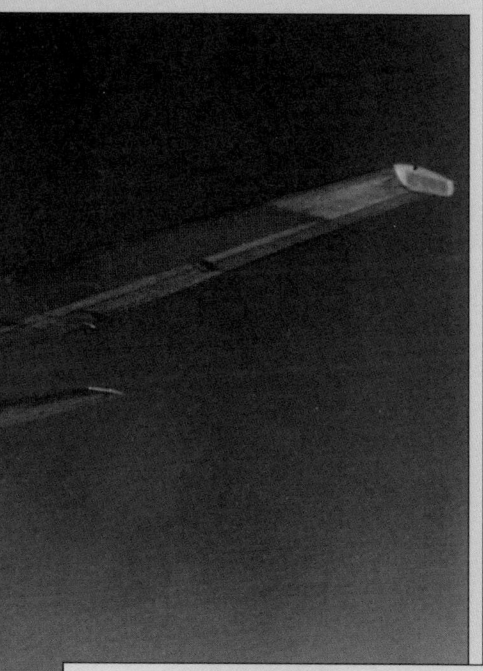

record set by a F-100 Super Sabre flown by Col. Haines reaching 822 mph

23 Aug 53 First flight of Short Seamew A.S.1 (GB)

Sept 53 First flight of Mikoyan MiG-19 (Farmer) (USSR)

3 Sept 53 First successful ejection from an aircraft at ground level carried out from a Meteor while travelling along a runway

11 Sept 53 First successful interception by a Sidewinder air-to-air missile

21 Sept 53 First flight of F.M.A. I.A.-35-11 Huanquero (AR)

24 Oct 53 First flight of Convair F-102 Delta Dagger (US)

***Convair F-102 Delta Dagger** (US) first flew 24 Oct 1953*

24 Nov 53 Indo China.Viet Minh increases the quantity of their AAA. In a two week period out of 51 French aircraft involved in bombing and strafing 45 are hit and three brought down

12 Dec 53 Capt Charles Yeager flies the air-launched Bell X-IA rocket-powered high-speed research aircraft at a speed of Mach 2.435, 1,650 mph, at an altitude of 21,340m (70,00ft)

***Mikoyan MiG-19 (Farmer)** (USSR) first flew Sept 1953*

16 Dec 53 First flight of Sud-Aviation S.O.1221 Djinn (F)
18 Dec 53 First flight of Grumman F9F-8 Cougar (US)
18 Dec 53 First flight of Sikorsky S-56 (US)

1954 First flight of Polikarpov Po-2 (U-2) (USSR)
1954 Aer Lingus acquires 4 Vickers Viscounts
10 Jan 54 Comet I breaks up in the air, the 35 persons on board perish; BOAC grounds the entire Comet fleet
15 Jan 54 First flight of Nord-SFECMAS 1402B Gréfaut I (F)
25 Feb 54 First flight of Convair R3Y-2 Tradewind (US)
28 Feb 54 First flight of Lockheed F-104 Starfighter (US)
Mar 54 First flight of Lockheed XFY-1 (US)
23 Mar 54 First flight of Comet fleet returned to service

BOEING 707 first flight 15 July 1954

Wingspan: 44.42 m (145ft 9in)
Overall Length: 46.61 m (152ft 11in)
Powerplant: 4 x Pratt & Whitney JT3D-7, 6818 kg (19,000 lb) st each
Payload: 189 passengers or 42,229 kg (93,098 lb) of freight
Maximum weight: 151,315 kg (333,600 lb)
Maximum speed: 645 mph at 25,000 ft
Cruising speed: 605 mph at 25,000 ft
Endurance: 3,630 miles with 36,287kg (80,000 lb) payload

Possibly the most important airliner ever developed. Together with the DC-8, the 707 helped forge today's world-wide pattern of air transport. Debut flight of the prototype Model 367-80, was in July 1954, with all development costs coming from Boeing. First sales were to the US Air Force of the smaller KC-135 tanker. The first civil variant was the 121/179 seat transcontinental Model 707-120 with 5897-kg (13,000-lb) JT3C-6 turbojets. The Model 707-138 was a subvariant for Qantas.

***Lockheed F-104 Starfighter** (US) first flew*
28 Feb 1954

The 'hot-and-high' Model 707-220 with 7167-kg (15,800-lb) thrust JT4A-4/5s, the 131/189 seat intercontinental Model 707-320 with 7938-kg (17,500-lb) JT4A-11 turbojets and the Model 707-420 with 7484-kg (16,500-lb) Rolls-Royce Conway Mk 505 turbofans were all later variants. Aircraft fitted with turbofans were indicated by suffix 'B', and those with convertible passenger/cargo interiors by suffix 'C'. Total production was 917.

13 Mar – 7 May 54 Indo-China. French defeat at Battle of Dien Bien Phu. French airlift troops and heavy equipment. 6,410 tons of supplies are transported in 6,700 sorties. Combat aircraft fly 3,700 sorties, with 48 shot down and 167 damaged and 14 destroyed on the ground. Leads to French pulling out of Indo-China

8 April 54 Comet I breaks up and falls into sea south of Naples with the loss of all on board. Type withdrawn from service

May 54 First flight of Myasishchev M-4 (USSR)

1 May 54 First flight of Revealed Ilyushin Il-37 (Bison) (USSR)

25 May 54 A US Navy ZPG-2 airship lands after being airborne for just over 200 hours

2 June 54 Belgian DC-3 civil freighter attacked by MiG-15 fighters over Yugoslavia. Makes an emergency landing with one crewman killed and and the other two wounded

22 June 54 First flight of Douglas A4D-1 Skyhawk (US)

26 June 54 First flight of Hunting Percival Jet Provost T.1 (GB)

28 June 54 First flight of Douglas B-66C Destroyer (US)

15 July 54 First flight of Boeing C-135/KC-135 (US)

15 July 54 First flight of Boeing 707 (US)

***Myasishchev M-4 (Bison)** (USSR) first flew*
May 1954

***Douglas A4D-1 Skyhawk** (US) first flew*
22 June 1954

LOCKHEED C-130 HERCULES first flight 23 August 1954

Powerplant: Four 4,050hp Allison T56-A-7A
Primary role: Transport
Dimensions: Wingspan 132ft 7in (40.41m); length 97ft 9in (29.79m)
Payload: 92 troops/64paratroops/74 litters (C-130H) and two medics/45,900lb (20,280kg) freight
Weights: Empty 72,892lb (33,058kg); loaded 175,000lb (79,365kg)
Speed: 384mph (618kph) max; 368mph (592kph) cruising
Range: 4,770 miles (7,680km); 2,450 miles (3,944km) with max payload
Crew: 4–7
Production total (all marks): 1,800
Variants: C-130B personnel and supplies transport; KC-130F flight refuelling tanker and transport; C-130H multi-role transport

The C-130 was developed as a turboprop transport for the US Air Force and the first prototype flew from Burbank, California, on 23 August 1953. The YC-130 was first flown on 23 August 1954 and the production C-130A on 7 April 1955. Service delivery began in December 1956, and the Hercules quickly became the USAF's standard tactical transport

***McDonnell F-101 Voodoo** (US) first flew 29 Sept 1954*

***Convair XFY-1** (US) first flew 2 Aug 1954*

2 Aug 54 First flight of Rolls-Royce 'Flying Bedstead' (GB)
2 Aug 54 First flight of Convair XFY-1 (US)
4 Aug 54 First flight of English Electric P.1A Lightning (GB)
23 Aug 54 First flight of Lockheed C-130 Hercules (US)
4 Sept 54 US Navy Neptune is shot down by two Soviet MiG-15s off Siberian coast outside Soviet airspace
20 Sept 54 First flight of Sikorsky S.58 (US)
29 Sept 54 First flight of McDonnell F-101 Voodoo (US)
6 Oct 54 First flight of Fairey Delta 2 (GB)
12 Oct 54 First flight of Cessna T-37A (A-37 Dragonfly) (US)
Nov 54 By now 60 turbo-prop Vickers Viscounts have entered service with American Airlines
30 Nov 54 Il-14 first enters service with Aeroflot (USSR)
10 Dec 54 First flight of Hispano HA-100-E1 Triana (SP)

1955 First flight of Antonov An-8 (USSR)
1955 First flight of Yakovlev Yak-24 (USSR)
1955 First flight of Sukhoi Su-7MF (Fitter) (USSR)

26 July 54 Two US Navy Skyraiders, which are searching for survivors of the Cathay Pacific DC-4 shot down on 23 July, are attacked by and shoot down two Chinese La-7s
29 July 54 First flight of Morane-Saulnier M.S.760 Paris (F)
30 July 54 First flight of Grumman F9F-9 Tiger (US)

***Fairey Delta 2** (GB) first flew 6 Oct 1954*

1 Jan 55 RAF Gaydon is the UK's first nuclear base. The first V-Bomber unit, No 138 Squadron flying the Valiant, is based there

2 March 55 First flight of Dassault Super Mystère B1 (F)

25 March 55 First flight of Chance Vought F8U-1 Crusader (US)

1 April 55 Lufthansa inaugurates first domestic route

27 May 55 First flight of SN Case S.E. 210 Caravelle (F)

June 55 First flight of Cessna 172 (US)

15 June 55 First flight of Tupolev Tu-104 (see overleaf) (Camel) (USSR)

DASSAULT SUPER MYSTÈRE first flight 2 March 1955

Powerplant: One 9,920lb (4,500kg) afterburning SNECMA Atar
Primary role: Fighter-bomber
Dimensions: Wingspan 34ft 5¾in (10.5m); length 46ft 1¼in (14.0m)
Armament: Two 30mm DEFA cannon; internal Matra launcher for 35 SNEB 68mm rockets; two wing pylons for tanks or weapons up to 2,000lb (907kg)
Weights: Empty 15,400lb (6,985kg); loaded 22,046lb (10,000kg)
Speed: 686mph (1,104kph, Mach 0.9) max at sea level; 743mph (1,200kph, Mach 1.125) max at altitude
Range: 540 miles (870km)
Crew: 1
Production total (all marks): 180

Dassault's Mystère IVB went supersonic in level flight on 24 February 1954, and Mystères were the first supersonic aircraft to go into production or service in Europe. A major advance, the Mystère IVB had tapered, milled and chem-milled sheets, integral tanks, flush aerials, a radar gunsight in a new nose, and introduced the more powerful and highly developed Atar 1010 with variable afterburner. It was followed by the bigger, heavier and more formidable Super Mystère B.2, which had new wing with 45 degrees of sweep and aerodynamics copied from the F-100 (but with outboard ailerons, inboard flaps and dogtooth leading edges). Production models were powered by the Atar 101G instead of the first SMB.2's Avon RA.7R. Twenty-four SMB.2s were bought by Israel and survivors remained in service until early 1977.

16 June 55 Argentine naval aircraft bomb Government House during a failed coup d'état against president Peron
25 June 55 First flight of Scottish Aviation Twin Pioneer (GB)
25 June 55 First flight of Dassault MD-550 Mirage (F)
27 June 55 Dornier Do 27B (SP/D)
3 July 55 Revealed Tupolev Tu-20 (Bear) (USSR)
3 July 55 First flight of PZL TS-8 Bies (PO)
3 July 55 First flight of Revealed Mil Mi-4 (Horse) (USSR)
14 July 55 First flight of Martin P6M-1 Seamaster (US)

SN CASE S.E. 210 CARAVELLE first flight 27 May 1955

Wingspan: 34.30m (112ft 6in)
Overall Length: 32.01m (105ft 0in)
Powerplant: 2 x Rolls-Royce Avon Mk 527, 5171kg (11,400 lb) st each
Payload: 80 passengers or 8400 kg (18,519 lb) of freight
Maximum weight: 46,000kg (101,411 lb)
Cruising speed: 500 mph at 32,810 ft
Endurance: 1,056 miles with maximum payload

World's first short-range jetliner, chosen from eight designs put forward for French consideration in 1951. Originally planned round three SNECMA Atar turbojets (one in the fin and two on the fuselage sides), the Caravelle was recast for a pair of more powerful Rolls-Royce Avons, the forward fuselage and flightdeck of the Comet, and a ventral airstair. Debut flight in May 1955. The 282 aircraft produced included 20 Caravelle Is with Avon RA.26 engines, 12 Mk IAs with Avon Mk 526 engines, 78 higher-weight Mk IIIs with Avon Mk 527 engines, 53 VINs with silencer-equipped Avon Mk 531s, 63 Mk VIRs with reverser-equipped Avon Mk 533s, 22 Mk 10Bs with Pratt & Whitney JT8D-7 turbofans, 20 Mk 10Rs with thrust reversers, six Mk 11Rs with a longer fuselage and five 140-seater Mk 12s with JT8D-9 engines. Alitalia, which ran 21 Caravelles in 1965, was one of the largest operators of the aircraft. When it was withdrawn from scheduled services, the Caravelle was used for charter work, and finally sold in Latin America.

TUPOLEV Tu-104 first flight 15 June 1955

Wingspan: 34.54m (113ft 4in)
Overall Length: 38.85m (127ft 5.5in)
Powerplant: 2 x Mikulin AM-3, 6,750 kg (14,881 lb) s.t. each
Payload: 70 passengers or 9,000 kg (19,841 lb) of freight
Maximum weight: 76,000 kg (167,549 lb)
Maximum speed: 635 mph at 25,000 ft
Cruising speed: 559 mph at optimum altitude
Endurance: 1,647 miles with maximum payload

The world's second jetliner to enter service, although largely forgotten today. Basic design adapted from the Tu-16 'Badger' bomber, with a revized nose landing gear unit, the wing in the low- rather than mid-set position, and a larger fuselage mounting. The prototype Tu-104G flew in June 1955, entering service with a 48-seat version in 1956. In the same fuselage, the 1958 Tu-104A carried 70 seats, and introduced in the same year, the 100-seater Tu-104B had a longer fuselage. The lower-rated AM-3 engine was replaced by the AM-3M in later versions, and the AM-3M-500 engine was introduced in 1959. Production then switched from the Tu-104A to the Tu-104C, and from the Tu-104B to the Tu-104D. Some 210 aircraft had been delivered when production ended in 1960. Most went to Aeroflot, who nicknamed the plane 'Krasnyii Shapochka' (Little Red Riding Hood). Czech airline CSA and the Soviet air force took delivery of small numbers.

***Republic F-105 Thunderchief** (US) first flew 22 Oct 1955*

18 July 55 First flight of Folland Gnat (GB)

27 July 55 An El Al Constellation airliner on route from Vienna to Tel Aviv shot down by Bulgarian MiG-15 fighters. All 58 people on board perish

1 Aug 55 Chinese agree to release 11 crewmen of a B-29 that was shot down during the Korean War

16 Aug 55 First flight of Hispano HA-200-R1 Saeta (SP)

23 Aug 55 First flight of Westland Widgeon (GB)

4 Sept 55 In the Aleutian Island region a US Navy Neptune makes a crash landing after being fired on by Soviet MiG-15s

16 Sept 55 In Argentina three Meteor fighters are used by rebels. One Meteor is shot down by a Navy SNJ-4. This revolt leads to the president, Peron, being forced into exile

20 Sept 55 First flight of Nord 1500 Griffon (F)

28 Sept 55 First flight of CASA 207 Azor (SP)

22 Oct 55 First flight of Republic F-105 Thunderchief (US)

25 Oct 55 First flight of Saab 35 Draken (SW)

1 Nov 55 A United Air Lines DC-6 explodes in mid-air and crashes near Longmont, Colorado, killing all 44 occupants. John Graham has planted the bomb in his mother's luggage in an effort to cash in on her life insurance

***Saab 35 Draken** (SW) first flew 25 Oct 1955*

24 Nov 55 First flight of Fokker F.27 Friendship (HO)

***Fokker F.27 Friendship** (HO) first flew 24 Nov 1955*

MIKOYAN MiG-21 (FISHBED) first flight March 1956

Powerplant: One afterburning 8,708lb (3,950kg) s.t. military (13,492lb/6,120kg max) Tumansky R11-F23-300
Primary role: Fighter, fighter-bomber and reconnaissance
Dimensions: Wingspan 23ft 5½in (7.15m); length 44ft 2in (13.46m)
Armament: Two K-13 heat-seeking AAMs; later models carried the fast-firing twin-barrelled 23mm GSh-23 cannon and two K-SM SARH AAMs, or two K-13s and two KM-5Ms
Weights: Empty c.12,015lb (5,450kg); loaded 17,086lb (7,750kg)
Speed: Mach 2.05 max
Range: 895 miles (1,440km)
Crew: 1
Production total (all marks): Over 20,000
Variants: 28

The first flight of the MiG-21 took place in February 1955. Designed as a fast-climbing point defence interceptor, it was an agile, lightweight and manoeuvrable aircraft of tailed delta configuration, which over the years has evolved into a multi-role fighter. More MiG-21s were built than any other jet fighter, with production lasting 28 years. The type served with 49 different air forces, but was on the losing side in many wars, notably the Arab/Israeli conflicts. It is still in frontline service with more than a dozen countries and an upgraded version, the MiG-21-2000, flew for the first time in 1995 and it should continue to serve well into the 21st century.

Dec 55 First flight of Edgar Percival E.P.9 (GB)
6 Dec 55 First flight of Convair CV-440 Metropolitan (US)
8 Dec 55 First flight of Auster B.8 Agricola (GB)
10 Dec 55 First flight of Ryan X-13 Vertijet (US)

1956 First flight of Antonov An-4 (USSR)
20 Jan 56 First flight of Supermarine Scimitar (GB)
March 56 First flight of Mikoyan MiG-21 (Fishbed) (USSR)
10 Mar 56 Lt Cdr Peter Twiss in a Fairey Delta 2 breaks the air speed record, flying 1,131 mph, becoming the first pilot to exceed 1,000 mph. This is the last time the UK holds an absolute speed record
26 Mar 56 First flight of Temco TT-1 Pinto (US)
21 April 56 First flight of Douglas F5D-1 Skylancer (US)
23 April 56 First flight of Douglas C-133 Cargomaster (US)
May 1956 The Sidewinder air-to-air missile enters service with the US
1 June 56 National Airlines, which has operated for the last 25 years without a single accident, is taken over by Eastern Airlines
8 June 56 Lufthansa opens its North Atlantic service with a Super Constellation, flying from Frankfurt to New York
30 June 56 Grand Canyon Disaster: A Super Constellation and a DC-7 collide in mid-air, both aircraft falling into the canyon. 128 people perish. As a result of this accident a formal system of commercial airways introduced in the USA
July 1956 Sparrow medium range air-to-air missile enters service with the US
24 July 56 First flight of Dassault Etendard IV (F)
6 Aug 56 First flight of Beech D95A Travel Air (US)
9 Aug 56 First flight of Fiat G-91 (IT)
7 Sept 56 The Bell X-2 research aircraft is flown by Capt Iven C Kincheloe to an altitude of 38,466m (126,200ft)
19 Sept 56 First flight of Aerfer Sagittario 2 (IT)
24 Sept 56 The official reformation of the Luftwaffe after the end of WW2
27 Sept 56 The Bell X-2 research aircraft crashes while on its approach to land, killing the pilot
Oct 56 First flight of Hughes 269A (US)
6 Oct 56 First flight of Bréguet Alizé (F)
11 Oct 56 Operation 'Totem'. An RAF Valiant bomber carries out the first air-dropping of a British nuclear bomb, in tests, over Maralinga

***Bréguet Alizé** (F) first flew 6 Oct 1956*

***Dassault Etendard IV** (F) first flew 24 July 1956*

BELL UH-1 IROQUOIS 'HUEY' first flight October 1956

Powerplant: One 1,342kW (1,800shp) Pratt & Whitney Canada T400-CP-400 flat-rated to 962kW (1,290shp)
Primary role: Light utility helicopter
Dimensions: Rotor diameter 48ft 2in (14.69m); length (rotors turning) 57ft 3¼in (17.46m)
Payload: 14 troops/4,000lb (1,814kg) freight carried internally or externally
Weights: Loaded 10,500lb (4,762kg)
Speed: 142mph (229kph) cruising at sea level
Range: 248 miles (399km)
Crew: 2
Production total (all marks): 10,000+
Variants: A/B/C/E/F/L/HH-1K/TH-1F/L

Developed for the US Army as a utility transport helicopter, the Model 204 Iroquois first flew in October 1956 as the XH-40. It entered service in 1959 as the HU-1A, powered by a 574kW (770shp) T53-L-1A. The helicopter is best known by its nickname 'Huey', even though the designation was revized in 1962 to UH-1A. Later Model 204 variants could carry ten passengers with a more powerful 1,044kW (1,400shp) engine. The US Marine Corps took the UH-1E assault support machine. In 1961, the Model 205 was launched. The UH-1D assault gunship, entering service with the US Army in 1963, could carry twelve troops, powered by an 820kW (1,100shp) T53-L-11; the 1044kW (1,400shp) UH-1H, entering service in 1967, could also carry twelve. Developed from the Model 205, the Model 212 appeared in 1969 as the UH-1N, featuring coupled turboshafts. Hueys gained HELMS rotor blade radar in 1971, allowing them to fly in all weather, as well as a radar-interface minigun armament.

***Convair B-58 Hustler** (US) first flew 11 Nov 1956*

***Lockheed Starliner** (US) first flew 11 Oct 1956*

11 Oct 56 First flight of Lockheed L-1649A Starliner (US)

22 Oct 56 First flight of Bell UH-1 Iroquois 'Huey' (US)

23 Oct–14 Nov 56 The Hungarian Uprising. During the course of which the USSR make use of assault helicopters and jet combat planes. The Hungarians manage to fly some sorties but are overwhelmed by their Soviet adversaries

29 Oct–7 Nov 56 SECOND ARAB-ISRAELI WAR and SUEZ CRISIS. Allied with Israel, the UK and France against Egypt. Heavy air attacks by both naval and airforce aircraft destroy a large part of Egyptian airforce. At night RAF Canberra and Valiant bombers attack the Egyptian airfields followed by daylight attacks by carrier and land based fighters. The alliance suffer light losses. It is a military victory on the part of alliance but a diplomatic defeat for the UK and France

8 Nov 56 World balloon altitude record: 23,165m/76,000ft by Lt Cdr Lewis and M. D. Ross

11 Nov 56 First flight of Convair B-58 Hustler (US)

17 Nov 56 First flight of Dassault Mirage III (see overleaf) (F)

26 Dec 56 First flight of Convair F-106 Delta Dart (US)

***Convair F-106 Delta Dart** (US) first flew 26 Dec 1956*

DASSAULT MIRAGE IIIC/IIIE first flight 17 November 1956

Primary role: Interceptor and light attack/strike, interdiction and multi-role fighter
Dimensions: Wingspan 26ft 11¾in (8.22m); length 50ft 10¼in (15.50m)
Armament: (IIIC) Two 30mm cannon plus provision for up to 3,000lb (1,360kg) of stores; (IIIE) two 30mm cannon plus provision for up to 8,800lb (4,000kg) of stores
Weights: Loaded (IIIC) 19,698lb (8,935kg); (IIIE) 30,200lb (13,700kg)
Speed: Mach 2.2 max
Range: 1,000 miles (1,610km)
Crew: 1
Production total (all marks): Over 1,250
Variants: See notes

Dassault's Mirage III, with an afterburning Atar 101G-2 turbojet and jettisonable rocket pack, first flew in November 1956. The Mirage IIIA was designed with a new, thinner wing, and was developed into the Mirage IIIC production fighter and the Mirage IIIB two-seat trainer. A development of the IIIC, the IIIE interdiction and strike machine had a longer fuselage, more fuel, Cyrano II radar matched to a new fire control system, Marconi Doppler navigation and five hardpoints for a greater disposable load. Its first flight was in April 1961, and more than 1,250 were produced, as multi-role fighters for export and as strike aircraft for the French Air Force. Variants included the two-seat Mirage IIID for Australia, the IIIR reconnaissance sub-family, the Mirage IIIS for Switzerland (with Hughes TARAN radar matched to Falcon AAMs), and the South African Z series. Many of these featured the higher-rated Atar 9K-SO, an engine offered in retrofit packages that could add modern electronics, a 'fly-by-wire' control system and canard foreplanes

1957 First flight of Tupolev Tu-28P (Fiddler) (USSR)
1957 First flight of Tupolev Tu-114 Rossiya (Cleat) (USSR)
1957 The Atoll air-to-air missile enters service with the USSR
23 Jan 57 First flight of Nord 1500-02 Griffin II
19 Feb 57 First flight of Bell X-14 (US)
27 Feb 57 First flight of Dassault Super Mystère B2 (F)
March 57 First flight of Antonov An-10 Ukrania (USSR)
28 March 57 First flight of Canadair CP-107 Argus (CA)
28 March 57 First flight of Canadair CL-44 Argus freighter (CA)
2 April 57 First flight of Shorts SC.1 (GB)
4 April 57 First flight of English Electric P.1B Lightning (GB)
8 April 57 First flight of Aero L-200A Morava (CH)

BAC LIGHTNING F.6 first flight 4 April1957

Powerplant: Two 15,680lb (7,112kg) thrust Rolls-Royce Avon 302
Primary role: All-weather interceptor
Dimensions: Wingspan 34ft 10in (10.6m); length 53ft 3in (16.23m)
Armament: Interchangeable packs for two all-attitude Red Top or stern-chase Firestreak guided missiles; option of two 30mm Aden cannon in forward part of belly tank; export versions up to 6,000lb (2,721kg) bombs or other offensive stores above and below wings
Weights: Empty 28,000lb (12,700kg); loaded 50,000lb (22,680kg)
Speed: 1,500mph (2,415km/h) at 40,000ft (12,200m) max
Range: 800 miles (1,290km)
Crew: 1
Production total (all marks): 338
Variants: F.1,F.1A, F.2, F.3, T.4, T.5, F.6, F.52, F.53, T.54, and T.55

The English Electric P.1B first flew on 4 April 1957 and the first production Lightning F.1 on 30 October 1959, the first F.6 following on 17 April 1964. Compared with the prototype P.1A, the P.1B had a new fuselage with a two-shock intake and Avon engines fitted with primitive after-burning. It achieved a speed of Mach 2 on 25 November 1958. With 20 pre-production aircraft, the Lightning F.1 was cleared for service in 1960, giving the RAF a modern supersonic fighter with radar and guided missiles. However, it was a complex machine, flying rates were poor and the maintenance burden heavy. In 1957 the British government believed that manned fighters were obsolete, but allowed production of the improved F.2, with fully variable afterburners and all-weather navigation, in 1961. In 1964 policy was overturned and the Mk 3 was produced, with more powerful engines, more fuel, a bigger fin, collision-course fire control, all-attitude Red Top missiles and no cannon. In 1965, on BAC's advice, fuel capacity was doubled and kinked and cambered wings were fitted. Variants included the T.4 and T.5 dual conversion trainers, equivalent to the F.2 and F.3. For export to Saudi Arabia and Kuwait, BAC developed 57 multi-role fighters and attack aircraft.

16 May 57 First flight of Saunders-Roe SR.53 (GB)

17 May 57 First flight of Westland Wessex (GB)

30 May 57 The USAF discloses a nuclear-tipped development of Hughes Falcon air-to-air missile, destined for the F-102 fleet

June 57 First flight of Ilyushin Il-18 Moskva (USSR)

5 June 57 First flight of Mil Mi-6/Mi-22 (Hook) (USSR)

29 June 57 A Bristol Britannia completes the first non-stop flight from London to Vancouver by

ANTONOV An-12 (CUB) first flight 16 December 1957

Powerplant: Four 4,000shp (2,983kW) Ivchyenko Al-20K
Primary role: Medium-range assault transport
Dimensions: Wingspan 124 ft 8in (38.0m); length 108ft 7½in (33.1m)
Armament/payload: Two 23mm cannon in tail turret; 100 paratroops/44,092lb (20,000kg) freight
Weights: Loaded 134,460lb (61,000kg)
Speed: 476mph (766kph) max
Range: 2,237 miles (3,600km) with max payload
Crew: 5-6
Production total (all marks): Over 850

Designed as a civil and military airlifter equivalent to the C-130 Hercules, the An-12 was based on the An-10 airliner, with the airframe modified for greater fuel capacity, larger-area vertical tail surfaces, ventral doors and a tail turret. The first flight in took place in 1957. Side-opening rear doors were full-width, allowing straight-in freight loading, but a separate ramp was needed to load vehicles. As an alternative to paratroops, a variety of assault vehicles could be carried, with a 14-seat pressurized compartment behind the flight deck for vehicle crews. When transporting paratroops, the unpressurized hold meant that the An-126P 'Cub A' had a ceiling of 16,400ft (5,000m). This model was replaced by the revized Il-76.

__Fairey Rotodyne__ (GB) first flew 6 Nov 1957

an airliner on a proving flight. 5,100 miles in 14hrs 40mins

9 July 57 First flight of Aviation Traders ATL.90 Accountant

26 July 57 First flight of Bréguet 1001 Taon (F)

1 Aug 1957 Joint US/Canadian NORAD (North Atlantic Air Defense Command) comes into being. The USA and Canada have more than 1,000 aircraft dedicated to air defense

13 Aug 57 First flight of Boeing Vertol VZ-2A (Model 76) (US)

19–20 Aug 57 Maj Simmons, USAF, sets a balloon world altitude record of 30,942m (101,516ft)

4 Sept 57 First flight of Lockheed CL-329 Jetstar (US)

3 Nov 57 Three B-52s make first non-stop round-the-world flight

6 Nov 57 First flight of Fairey Rotodyne (GB)

26 Nov 57 First flight of Piaggio P.166 (IT)

6 Dec 57 First flight of Lockheed L-188 Electra (US)

10 Dec 57 First flight of Macchi M.B.326A (IT)

16 Dec 57 First flight of Antonov An-12 (Cub) (USSR)

19 Dec 57 An Israeli El Al Britannia makes a record-breaking non-stop flight from New York to Tel Aviv of 6,100 miles (9,817 km) at an average speed of 401 mph

1958 First flight of SNECMA C-450 Coléoptère (F)

1958 First flight of Piper PA-25 Pawnee (US)

1958 Firestreak, the first British air-to-air missile enters service

19 Jan 58 First flight of Fuji T1F2 (J)

20 Jan 58 First flight of Nord 3400 (F)

5 Feb 58 A BEA Ambassador airliner crashes while attempting take-off at Munich airport, killing 23 passenger and crew including 8 members of Manchester United soccer team

10 Feb 58 First flight of North American T2J-2 Buckeye (US)

21 Feb 58 RAF Canberra bombers given nuclear strike capability, initially with US weapons

22 Feb 58 First flight of Auster J/1U Workmaster (GB)

March 1958 First flight of Antonov An-14 Ptchelka (USSR)

11 Mar 58 First flight of Handley Page Herald (GB)

25 March 58 First flight of Avro Canada Arrow (CA)

27 March 58 First flight of Aerfer Ariete (IT)

27 May 58 First flight of McDonnell F4 Phantom (see overleaf) (US)

30 May 58 First flight of Douglas DC-8 (US)

22 June 58 First flight of Boeing-Vertol CH-46 Sea Knight (US)

__Douglas DC-8 (US)__ first flew 30 May 58

__Boeing-Vertrol CH-46 Sea Knight (US)__ first flew 22 June 58

MCDONNELL DOUGLAS F-4 PHANTOM II first flight 27 May 1958

Powerplant: Two 17,900lb (8,119kg) J79-GE-17
Primary role: Multi-role fighter
Dimensions: Wingspan 38ft 5in (11.79m); length 63ft (19.2m)
Armament: One 20mm cannon and up to 16,000lb (7,256kg) of disposable stores
Weights: Empty 29,000lb (13,150kg); loaded 60,630lb (27,500kg)
Speed: Mach 2.17 max at altitude
Range: 1,750 miles (2,820km)
Crew: 2
Production total (all marks): 5,057
Variants: F-4A–G, K, M, N, S, RF-4

Developed as a carrier fighter for the US Navy, the Phantom was one of the world's most successful warplane designs and proved to be the USAF's most important fighter in the late 1960s and 1970s. The first flight by the prototype XF4H-1 was made in May 1958. The naval F-4A and B (fighter and strike fighter) marks were followed by the USAF's F-4C, D and E, which introduced more powerful engines, smaller APQ-120 radar, manoeuvring wing slats and a 20mm multi-barreled cannon. The US Air Force, Navy and Marine Corps

employed F-4s throughout the Vietnam War, and Phantoms were also engaged in air-to-air and air-to-ground fighting in various Middle East conflicts. As well as export, production was licensed in various countries, with British marks (F-4K and M) equipped with Rolls-Royce Spey engines. Production ended in 1979. The Phantom saw service with Britain, Germany, Greece, Israel, Iran, Japan, Saudi Arabia, South Korea, Spain, Turkey, and the US.

18 July 58 USAF Super Sabres and Voodoos flying from Turkey as well as Navy Demons, Crusaders, Skyrays, Furies and Skyraiders from the 6th Fleet, in support of the US landings in Lebanon

30 July 58 First flight of de Havilland Canada DHC-4 Caribou (CA)

De Havilland Canada DHC-4 Caribou (CA) *first flew 30 July 1958*

Blackburn Buccaneer (GB) *first flew 26 Aug 1958*

14 Aug 58 First flight of Grumman Gulfstream (US)

26 Aug 58 First flight of Blackburn Buccaneer (GB)

28 Aug 58 First flight of Cessna 210 (US)

29 Aug 58 First flight of Lockheed P3V-1 Orion (US)

31 Aug 58 First flight of North American A3J-1 Vigilante (US)

9 Sept 58 First flight of Lockheed X-7 (US)

16 Sept 58 First flight of North American T-39 Sabreliner (US)

24 Sept 58 Communist and Nationalist Chinese fighters clash. The first time air-to-air missiles (Sidewinder) successfully used in combat, four communist MiGs claimed destroyed

26 Oct 58 Pan Am opens first Boeing 707 service, between New York and Paris

Oct 58 Malayan Emergency. During Operation 'Tiger' 4, 133 fully equiped British troops are

ARMSTRONG WHITWORTH ARGOSY first flight 8 Jan 1959

Powerplant: Four 2,680shp Rolls-Royce Dart RDa.8 Mk 101
Primary role: Medium-range tactical transport
Dimensions: Wingspan 115ft (35.05m); length 89ft 2in (27.2m)
Payload: 69 troops/54 paratroops/48 litters/20,000lb (13,154kg) freight
Weights: 103,000lb (46,712kg) loaded
Speed: 266mph (428kph) max at 20,000ft (6,100m)
Range: 345 miles (555km)
Crew: 4
Production total (all marks): 56

Developed to replace the Vickers Valetta, the Argosy was the military counterpart to the AW.660 civil transport. The first flight took place in March 1961, more than two years after that of the civil prototype. The design featured a high set wing with a twin boom tail extending from the inner engine nacelles. Straight-in loading and airdrops were permitted through upward/downward-opening rear 'crocodile doors' at the end of a circular-section fuselage. For paratrooping, the volume inside the doors was used for kit stowage. With a strong tricycle landing gear, the Argosy could operate from semi-prepared surfaces. The type served with six RAF squadrons (three at home and one each in Cyprus, Aden and the Far East) before its withdrawal in 1975 as an economy measure.

airlifted in and out of operational areas

26 Oct 58 Although designed for domestic routes a Pan Am Boeing 707-121 leaves Idlewild, New York for Le Bourget, France with 111 passengers and 11 crew, on a promotional transatlantic flight

13 Dec 58 First flight of Kaman H-43B Huskie (US)

Dec 58 First flight of Dornier Do 29 (G)

1959 First flight of Kamov Ka-18 (Hog) (USSR)

1959 First flight of Piper UO-1 Aztec (US)

1959 MiG-21 enters service with Soviet Airforce

1959 First flight of Cessna 210 (US)

8 Jan 59 First flight of Armstrong Whitworth AW.660 Argosy (GB)

20 Jan 59 First flight of Vickers Vanguard (GB)

27 Jan 59 First flight of Convair CV-880 Coronado (US)

11 Feb 59 A US weather balloon climbs to a record of 146,00ft (44,500m)

3 Mar 59 US Chief of Naval Operations stresses danger to US warships from growing Soviet submarine strength. This leads to development of more effective ASW aircraft

10 March 59 First flight of Northrop T-38A Talon (US)

13 April 59 First flight of Grumman AO-1AF Mohawk (US)

23 Apr 59 The US Hound Dog thermo-nuclear stand-off missile makes 1st flight, launched from a B-52 bomber

29 April 59 First flight of Dornier Do 28 (G)

15 May 59 Last use of water-based aircraft (a Sunderland) by RAF

17 June 59 First flight of Dassault Mirage IV-A (F)

30 July 59 First flight of Northrop N-156A (F-5 Freedom Fighter) (US)

Sept 59 Revealed Cessna 407 (US)

30 Oct 1959 26 people are killed when a Piedmont Airline aircraft crashes. Uniquely, there is one survivor

16 Nov 59 Capt Joseph W. Kittinger Jr makes a balloon ascent from White Sands, New Mexico. After gaining an altitude of 23,285m he parachutes to the ground, a free-fall of 19,505m.

20 Dec 59 First flight of Antonov An-24 (Coke) (USSR)

1960 First flight of Tupolev Tu-124 (Cookpot) (USSR)

Antonov An-24 (Coke) *(USSR) first flew 20 Dec 1959*

Northrop T-38 Talon *(US) first flew 17 March 1961*

Grumman A-6A Intruder *(US) first flew 19 April 1960*

Avro 748 (H.S.748) *(GB) first flew 24 June 1960*

Hawker Siddeley P.1127 *(GB) first flew 21 Oct 1960*

6 Jan 60 A National Airlines DC-6 is destroyed by a bomb in flight from New York to Miami, killing all 34 people on board

13 Jan 60 First flight of Canadair CL-41A Tutor (CA)

14 Jan 60 First flight of Piper PA-28 Cherokee 235B (US)

16 Feb 60 In a change of policy, announcement that UK will rely on ballistic nuclear missiles launched by aircraft or from submarines

29 Feb 60 First flight of Beech C-55 Baron (US)

19 April 60 First flight of Grumman A2F-1 (A-6A) Intruder (US)

7 May 60 Lockheed U-2 high-altitude reconnaissance aircraft flying over Soviet Union, piloted by Gary Powers, shot down by a Soviet SAM

3 June 60 Maj Robert White, USAF, pilots the North American X-15A research aircraft to a height of 41,600m (136,500ft)

24 June 60 First flight of Avro 748 (H.S.748) (GB)

29 June 60 No 74 Squadron RAF, operates the first British supersonic fighter, the Lightning F.Mk 1

1 July 60 Soviet MiG-19 shoots down a US RB-47E Stratojet reconnaissance aircraft over the Barents Sea

16 Aug 60 Capt Joseph W. Kittinger Jr USAF jumps from a balloon at 31,150m (102,200 ft) making a free fall of 25,815m (84,700ft)

10 Sept 60 NORAD carries out operation Sky Shield, air exercize to test capability and preparedness of US/Canadian radar and electronics early warning system.

4 Oct 1960 Major aircraft accident blamed on a bird strike when an Eastern Airlines jetliner crashes into Boston Harbor. 62 people are killed

18 Oct 60 First flight of Beriev Be-12/Be-14 (Mail) (USSR)

***Kamov Ka-25 (Hormone)** (USSR) first flew 26 April 1961*

21 Oct 60 First flight of Hawker Siddeley P.1127 (GB)

21 Oct 60 First flight of Grumman W2F-1 Hawkeye (US)

16 Dec 1960 A United Airlines DC-8 collides with a TWA Super Constellation over New York City, killing all 134 people on board

VIETNAM WAR

Vietnam (US involvement 1961–73) is the first major war for a decade and sees many technical and operational innovations, including use of helicopters to deploy troops en masse as well as for find and search operations. Development of dedicated helicopter gunships (HueyCobra). Laser-guided bombs. Surface-to-air missiles on a large scale

30 March 61 NASA pilot Joe Walker attains a height of 51,695m (169,600ft) in the North American X-15A research aircraft

12 April 61 Russian Yuri Gagarin is the first man to enter space

15 Apr 61 Cuba. 16 B-26 bombers support the unsuccessful Bay of Pigs invasion. In heavy fighting the invaders lose over half the B-26s deployed which are opposed by Castro's B-26s, T-33s and Sea Furies.

26 April 61 First flight of Kamov Ka-25 (Hormone) (USSR)

May 61 First flight of Soko Galeb (JU)

1 May 1961 The first occurrence of a US airliner to be hijacked to Cuba

5 May 61 Alan Shepard is the first American to enter space

June 61 First flight of Tupolev Tu-22 (Blinder) (USSR)

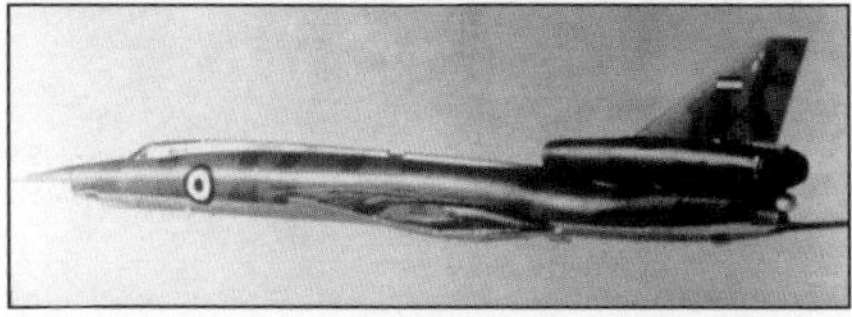

***Tupolev Tu-22 (Blinder)** (USSR) first flew June 1961*

MIL Mi-8 first flight 1961

Powerplant: Two 1267kW (1,700shp) Isotov TV2-117A
Primary role: Medium general-purpose
Dimensions: Main rotor diameter 69ft 10½in (21.29m); length (rotors turning) 82ft 9½in (25.24m)
Payload: 28–32 passengers or 8,818lb (4,000kg) of freight carried internally, or a 6,614lb (3,000kg) slung load
Weights: Loaded 26,455lb (12,000kg)
Speed: 140mph (225kph) cruising at optimum altitude

Range: 311 miles (500km) with 28 passengers
Crew: 2
Production total (all marks): 12,000 (major part for military service)
Variants: See notes
Developed in parallel with military versions, the civil Mi-8 has rectangular instead of circular cabin windows, but all Aeroflot's passenger versions can be quickly converted for military operations. Soot from hot gas marks the surface around the engine jetpipes, so Aeroflot's models feature a black area to hide this. Best known as the 'Hip' military series, the Mi-8 first flew in 1961 with a single 2013kW (2,700shp) Soloviev turboshaft and a four-blade main rotor. In September 1962 the second prototype 'Hip-B', with a definitive twin-turbine powerplant plus five-blade main rotor, was flown. The Mi-8 Salon variant was designed for eleven VIP passengers, and the Mi-8T utility type, with 24 tip-up seats, can carry freight internally or externally. The Mi-17 was designed for improved 'hot and high' performance, with upgraded transmission and two 1417kW (1,900shp) Isotov Tv3-117 turboshafts.

24 June 61 First flight of Hindustan HF-24 (IN)
24 June 61 First flight of Mil Mi-8 (Hip) (USSR)
July 61 The Mirage III becomes operational with the French Airforce, their first Mach 2 fighter
July 61 Phantom II becomes operational with US Navy
16 Aug 61 First flight of Bell UH-1D Iroquois (US)
18 Sept 61 United Nations Secretary General Dag Hammarskjold killed in an air crash in Africa
21 Sept 61 First flight of Boeing-Vertol CH-47A Chinook (US)
5 Oct 61 The US Air Force's 507th Tactical Control Group arrives in South Vietnam to begin US training assistance for the South Vietnamese Air Force
14 Oct 61 North American Air Defense Command (NORAD) exercize involving thousands of aircraft, largest air defense exercize to that date in western hemisphere
21 Oct 61 First flight of Bréguet 1150 Atlantic (F)
9 November 61 In the last high-speed flight made by the X-15A during 1961, Maj Robert White USAF, attains a speed of 6,587 km/ph (4,093 mph) at 30,970m (101,600ft)
11 Dec 61 First direct US military support for South Vietnam – two US Army helicopter companies
15 Dec 61 NORAD's SAGE system becomes fully operational (21 control centres)

1962 First flight of L-29 Delfin (CH)
9 Jan 62 First flight of de Havilland Trident (GB)
2 Feb 62 US Air Force suffers its first loss of the Vietnam War, a C-123 Provider transport

***De Havilland Trident** (UK) first flew 9 Jan 1962*

27 Feb 62 Two South Vietnamese aircraft attack the Presidential Palace in attempt to kill President Diem
28 Feb 62 In the first manned test of the steel cocoon-type escape capsule carried by the General Dynamics/Convair B-58A Hustler, WO Edward J Murra is ejected from the aircraft which is travelling at 909 kph at 6,100m

BOEING VERTOL CH-47 CHINOOK first flight 21 September 1961

Powerplant: Two 3,356kW (4,500shp) Avco Lycoming T55-L-712
Primary role: Medium transport
Dimensions: Rotor diameter 60ft 0in (18.29m); length overall 99ft 0in (30.18m)
Payload: 44 troops or 18,000lb (8,164kg) freight, or 20,700lb (9,389kg) freight carried externally
Weights: Loaded 50,000lb (22,680kg)
Speed: 185mph (298kph) cruising at sea level
Range: 115 miles (185km) with 18,000lb (8,164kg) load
Crew: 2–3
Production total (all marks): 1,173
Variants: A/B/C/D/HT-17/HC.1

Developed for the US Army as a medium transport helicopter, the YHC-1B prototype first flew in September 1961, with CH-47A production models entering service in 1962. A more powerful version of the Model 107, the CH-47A had quadricycle instead of tricycle landing gear, and 1,641kW (2,200shp) T55 L-5 turboshafts for a payload of 44 troops or a

slung load of 16,000lb (7,257kg). CH-47Bs and -47Cs were even more powerful, and earlier variants were often upgraded to CH-47D standard with advanced avionics, crash-resistant systems, a three-point suspension and composite rotor blades. The Chinook can lift heavy loads either internally or from three underslung cargo hooks, and with a rear ramp vehicles can be loaded inside. It is in service with several countries.

March–June 62 USA. A bear and a chimpanzee used as 'guinea pigs' for high-speed tests of the B-58 escape capsule

22 May 1962 45 people are killed when a Continental Boeing 707 crashes after a bomb explodes as it flies over Kansas

19 June 62 A USAF superpressure balloon lands near Iwo Jima after a 19 day flight from Bermuda at a constant height of 20,725m (68,000ft)

29 June 62 First flight of Vickers VC-10 (GB)

Vickers VC-10 *(GB) first flew 29 June 1962*

12 Oct 62 First flight of Dassault Balzac (F)

22 Oct 62 President Kennedy announces US reconnaissance aircraft have identified offensive missile sites being constructed in Cuba

19 Sept 62 First flight of Aero Spacelines Pregnant Guppy (US)

15–28 Oct 62 Cuban Missile Crisis brings the world to the brink of nuclear war

7 Nov 62 First flight of Piper PA-30-160 Twin Comanche B (US)

7 Dec 62 First flight of Sud-Aviation SA 3210 Super Frelon (F)

31 Dec 62 US announces cancellation of air-launched ballistic Skybolt missile programme upon which UK deterrent capability was to be based

1963 NASA pilot Joe Walker flies the North American X-15A to a height of 107,955m (354,200ft). He qualifies for 'astronaut's wings' having exceeded a height of 80km (50miles)

7 Jan 63 First flight of Short Skyvan (GB)

Short Skyvan *(GB) first flew 7 Jan 1963*

TRANSALL C-130 first flight March 1963

Name: Transall C-160
Powerplant: Two 6,100shp (4,549kW) Rolls-Royce Tyne Mk 22
Primary role: Short/medium-range medium assault transport
Dimensions: Wingspan 131ft 2¾in (40m); length 106ft 3½in (32.4m)
Payload: 93 troops/88 paratroops/35,273lb (16,000kg) freight
Weights: Loaded 112,438lb (51,000kg)
Speed: 319mph (514kph) max at 16,000ft (4,875m)
Range: 1,150 miles (1,850km) with max payload
Crew: 4
Production total (all marks): 169 production versions
Variants: Transall II

Designed by partnership in France and West Germany as a tactical airlift alternative to the American Hercules, the C-160 first flew in March 1963 as a conventional high-wing transport, with multi-wheel landing gear, an upswept tail and a rear ramp/door accessing a hold 44ft 4in (13.51m) long. Initial production amounted to 169 aircraft, 90 C-130Ds for the West German Luftwaffe, 50 C-130Fs for France, 20 C-160Ts for Turkey and nine C-160Zs for South Africa. In 1977 France placed a second order to include command post and electronic reconnaissance versions, and the first of these flew in 1980. The second-batch machines have modernized electronics, extra centre-section tankage and a refuelling probe. Ten were configured as single-point tankers, and others as communications relay aircraft and signals intelligence-gatherers.

Lockheed C-141A Starlifter *(US) first flew 17 Dec 1963*

9 Feb 63 First flight of Boeing 727 (US)
25 Feb 63 First flight of Transall C-160 (F/G)
26 Mar 63 First flight of Hunting H.126 (GB)
4 May 63 First flight of G.A.M.Dassault Falcon (Mystère 20) (F)
29 June 63 First flight of Saab 105 (SW)
Mid 63 The British nuclear armed Blue Steel missile becomes operational with the RAF
20 Aug 63 First flight of BAC One-Eleven (GB)
14 Sept 63 First flight of Mitsubishi MU-2 (J)
16 Sept 63 First flight of Yakovlev Yak-36 (Freehand) (USSR)
7 Oct 63 First flight of Learjet Model 23 (US)
20 Nov 63 USAF formal acceptance of 1st McDonnell F-4C Phantom II fighters
17 Dec 63 First flight of Lockheed C-141A Starlifter (US)
21 Dec 63 First flight of Hawker Siddeley H.S.748MF Andover (GB)
24 Dec 63 New York International Airport re-dedicated as John F. Kennedy Airport

1964 First flight of Helio HST-550 Stallion (US)
1964 Red Top air-to-air missile enters service (GB)
5 Jan 64 First flight of Short SC-5/10 Belfast C. Mk 1 (GB)
17 Feb 64 American Jarrie Mock is the first woman to complete a solo flight around the world, taking 29 days in a Cessna 180
6 March 64 First flight of Mikoyan MiG-25 (Foxbat) (USSR)
9 April 64 First flight of de Havilland Canada

Mikoyan MiG-25 (Foxbat) *(USSR) first flew 6 March 1964*

LOCKHEED SR-71 BLACKBIRD first flight 22 December 1964

Powerplant: Two 32,500lb (14,740kg) s.t. Pratt & Whitney J58
Primary role: High-altitude strategic reconnaissance
Dimensions: Wingspan 55ft 7in (16.94m); length 107ft 5in (32.74m)
Armament: None
Weights: Empty 60,000lb (27,210kg;) loaded 170,000lb (77,110kg)
Speed: Mach 3+ max
Range: c.3,000miles (4,830km)
Crew: 2
Production total (all marks): 32

Variants: A11/A/B
Blackbirds were designed for speeds greater than Mach 3 at 85,000ft altitude, featuring huge engines which acted almost at ramjets, with movable inlet spikes and auxiliary intakes to optimize airflow. The type entered clandestine reconnaissance service in 1966, employed in overflying lightly defended countries. Electronic, optical, radar and infrared sensors were located in the nose cone and along the fuselage sides. Two machines were based at RAF Mildenhall in Britain.

***Sikorsky CH-53A Sea Stallion** (US) first flew 14 Oct 1964*

DHC-5 Buffalo (CA)
7 May 64 First flight of BAC Super VC-10 (GB)
2 Aug 64 US Navy aircraft from the aircraft carrier USS *Ticonderoga* sink a North Vietnamese torpedo-boat, one of a number which have tried to attack the destroyer USS *Maddox* in the Gulf of Tonkin
5 Aug 64 US carrier-based aircraft attack North Vietnamese naval bases
4 Sept 64 First flight of HAL HJT-16 Kiran (IN)
21 Sept 64 First flight of North American XB-70A Valkyrie (US)
27 Sept 64 First flight of BAC TSR-2 (GB)
14 Oct 64 First flight of Sikorsky CH-53A Sea Stallion (US)
18 Nov 64 First flight of Grumman C-2A (US)
21 Nov 64 First flight of Agusta A 105 (IT)
21 Dec 64 First flight of General Dynamics F-111A (US)
22 Dec 64 First flight of Lockheed SR-71A Blackbird (US)
1965 First flight of Sukhoi Su-15 (Flagon-A) (USSR)
11 Jan 65 First flight of Aero Commander Jet Commander 1121 (US)
7 Feb 65 US Air Force and South Vietnam aircraft attack military targets in North Vietnam
23 Feb 65 First flight of Douglas DC-9 (US)
27 Feb 65 First flight of Antonov An-22 Antei (Cock) (USSR)

Vietnam: Operation 'Rolling Thunder'

12 March 65–31 Oct 68 The sustained aerial bombardment of North Vietnam. During the 45-month campaign 645,000 tons of ordnance were released in the course of over 306,000 aircraft sorties
6 April 65 UK cancels the TSR.2
15 April 65 First flight of Sud-Aviation SA.330 Puma (F)
1 May 65 World speed record set by the YF-12 at 2,070mph/3331km/ph (US)
20 May 65 First flight of de Havilland Canada

***Sud-Aviation SA.330 Puma** (F) first flew 15 April 1965*

***North American OV-10A Bronco** (US) first flew 16 July 1965*

DHC-6 Twin Otter (CA)

20 May 65 At Cairo Airport, in Egypt, a Pakistani Boeing 720 crashes, killing 121 people

12 June 65 First flight of Britten-Norman BN-2 Islander (GB)

18 June 65 B-52 bombers make their first strikes of the Vietnam War in South Vietnam

10 July 65 F-4 Phantoms are the first US aircraft to score air-to-air victories during Vietnam War

July 65 First launch site for Soviet-built SA-2 Guidleine SAMs in North Vietnam

16 July 65 First flight of North American OV-10A Bronco (US)

16 Aug 65 Operational debut of AGM-45 Shrike anti-radar missile in Vietnam

1–25 Sept 65 India and Pakistan make considerable use of air power during their war over the sovereignty of Kashmir

11 Sept 65 Equipped with more than 400 helicopters and numerous other aircraft, the 1st US Cavalry Division arrives in South Vietnam

13 Sept 65 A hot-air balloon was flown to an altitude of 9,770ft (2978m) by B. Boagan, the first ratified record set by this type of craft

27 Sept 65 First flight of LTV A-7A Corsair (US)

Nov 65 First flight of Agusta A 106 (IT)

1966 First flight of Harbin H-5 (Il-28 Beagle) (CHI)

1966 First flight of Sukhoi Su-11 (Flagon A) (USSR)

***LTV A-7A Corsair** (US) first flew 27 Sept 1965*

10 Jan 66 First flight of Bell 206A JetRanger (US)

17 Jan 66 First flight of Chengdu J-7 (MiG-21) (CHI)

8 February 66 Freddie Laker announces the formation of his low-cost airline, Laker Airways

23 Feb 66 First flight of Dornier Do 28D Skyservant (G)

17 March 66 First flight of Bell X-22A (US)

12 April 66 B-52s bomb targets in North Vietnam for the first time

24 June 66 A Bombay to New York Air India flight crashes into Mont Blanc in Switzerland. 117 people die in the crash

1 July 66 US Navy aircraft from the aircraft carriers, USS *Constellation* and USS *Hancock* sink three North Vietnamese torpedo-boats which have tried to attack US Naval vessels in the Gulf of Tonkin

2 Aug 66 First flight of Sukhoi Su-17/Su-20/Su-22 (Fitter) (USSR)

12 Aug 66 First flight of Learjet 25 Transporter (US)

31 Aug 66 First flight of Hawker Siddeley Harrier (GB)

2 Oct 66 First flight of Grumman Gulfstream II (US)

Nov 66 First flight of Bushmaster Aircraft Bushmaster 2000 (US)

23 Dec 66 First flight of Dassault Mirage F.1 (F)

4 Jan 67 Luftwaffe F-104G Starfighters returned to service after modifications

22 Feb 67 Operation 'Junction City', first airborne assault in Vietnam

29 March 67 First flight of HAL HF-24 Marut (IN)

7 April 67 First flight of Sud-Aviation SA.321F Civil Super Frelon (F)

7 April 67 First flight of Eurocopter SA 342 Gazelle (INT)

9 April 67 First flight of Boeing 737-100 (US)

20 April 67 A Swiss Britannia crashes at Nicosia, Cyprus, killing 126 people

Grumman Gulfstream II *(US) first flew 2 Oct 1966*

Boeing 737 *(US) first flew 9 April 1967*

Dassault Mirage F.1 *(F) first flew 23 Dec 1966*

Bell AH-1G HueyCobra (US) first flew May 1967

May 67 First flight of Bell AH-1G HueyCobra (US)
May 67 First flight of Handley Page HP.137 Jetstream (GB)
23 May 67 First flight of Hawker Siddeley Nimrod (GB)
5–10 JUNE 62: ARAB-ISRAELI 'SIX-DAY WAR'
5–10 June 67 Pre-emptive air strikes by Israeli Air Force render air forces of Egypt, Jordan, Syria almost ineffective. Some 380 Arab and 60 Israeli planes are lost
10 June 67 First flight of Mikoyan MiG-23 (Flogger) (USSR)
2 July 67 First flight of Sukhoi Su-24 (Fencer) (USSR)
10 Oct 67 First flight of Lockheed AH-56A Cheyenne (US)
17 Oct 67 First flight of Zlin Z 42 (CH)
26 Oct 67 First flight of BAC 167 Strikemaster (GB)
8 Nov 67 RAF uses 50 transport aircraft to withdraw troops from Aden, its biggest transport operation since Berlin airlift
18 Nov 67 First flight of Dassault Mirage G (F)
28 Nov 67 First flight of Pilatus PC-8 Twin Porter (SWI)
22 Dec 67 First flight of MBB Bö 209 Monsun (G)

1968 First flight of Cavalier Turbo Mustang (US)
1968 First flight of Mil Mi-12 (Homer) (USSR)
1968 First flight of IS-23 (RO)
1968 First flight of IAR-821 (RO)
March 68 First flight of Piper PA-31P (US)
17 March 68 1st operational use of USAF F-111As in Vietnam
29 March 68 First flight of LFU 205 (G)
30 April 68 RAF Fighter Command and Bomber Command merge as RAF Strike Command
13 May 68 First flight of Piper PA-35 Pocono (US)
25 May 68 First flight of Grumman EA-6B Prowler (US)
30 June 68 First flight of Lockheed C-5A Galaxy (US)
23 July 68 First flight of Nord 500 (F)
8 Sept 68 First flight of SEPECAT Jaguar (F/GB)
11 Sept 68 First flight of Dassault MD 320 Hirondelle (F)
4 Oct 68 First flight of Tupolev Tu-154 (USSR)
26 Oct 68 First flight of Embraer EMB-110 Bandeirante (BR)
31 Oct 68 US halt of the bombing of North Vietnam
4 Nov 68 First flight of Aero L-39 Albatross (CH)

Mikoyan MiG-23 (USSR) first flew 10 June 1967

Lockheed C-5 Galaxy *(US) first flew 30 June 1968*

SEPECAT Jaguar *(F/GB) first flew 8 Sept 1968*

BOEING 747 first flight 9 February 1969

Powerplant: Four 50,000lb (22,675kg) s.t. class turbofans (e.g. General Electric CF6-50/80, Pratt & Whitney JT9D, Rolls-Royce RB211-524)
Primary role: Passenger transport
Dimensions: Wingspan 195ft 8in (59.63m); length 231ft 4in (70.51)
Payload: 452–516 passengers/142,900lb (64,818kg) freight
Weights: Max take-off 833,000lb (377,840kg)
Speed: 522kts (965kph) cruising
Range: 7,600 miles (12,250km)
Crew: 3
Production total (all marks): 1,290
Variants: See notes

The original 'Jumbo Jet', the Boeing 747 was launched on 13 April 1966 with an order for 21 aircraft from Pan American. The prototype first flew on 9 February 1969 and the aircraft entered service in January 1970, more than doubling passenger and cargo transport capacities. Passenger versions include the 747-100 and -200; the 747SP, a lighter weight, short-bodied, long-range version of the 747-100;

and the 747-300, with increased passenger accommodation and crew rest areas in an extended upper deck. The latest version of the aircraft is the 747-400, an advanced long-range variant of the 747-300 with 58,000lb (26,300kg) s.t. class engines, a two-crew all-digital flight deck, a tailplane fuel tank and winglets.

24 Dec 68 First flight of Xi'an Aircraft Co H6 (Tu-16 Badger) (CHI)

1969 A total of 57 planes hijacked to Cuba this year

9 Feb 69 First flight of Boeing 747 'Jumbo Jet' (US)

2 March 69 First flight of Aerospatiale/BAC Concorde (see overleaf) (F/GB)

7 May 69 First flight of Westland Sea King/Commando HAS Mk I (GB)

Westland Sea King/Commando *(GB) first flew 7 May 1969*

5 June 69 The first retaliatory air strikes made into North Vietnam since the bombing halt of November of previous year. They recur from time to time

5 June 69 First flight of Tu-144 'Concordski' beats Concorde in going supersonic (see overleaf)

21 July 69 An American, Neil Armstrong, is the first man to step on the Moon

10 Aug 69 First flight of Tupolev Tu-22M (Backfire) (USSR)

20 Aug 69 First flight of FMA IA 58 Pucará (AR)

20 Aug 69 First flight of Piper PA42 Cheyenne (US)

Tupolev Tu-22M (Backfire) *(USSR) first flew 10 Aug 1969*

AÉROSPATIALE/BAC CONCORDE first flight 2 March 1969

Powerplant: Four 38,050lb (17,256kg) Rolls-Royce/SNECMA Olympus 593 Mark 610
Primary role: Supersonic airliner
Dimensions: Wingspan 83ft 10in (25.6m); length 202ft 4in (61.66m)
Payload: 131 (BA 100) passengers/29,000lb (13,150kg)
Weights: Loaded 408,000lb (185,070kg)
Speed: Mach 2.04 at 53,000ft (16,150m) max
Range: 4,092 miles (6,582km)
Crew: 6
Production total (all marks): 16, plus 2 prototype/pre-production models

Concorde was the more successful of the only two supersonic passenger airliners to have ever operated commercially, the other being the Tupolev Tu-144. The program was developed as a cooperative French/British project from 1962, and the prototypes first flew in 1969; pre-production models appeared in 1971 and the production standard aircraft flew in 1974. Because the aircraft needed afterburning engines to cruise supersonically, the project was economically threatened by rising fuel costs in the 1970s. Concorde was required by anti-noise pollution laws to fly at subsonic speeds over land, and the service was thereby effectively restricted to transatlantic crossings. Only British Airways and Air France operated Concorde, but these unique airliners proved popular and profitable for the carriers. Unusual features included the drooping nose to allow the pilot to see the ground during his landing approach. In flight, Concorde's outer fuselage temperature reached 1,800°F (1,000°C) with the friction causing the fuselage to stretch. Tragically, on 25 July 2000, 109 passengers and crew died when an Air France Concorde crashed on take-off at Paris, and the aircraft was grounded. Commercial operations resumed on 7 Nov 2001, but on 10 April 2003 British Airways and Air France simultaneously announced that they would retire Concorde later that year, citing low passenger numbers.

Tupolev Tu-144 *(USSR) first flew 5 June 69. 'Concordski' beat Concorde in going supersonic*

MIL Mi-24 (HIND) first flight 15 September 1969

Powerplant: Two 1,640kW (2,200shp) Isotov Tv3-117 turboshafts
Primary role: Assault
Dimensions: Rotor diameter 55ft 0in (16.76m); fuselage length 55ft 6in (16.9m)
Payload/armament: 8 troops; one 4-barrelled 12.7mm machine gun in nose, plus four 57mm rocket launcher pods
Weights: Loaded 24,100lb (10,940kg)
Speed: 200mph (322kph) max
Range: 140 miles (225km)
Crew: 2 plus 8 troops or 4 litters for wounded
Variants: Mi-25 (export variant). In service with over 20 countries

From 1972, early versions of the Mi-24 'Hind' saw service supporting Soviet ground troops. With a redesigned nose, the assault and anti-

armour 'Hind-D' appeared in 1976. Weapons included a turreted, four-barrelled 12.7mm machine gun and provision for four UV-32-57 57mm wing-mounted rocket pods. The 'Hind-E' appeared in 1981, with an IR jammer, IR-suppression exhaust mixers and provision for four AT-2 'Swatter' anti-armour missiles. Although well armed, 'Hinds' are large and cumbersome.

15 Sept 69 First flight of Mil Mi-24/ Mi-25/Mi-35 (Hind) (USSR)
27 Nov 69 First flight of IAI Arava (IS)
Arab-Israeli 'War of Attrition'
1969–70 Egyptian and Israeli continual skirmishing in the skies above the Suez Canal and Sinai. Russian pilots participate on the Egyptian side

22 Jan 70 First 'wide body' airline service begins with a Pan American Boeing 747 between JFK and Heathrow airports
1 February 70 Capt Raymond Munro makes the first hot air balloon crossing of the Irish Sea.
18 March–26 May 70 Major bombing campaign by US of targets in Cambodia in support of invading ground force
29 May 70 First flight of Dassault Milan (F)
2 July 70 First flight of Saab Sk 37 Viggen (SW)

***Saab Sk 37 Viggen** (SW) first flew 2 July 1970*

17 July 70 New Orleans Airport is first to introduce a passenger screening system to combat hijacking
18 July 70 First flight of Aeritalia (Fiat) G.222 (IT)
20 Aug 70 First flight of Mikoyan MiG-27 (Flogger) (USSR)
22 Aug 70 First flight of Aermacchi MB.326K/ MB.326G (IT)
29 Aug 70 First flight of McDonnell Douglas (see overleaf) DC-10 (US)
11 Sept 70 First flight of Britten-Norman Trislander (GB)
12 Sept 70 After hijacking them, Palestinian terrorists blow up a BOAC Super VC10, a TWA 707 and a Swissair DC-8, Dawson's Field, Jordan
16 Nov 70 First flight of Lockheed TriStar (US)

McDONNELL DOUGLAS DC-10 first flight 29 August 1970

Powerplant: Three 40,000lb (18,140kg) General Electric CF6-6D
Primary role: Passenger transport
Dimensions: Wingspan 165ft 4in (50.39m); length 181ft 7in (55.34m)
Payload: 208–380 passengers
Weights: Max take-off 555,000lb (251,742kg)
Speed: Mach 0.88 max; 498kts (925kph) cruising
Range: 6,850 miles (11,030km)
Crew: 3
Production total (all marks): 380
Variants:
Developed to satisfy US trunk carriers' short, medium and long-range needs, the DC-10C had the same innovative engine configuration, with two underwing pods and the third engine mounted at the base of the fin, as its rival Lockheed L-1011 TriStar. The first DC-10 Series 10 flew on 29 August 1970, and the type entered service with American Airlines in 1971. The DC-l0 Series 30, first flying on 21 June 1972, introduced intercontinental capability and served first with KLM and Swissair. Other models included the DC-10-30ER, with further increased range, the 30CF convertible passenger/cargo aircraft, the dedicated all-cargo Series 30F and the intercontinental Series 40, powered by three Pratt & Whitney JT9D-20 or -59A engines. An advanced development of the DC-10, the MD-11, features a fuselage 18ft 7in (5.66m) longer than that of the DC-10-30, aerodynamic improvements including winglets, an all-digital, two-crew flight deck, GE CF6-80 or P&W PW4000 series turbofans and restyled passenger cabins.

21 Dec 70 First flight of Grumman F-14A Tomcat (US)
25 Dec 70 First flight of Xi'an Y7 (CHI)

15 Jan 71 First flight of Yakovlev Yak-36MP (Forger-A) (USSR)
15 March 71 First flight of VFW-Fokker H3 Sprinter (G)
21 March 71 First flight of Westland WG.13 Lynx (GB)
25 March 71 First flight of Ilyushin Il-76 (Candid) (USSR)
29 April 71 First flight of Piper PE-1 Enforcer (US)
8 May 71 First flight of Dassault Mirage G8 (F)
18 May 71 First flight of Wassmer WA-43 Guépard (F)
28 May 71 First flight of Dassault/ Bréguet Mercure (F)
30 June 71 First flight of Robin HR 200 Acrobin (F)

Grumman F-14 Tomcat *(US) first flew 21 Dec 1970*

3 July 71 First flight of GAF N2 (AU)
14 July 71 First flight of VFW-Fokker VFW 614 (D)
4 Aug 71 First flight of Agusta A 109 Hirundo (see overleaf) (IT)
6 Aug 71 First flight of SA 341 Gazelle (F)
3 Sept 71 First flight of Embraer/ Aermacchi EMB-326 Xavante (BR/IT)
13 Sept 71 First flight of Bede BD-5 Micro (US)
Sept 71 First flight of IAI Kfir C2 (IS)

1972 First flight of Sukhoi Su-20 (Fitter) (USSR)
21 Jan 72 First flight of Lockheed S-3A Viking (US)

Lockheed S-3A Viking *(US) first flew 21 Jan 1972*

SA 341 Gazelle *(F) first flew 6 Aug 1971*

AGUSTA A109A Mk II first flight August 1971

Powerplant: Two 313kW (420shp) Allison 250-C20B
Primary role: Light general-purpose
Dimensions: Main rotor diameter 36ft 1in (11.0m); length (rotors turning) 42ft 9½in (13.05m)
Payload: 6 passengers or freight in the cabin, or a 2,000lb (907kg) slung load
Weights: Loaded 5,732lb (2,600kg)
Speed: 174mph (280kph) at sea level cruising
Range: 363 miles (585km)
Crew: 2
Production total (all marks): 600
Variants: 3

First proposed in the late 1960s as the single-turboshaft Hirundo (Swallow), the A109 was redesigned with a more reliable twin-turbine engine and developed as a high-speed civil helicopter. The first flight by the prototype was in August 1971, but the sleek production model A109A, with fully retractable tricycle landing gear, was delayed by problems and tests until 1975. The A109A Mk II appeared in September 1981, featuring improvements such as reduced vibration and noise, an uprated transmission, a new tail rotor to reduce vibration to a minimum, revized engine mountings, again to reduce vibration and noise, and a number of other operating improvements.

28 Jan 72 Singapore Airlines formed
9 Feb 72 First flight of Boeing E-3 Sentry (US)
21 Feb 72 First flight of AESL CT-4 Airtrainer (NZ)
8 March 72 First flight of *Goodyear Europa* (GB)
30 March 72 First flight of HAL HA-31 Mk II Basant (IN)
1 April 72 BEA and BOAC combine to form British Airways
29 April 72 A specially equipped F-4 Phantom II becomes the first aircraft to be flown in the US with a fly-by-wire control system
8 May – 22 Oct 72 ***Linebacker I.*** Intense US bombing campaign against North Vietnam
10 May 72 First flight of Fairchild-Republic A-10 Thunderbolt II (US)
25 May 72 First flight of Westland/Aérospatiale Lynx HAS Mk 2 (GB/F)
2 June 72 First flight of Aérospatiale SA 360 Dauphin (F)
27 July 72 First flight of McDonnell Douglas F-15 Eagle (US)
18–29 Dec 72 ***Linebacker II.*** Intense US bombing campaign against North Vietnam

McDONNELL DOUGLAS F-15 EAGLE first flight 27 July 1972

Powerplant: Two 14,370lb (6,518kg) s.t. military (23,450lb/10,637kg max) Pratt & Whitney F100-220 afterburning turbofans
Primary role: Air combat fighter
Dimensions: Wingspan 42ft 9¾in (13.05m); length 63ft 9in (19.43m)
Armament: One 20mm M61A Vulcan cannon, four AIM-7 Sparrow, four AIM-9 Sidewinder
Weights: Empty 29,180lb (13,236kg); loaded 44,500lb (20,185kg)
Speed: Mach 2.5+ max
Range: (Ferry) over 3,450 miles (5,550km)
Crew: 1

The F-15 was developed to counter the Mig-25 'Foxbat' under the mistaken impression that the latter was a fully manoeuvrable tactical fighter capable of Mach 3, and performance and manoeuvrability outclassed those of Russian machines. The first flight took place in July 1972. With the help of air refuelling, the F-15 is able to deploy anywhere in the world. Systems include HOTAS (hands-on-throttle-and-stick), where radar mode, missile switches and other critical commands are mounted on the two main controls. The aircraft's combat debut was made with the Israeli Air Force on 27 June 1979, when it shot down four Syrian MiG-21s over Lebanon. On 13 March 1981 an Eagle claimed a super-fast Syrian MiG-25 interceptor, and in June 1982 F-15s took part in the Israeli defeat of Syria over the Beka'a. The F-15 also performed superbly for the USAF in the 1991 Gulf War, Yugoslavia in 1999 and subsequent operations over Iraq and Afghanistan. The F-15E Strike Eagle is the two-seat derivative which is an all-weather strike fighter, entering service in 1989. It has also performed superbly in combat. All F-15 aircraft were grounded by the U.S. Air Force after a Missouri Air National Guard F-15C crashed on 2 November 2007 due to structural problems. By January 8, 2008, the USAF cleared a portion of its F-15A-D fleet to return to flying status. But subsequently other F-15s have been identified to have similar problems with their structure. As a result of this the long-term future of the F-15 is in question.

AIRBUS A300-600 first flight 28 October 1972

Powerplant: Two 52,000lb (23,580kg) s.t. General Electric CF6-50 (optionally Pratt & Whitney JT9D-59)
Primary role: Passenger transport
Dimensions: Wingspan 147ft 1¼in (44.83m); length 177ft 5in (54.07m)
Payload: 287–375 passengers/98,060lb (43,571kg) freight
Weights: Max take-off 363,800lb (165,016kg)
Speed: Mach 0.82 max; 472kts (875kph) cruising
Range: 5,000 miles (8,050km)
Crew: 2
Production total (all marks): 268

Airbus Industrie was set up in 1970 to develop a twin-engine, large-capacity 'European Airbus'. Its partners came from Belgium, France, West Germany, the Netherlands, Spain and Britain. The prototype Airbus A300 first flew on 28 October 1972, and the first production A300B2 on 28 June 1973. The current production model is the A300-600, with a longer fuselage and increased capacity, A310 rear fuselage section and tailplane, all-digital two-crew flight deck with fly-by-wire controls, and improved handling and payload/range performance.

***General Dynamics F-16 Fighting Falcon** (US) first flew 20 Jan 1974*

28 Oct 72 First flight of Airbus A300B1 (INT)

7 Jan 73 First flight of Cameron Balloons D-96 (GB)

1 March 73 First flight of Sportavia RF6-180 Sportsman (G)

24 March 73 First flight of Dassault-Bréguet Falcon 30 (F)

3 June 73 First flight of Tu-144 SST crashes at Paris Air Show killing all 6 crew

8 Aug 73 First flight of Kamov Ka-27/Ka-28 (Helix) (USSR)

22 Aug 73 First flight of Gates Learjet 35 (US)

12 Sept 73 First flight of Westland Commando Mk 1 (GB)

6–24 Oct 73 ARAB-ISRAELI 'YOM KIPPUR WAR': Initially many Israeli aircraft are lost to SAMs but Israel eventually maintains its ascendancy and defeats its Arab foes. Some 270 Arab and 120 Israeli combat aircraft are lost

26 Oct 73 First flight of Dassault-Bréguet/ Dornier Alpha Jet (F/G)

20 Jan 74 First flight of General Dynamics F-16 Fighting Falcon (US)

16 Feb 74 First flight of Atlas C4M Kudu (SA)

9 June 74 First flight of Northrop YF-17 (US)

14 Aug 74 First flight of Panavia Tornado (INT)

21 Aug 74 First flight of Hawker Siddeley Hawk (GB)

***Panavia Tornado** (INT) first flew 14 Aug 1974*

AH-64 APACHE first flight 30 September 1975

Powerplant: Two 1,265kW (1,696shp) General Electric T700-GE-701 turboshafts
Primary role: All-weather attack
Dimensions: Rotor diameter 48ft (14.63m); length overall 58ft 3in (17.76m)
Armament: One MD 30mm Chain Gun, plus up to 16 Hellfire anti-armour missiles or 76 2.75in (7cm) folding-fin air-to-ground rockets
Weights: Loaded 21,000lb (9,525kg)
Speed: 227mph (365kph) max
Range: 300 miles (482km)
Crew: 2
Production total (all marks): Over 800
Variants: A/D

Developed by McDonnell Douglas from the Hughes Model 77, the AH-64 was designed for the US Army as a day or night, all-weather, anti-armour, ground support helicopter. The first flight by the prototype YAH-64 was in 1975 and the first production AH-64 model was delivered in January 1984, featuring a lightweight Doppler navigation system, IR and radar jammers, a Martin TADS/PNVS, a passive radar warning receiver, a Bendix rocket control system, an International laser rangefinder/designator, and provision for Honeywell integrated helmet and display sighting. Using sophisticated long-distance sensors, Apaches can identify and shoot their targets even in the dark.

***Sikorsky YUH-60A Black Hawk** (US) first flew 17 Oct 1974*

22 Aug 74 First flight of Short SD.330 (GB)
17 Oct 74 First flight of Sikorsky YUH-60A Black Hawk (US)
28 Oct 74 First flight of Dassault Super Etendard (F)
31 Oct 74 First flight of SC/Soko/UTVA Orao (INT)
20 Dec 74 First flight of Gulfstream American GA-7 Cougar (US)
23 Dec 74 First flight of Rockwell B-1 (US)
26 Dec 74 First flight of Airbus A300B4 (INT)

6 Feb 75 First flight of Beechcraft Skipper 77 (US)
22 Feb 75 First flight of Sukhoi Su-25 (Frogfoot) (USSR)
26 Feb 75 First flight of Cessna 404 Titan (US)
7 March 75 First flight of Yakovlev Yak-42 (USSR)
27 March 75 First flight of de Havilland Canada DHC-7 Dash 7 (CA)
30 April 75 Saigon falls to North Vietnamese. Vietnam War ends
28 Aug 75 First flight of Robinson R22 HP (US)
16 Sept 75 First flight of MiG-31 (Foxhound) (USSR)
30 Sept 75 First flight of AH-64 Apache (US)

May 76 First flight of Piper PA-44 Seminole (US)
24 May 76 Concorde begins passenger services from Europe to USA
19 July 76 First flight of Antonov An-32 (Curl) (USSR)

***Dassault Super Etendard** (F) first flew 28 Oct 1974*

ILYUSHIN IL-86 first flight 22 December 1976

Powerplant: Four 28,660lb (13,000kg) Kuznetsov NK-86 turbofans
Primary role: Passenger transport
Dimensions: Wingspan 157ft 8in (48.0m); length 198ft 4in (60.45m)
Payload: 350–375 passengers/ 92,600lb (42,002kg) freight
Weights: Max take-off 454,150lb (205,997kg)
Speed: 512kts (950kph) cruising
Range: 2,855 miles (4,600km)
Crew: 3
Production total (all marks): 103
Variants: see notes

The Il-86 was the Soviet Union's first wide-bodied turbofan airliner. The prototype first flew on 22 Dec 1976, but the production-standard Il-86 did not enter service with Aeroflot until 26 December 1980, serving on the Moscow–Tashkent internal route. The Il-86 was the first Soviet jet airliner to adopt a 'conventional' configuration but was otherwise a unique large civil transport. With self-contained boarding stairs, there was no need for airport 'airbridges' and passengers boarded at ground level. They placed their own baggage on the lower deck and climbed internal staircases to the three cabins, each with nine-abreast seating. The Il-86-300 is the long-range model.

BOEING E-3A SENTRY first flight March 1977

Powerplant: Four 21,000lb (9,526kg) Pratt & Whitney TF33-P-100/100A
Primary role: Airborne early warning and control
Dimensions: Wingspan 145ft 9in (44.42m); length 152ft 11in (46.61m)
Armament: None
Weights: Loaded 325,000lb (147,240kg)
Speed: 520mph (853kph) max
Endurance: 6 hours at 1,000 miles (1,600km) radius
Crew: 17
Production total (all marks): 68
Variants: A/B/C/E/D/F

Entering service in 1977, the Sentry was developed to control friendly aircraft and to carry out surveillance of air activity within a 230-mile (370km) radius. Based on the Model 707-300 airliner airframe, the Sentry has a 30ft (9.14m) diameter rotodome above the fuselage housing the antennae of its APY-1 radar and APX-103 IFF. Equipped with an IBM computer to handle data, the tactical compartment contains nine display consoles and two auxiliary units. Early models were improved to E-3B standard with a more powerful computer, radar modification for limited overwater capability and the Joint Tactical Information Distribution System. The later E-3Cs are capable of firing Sidewinder AAMs and feature five extra display consoles. Sentries serve with the USAF, the RAF and the French Armée de l'Air as well as a multinational squadron (under the flag of Luxembourg) for NATO.

28 July 76 World speed record: 3,529.56 km/h/2,193.17 mph by Capt Joersz and Maj Morgan (Lockheed SR-71A)
12 Aug 76 First flight of Aermacchi MB 339 Veltro (IT)
13 Aug 76 First flight of Bell 222 (US)
7 Nov 76 First flight of Dassault-Bréguet Mystère-Falcon 50 (F)
22 Dec 76 First flight of Ilyushin Il-86 (Camber) (USSR)

6 Jan 77 First flight of HAL HPT-32 (IN)
March 77 First flight of Boeing E-3A Sentry (US)
13 March 77 First flight of Sikorsky S-76 (see overleaf) (US)
24 March 77 First flight of Lockheed C-141B Starlifter (US)
27 March 77 579 people die when two Boeing 747s collide on runway at Santa Cruz, Tenerife, the largest number in an aircraft accident
20 May 77 First flight of Sukhoi Su-27 (Flanker) (USSR)
24 May 77 First flight of Beechcraft Duchess 76 (US)

***Sukhoi Su-27 (Flanker)** (USSR) first flew 20 May 1977*

SIKORSKY S-76 first flight 13 March 1977

Powerplant: Two 508.5kW (682shp) Allison 250-C305
Primary role: Light/medium general-purpose and transport
Dimensions: Main rotor diameter 44ft 0in (13.41m); length 43ft 4in (13.22m)
Payload: 12 passengers or freight carried internally, or a 4,000lb (1,814kg) slung load
Weights: Loaded 10,300lb (4,672kg)
Speed: 178mph (287kph) cruising
Range: 465 miles (750km) with 12 passengers
Crew: 2
Production total (all marks): 480

Designed in the mid-1970s to increase Sikorsky's share of the corporate and civil helicopter market, the S-76 first flew in March 1977 and soon revealed an excellent performance as a result of its careful streamlining combined with two 485kW (650shp) Allison 25C-C30 turboshafts driving a rotor system derived from that of the S-70 (UH-60 Black Hawk) military helicopter. The basic type is certificated

for flight in IFR conditions, and can be configured without difficulty for a number of applications as diverse as corporate transport and support of offshore resources exploitation. From 1982 deliveries have been of the S-76 Mk II variant, which had forty improvements to the standard airframe, improved ventilation and dynamic systems and uprated Allison turboshafts. The S-76 Spirit has proved itself a successful competitor in the commercial market and at least some of this success must be attributed to the benefits reaped from the research carried out on Sikorsky's UH-60A. The S-76 Mk II has established twelve records for speed, rate of climb and sustained altitude, and this helicopter's versatility has been further enhanced by the availability of three different quick-change kits enabling speedy conversion to the ambulance configuration.

AÉROSPATIALE SUPER PUMA first flight September 1977

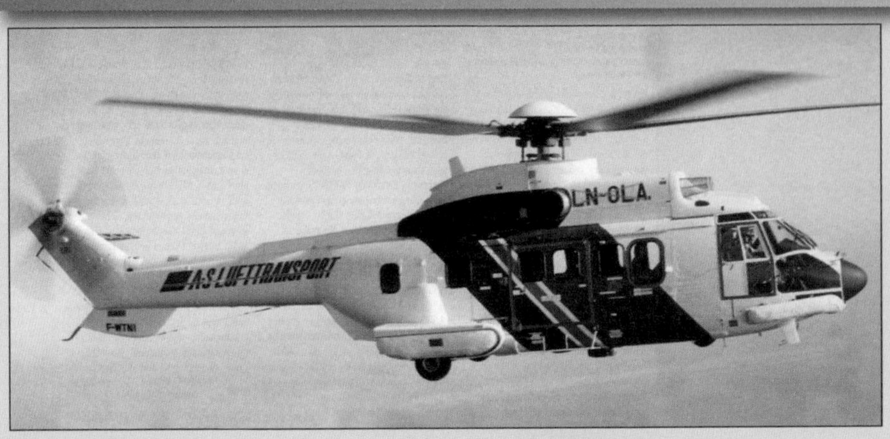

Powerplant: Two 1,324kW (1,725shp) Turboméca Makila lA
Primary role: Medium general-purpose and transport
Dimensions: Main rotor diameter 49ft 5½in (15.08m); length (rotors turning) 61ft 5½in (18.73m)
Payload: 20–24 passengers or 6,012lb (2,727kg) of freight carried internally, or a 9,921lb (4,000kg) slung load
Weights: Loaded 18,410lb (8,350kg)
Speed: 173mph (278kph) cruising at sea level
Range: 394 miles (634km)
Crew: 2
Production total (all marks): 696 (including military)

Variants: 3
Produced in both military and civil versions, the Super Puma AS 331 prototype first flew in September 1977, leading to the improved AS 332 with reduced vibration and noise and greater capacity. A direct development of the SA 330 Puma, the more powerful Super Puma featured revized air inlets, improved transmission, a Starflex lightweight rotor head and thermally de-iced main rotor blades. Civil variants are the AS 332C with a cabin seating 17 persons, and the 29.9in (0.76m) longer AS 332L carrying an extra four passengers and featuring two more cabin windows and greater fuel capacity. The Bristow Helicopters Tiger variant was specially designed for over-water operations.

27 June 77 First flight of CASA C-101 Aviojet (SP)

24 Aug 77 First flight of Gates Learjet 28 Longhorn (US)

31 Aug 77 World altitude record for air-breathing aircraft: 37,650m/123,524ft by A. Fedotov (Mikoyan Ye-266M)

Sept 77 First flight of Aerpspatiale Super Puma (F)

6 Oct 77 First flight of Mikoyan MiG-29 (Fulcrum) (USSR)

27 Oct 77 First flight of RFB Fantrainer ATI-2 (G)

14 Nov 77 First flight of Mil Mi-26/Mi-27 (Halo) (USSR)

22 Dec 77 First flight of Antonov An-72 (Coaler) (USSR)

1978 – to date Ongoing Israeli Air Force incursions over Lebanon, mainly opposed by Syrian combat aircraft

10 March 78 First flight of Dassault Mirage 2000 (F)

17 July 78 First flight of UTVA G-4/G-5 Galeb (JU)

MIKOYAN MiG-29 (FULCRUM) first flight 6 October 1977

Powerplant: Two 11,111lb (5,040kg) s.t. military (18,300lb/8,300kg max) Klimov RD-33 afterburning turbofans
Primary role: Air combat fighter
Dimensions: Wingspan 37ft 3¼in (11.36m); length 56ft 10in (17.32m)
Armament: One 30mm Gsh-30L cannon; six AAMs including SARH and IR AA-10 and AA-11
Weights: Empty 22,487lb (10,200kg); loaded 33,598lb (15,240kg)
Speed: Mach 2.3 max
Range: 932 miles (1,500km)
Crew: 1

The MiG-29 was designed as a rival to the American F-16 and F-18 fighters and its first flight took place in October 1977 in the hands of Alexandr Fedotov. Agile and delivering high performance with a high thrust-to-weight ratio, the aircraft featured a number of innovations, including engine doors which could be closed to prevent accidental compressor damage, a helmet-mounted sight allowing dogfight missiles to be launched as high as 45 degrees off-boresight, and a sighting system linked to an IR sensor and radar. However, the 'Fulcrum' proved difficult to maintain and lacked endurance. It saw action with the Iraqi Air Force during the 1991 Gulf War, also with the Serbians during the Wars of Yugoslavian Dissolution and with the Eritrean Airforce in their war with Ethiopia.

BRITISH AEROSPACE SEA HARRIER FRS.1 first flight 20 August 1978

Powerplant: One 21,500lb (9,752kg) s.t. Rolls-Royce Pegasus 11 Mk 104
Primary role: Carrier-borne reconnaissance/strike attack
Dimensions: Wingspan 25ft 3in (7.7m); length 47ft 7in (14.5m) overall
Armament: Two 30mm cannon, and 5,000lb (2,268kg) weapons on five external points
Weights: Loaded 26,190lb (11,880kg)
Speed: 735mph (1,185kph) max at sea level
Range: 920 miles (1,480km)
Crew: 1
Production total (all marks): 96 (650 approx. of all types of Harrier)
Variants: FRS.1/51/FA.2

Developed from the very similar Harrier specifically for the *Invincible* class carriers, the Sea Harrier entered service in 1981 as a STOVL fighter, reconnaissance and strike/attack aircraft. To prevent sea-salt corrosion, Sea Harriers had some aluminium components compared with their predecessors.

Other design features included a high bubble canopy for the pilot and Blue Fox multi-role radar. Agile in close fighting, the aircraft saw successful action in the Falklands War. The FRS Mk 2 update is equipped with AMRAAM medium-range missiles and look-down/shoot-down Blue Vixen radar. The Sea Harrier was withdrawn from Royal Naval service in March 2006 but is still in service with the Indian Navy.

18 Aug 78 First flight of Pilatus PC-7 Turbo Trainer (SWI)

20 Aug 78 First flight of Hawker Siddeley Sea Harrier FRS.1 (GB)

Canadiar CL-600 Challenger *(CA) first flew 8 Nov 1978*

McDonnell Douglas AV-8B Harrier *(US) first flew 9 Nov 1978*

8 Nov 78 First flight of Canadair CL-600 Challenger (CA)

9 Nov 78 First flight of McDonnell Douglas AV-8B Harrier (US)

18 Nov 78 First flight of McDonnell Douglas F/A-18 Hornet (see overleaf) (US)

19 Dec 78 First flight of Ilyushin IL-76 (see overleaf) (USSR)

19 Dec 78 Britons David Williams and Fred To fly Solar One, the world's first solar powered aircraft

3 Feb 79 First flight of Aerospace Developments AD 500 (GB)

9 March 79 First flight of Dassault Super Mirage 4000 (F)

19 April 79 First flight of Gates Learjet 55 (US)

5 June 79 First flight of Massachusetts Institute of Technology *Chrysalis* (US)

12 June 79 The *Gossamer Albatross* wins the Kremer Prize for a first crossing of the English Channel by a man-powered aircraft

27 Jun 79 First combat use of McDonnell Douglas F-15 Eagle; Israeli Air Force destroys five Syrian MiG-21s

Aug 79 Successful test firing of a Sky Flash air-to-air missile (GB)

17 Oct 79 First flight of Cessna 303 Crusader (US)

1980 First flight of Piper PA-46-310P Malibu (US)
11 Jan 80 First flight of Kamov Ka-32 (Helix-C) (USSR)
24 Apr 80 Disaster at 'Desert One'. Unsuccessful attempt to rescue US hostages in Iran involving C-130 transports and Sikorsky RH-53 Sea Stallion helicopters from USS *Nimitz*
10 July 80 First flight of McDonnell KC-10A Extender (US)
16 Aug 80 First flight of Embraer EMB-312 (T-27) Tucano (BR)

IRAN–IRAQ WAR
22 Sept 80–July 88 Intermittent air combat in what is essentially a ground war
20 Nov 80 First flight of MacCready Solar *Challenger* (US)

28 March 81 First flight of Dornier 228-100 (G)

McDONNELL DOUGLAS F-18 HORNET first flight 18 November 1978

Powerplant: Two 16,000lb (7,256kg) F404 General Electric afterburning turbofans
Primary role: Multi-role fighter
Dimensions: Wingspan 37ft 6in (11.43m); length 56ft 0in (17.07m)
Armament: One M61A1 Vulcan 20mm cannon; AIM-120 AMRAAM, AIM-7 Sparrow, AIM-9 Sidewinder guided and unguided missiles
Weights: Empty 23,050lb (10,455kg); loaded 56,000lb (25,401kg)
Speed: 1,190mph (1,915kph) max
Range: (Ferry) 2,073 miles (3,336km)
Crew: 1
Production total (all marks): 410

A development of Northrop's YF-17, the F/A-18 was the first 'digital' warplane, with display screens rather than dials in the cockpit. The aircraft was developed to meet varying roles – light attack, air defence and ground attack, operating from aircraft carriers or short airstrips for the US Marine Corps. Reliable and accurate, the Hornet is also popular with land-based air forces. The first flight took place on 18 November 1978 and the aircraft entered service with US Navy and Marine Corps units in 1983. Production switched to the -18C/D models, with enhanced technology, in 1987, and redesigned -18E/F models have a 25% larger airframe and the more powerful F414 engine. Hornets saw action with US forces in Libya in 1986 and in the 1991 Gulf War, for the UN in the Yugoslavian conflict in 1995 and with the Royal Australian Air Force in peace-keeping operations over East Timor in 1999. The aircraft is also in service in Canada (CF-188), Kuwait, Finland, Malaysia, Thailand, Switzerland and Spain.

ILYUSHIN IL-76 (MAINSTAY) first flight 19 December 1978

Powerplant: Four 26,455lb (12,000kg) s.t. Soloviev D-30KP
Primary role: Airborne early warning and control
Dimensions: Wingspan 165ft 8in (50.5m); length 152ft 10in (46.5m)
Armament: None
Weights: Loaded c.374,786lb (170,000kg)
Speed: c.500mph (800kph) max at 36,000ft (11,000m)
Range: 4,000 miles (7,300km)
Crew: 15
Production total (all marks): 25

Based on the airframe of the Il-76 logistic freighter, the 'Mainstay' entered service in the USSR in the late 1980s as the new-generation Soviet tactical AEW platform. Versatile and capable, with four turbofans and a radar capable of overland and overwater use, the 'Mainstay' can detect and track targets as small as low-flying cruise missiles. Western observers predicted the production of 50 machines. The Iraqi AF employed a smaller AWACS version of the Il-76 with rear-fuselage radome and no dorsal rotodome.

LOCKHEED F-117 NIGHTHAWK first flight 15 June 1981

Powerplant: Two 10,800lb (48.04kN) max General Electric F404-GE-F1D2 non-afterburning turbofans
Primary role: Bomber
Dimensions: Wingspan 43ft 4in (13.2m); length 65ft 11in (20.08m) overall
Armament: Two 2,000lb (907kg) or two GBU-10/GBU-27 laser-guided bombs; potential for other weapons, including AGM-88 HARM and B61 free-fall nuclear bomb
Weights: Empty 29,000lb (13,154kg); loaded 54,000lb (24,494kg)
Speed: Mach 0.9 max at optimum altitude; Mach 0.81 (562mph/904kph) cruising at 30,000ft (9,144m)
Range: 535 miles (862km)
Crew: 1
Production total (all marks): 59
Nicknamed the 'Black Jet', the F-117 was developed in secrecy as part of a Cold War 'black' programme at the USAF's hidden Tonopah base. Some of its technology is still classified, and some components were hybridized from existing aircraft to maintain project secrecy. Development began in 1978 and the F-117 first flew some eight years before the USAF publicly admitted to the project in November 1988. The Nighthawk's main role is to precision-bomb critical, well-protected targets at great distances. Low-observable or stealth technology includes a radar-absorbent composite external material, to convert radar waves into heat and dim the radar signature; a V-shape built entirely of flat plates to scatter radar beams irregularly away from the detector; serrated door and turret cover edges to reduce the radar cross-section; and exhaust nozzles that bleed over the fuselage to screen heat emissions from below. Weapons are carried in internal trapezes, and are released directly from the bomb bay. The aircraft saw service during the US invasion of Panama in 1989, the 1991 Gulf War the 1999 Kosovo campaign, when a F-117 was lost, and during Operation 'Iraqi Freedom' in 2003. The F-117 was retired from service on 22 April 2008, due to the deployment of the more effective F-22 Raptor.

10 April 81 First flight of SIAI-Marchetti S.211A (IT)
12 April 81 The first Space Shuttle *Columbia* is launched
1 June 81 First flight of Short 360 (GB)
7 June 81 Two US Navy F-14 Tomcats shoot down two Libyan Sukhoi Su-22s over Gulf of Sirte, claiming they showed hostile intent
7 Jun 81 First flight of Israeli F-16s, escorted by F-15s, attack Osirak nuclear reactor near Baghdad, Iraq
15 June 81 First flight of Lockheed F-117A Nighthawk (US)
1 Aug 81 First flight of Lockheed TR-1A (US)
3 Sept 81 First flight of British Aerospace 146 100 (GB)
26 Sept 81 First flight of Boeing 767 (US)
28 Sept 81 First flight of Airship Industries Skyship 500 (GB)
17 Dec 81 First flight of Tupolev Tu-160 (Blackjack) (USSR)

19 Feb 82 First flight of Boeing 757 (US)

***Boeing 757** (US) first flew 19 Feb 1982*

18 March 82 First flight of BAe Jetstream 31 (GB)

FALKLANDS WAR

2 April–14 June 82 Successful attempt by UK to retake Falkland/Malvinas Is, involving heavy air combat between the UK and Argentine forces. First combat use of Harrier V/STOL aircraft
June–Dec 82 Lebanon. Israel claims over 80 Syrian high-performance combat jets shot down for the loss of possibly 14/15 of their own. Two USN ground attack jets shot down by anti-Israeli ground forces
17 June 82 First flight of Kamov Ka-50/52 (Hokum) (USSR)
5 Aug 82 First flight of Airbus S310 (INT)
30 Aug 82 First flight of Northrop F-20 Tigershark (F-5G) (US)
3 Sept 82 First flight of Beechcraft Commuter 1900 (US)
6 Sep 82 Soviet Air Force Sukhoi Su-15 interceptor shoots down Korean Air Lines 747. It had flown off course over Sakhalin Island
10 Nov 82 First flight of Mil Mi-28 (Havoc) (USSR)

Antonov An-124 Condor *(USSR) first flew 26 Dec 1982*

9 Dec 82 First flight of Cessna Caravan (US)
23 Dec 82 First flight of Short 330-200/Sherpa (GB)
26 Dec 82 First flight of Antonov An-124 Condor (USSR)

25 April 83 First flight of Dornier Do 24TT (Technologieträger) (G)
17 June 83 First flight of Robin ATL (F)
20 June 83 First flight of de Havilland Canada DHC-8 Dash 8 (CA)
27 July 83 First flight of Embraer EMB-120 Brasilia (BR)
15 Sept 83 First flight of Agusta A 129 Mangusta (IT)
5 Dec 83 First flight of Slingsby T67M Firefly 160M (GB)

6 March 84 First flight of Airship Industries *Skyship 600* (GB)
19 March 84 First flight of IAI 1125 Astra SP (IS)
4 May 84 First flight of Hawker 800 (GB)
7 May 84 First flight of Pilatus PC-9 (SWI)
15 May 84 First flight of Aeritalia-Aermacchi-Embraer AMX (IT/BR)
June 84 First flight of Sukhoi Su-26 (USSR)
13 June 84 First flight of Lockheed P-3 Sentinel (US)
22 June 84 First flight of Voyager Aircraft Inc *Voyager* (US)
22 June 84 Virgin Atlantic formed
17 Sept 84 First flight of AVTEK 400 (US)
21 Sept 84 First flight of Dassault Falcon 900B (F)

Airship Industries Skyship 600 *(GB) first flew 6 March 1984*

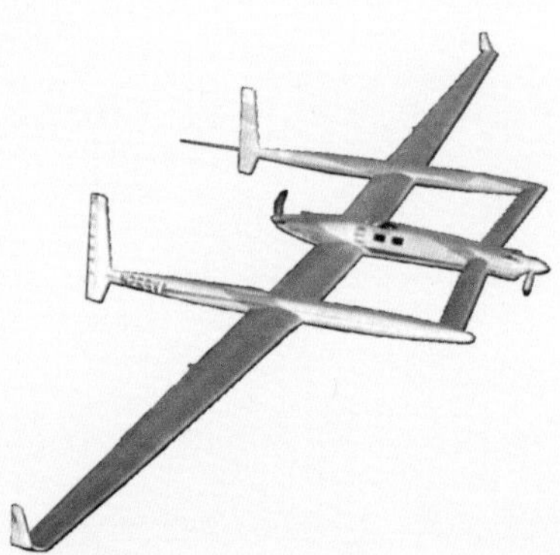

Voyager Aircraft Inc Voyager *(US) first flew 22 June 1984*

ROCKWELL B-1B first flight 18 October 1984

Powerplant: Four 30,760lb (13,950kg) General Electric F101GE-102 turbofans
Primary role: Strategic heavy bomber
Dimensions: Wingspan spread 136ft 8½in (41.67m), fully swept 78ft 5in (23.9m); length 150ft 3in (45.8m)
Armament: Up to 73,860lb (33,500kg) weapons load in three fuselage bays, plus external carriage; (nuclear role) up to 12 B28 or 14 B23 or 24 B61 or B83 free-fall bombs or 24 AGM-69 SRAM or eight AGM-86B SRAM; (conventional weapons) up to 84 Mk 82 or 24 Mk 84 GP bombs or 8 AGM-86C ALCMs internally or 44 Mk 82 or 14 Mk 84 or 14 AGM-86C ALCMs externally
Weights: Empty 180,000lb (81,641kg); loaded 477,090lb (216,367kg)
Speed: 1,450mph (2,335kph, Mach 2.2) max at 40,000ft (12,200m); Mach 0.72–0.8 cruising
Range: (Ferry) 7,450 miles (12,000km)
Crew: 4
Production total (all marks): 4 prototypes, 100 production models
Variants: B-1A (prototypes only)
The prototype B-1 first flew on 23 December 1974; the simplified and heavier B-1B Lancer was first flown on 18 October 1984 and delivered to US Strategic Air Command on 7 July 1985. In November 1998 the aircraft made its combat début against Iraq in 'Desert Fox', with two aircraft flying from Oman and bombing a Republican Guard barracks with 500lb Mk 82s. The B-1B also saw action in the air campaign against Serbia from 24 March to 9 June 1999 and the operations over Afghanistan during 'Enduring Freedom' and Iraq during 'Iraqi Freedom'.

6 Oct 84 First flight of FMA IA.63 Pampa (AR)
18 Oct 84 First flight of Rockwell B-1B Lancer (US) (see previous page)
14 Dec 84 First flight of Grumman X-29A (US)

1985 First flight of UTVA Lasta (JU)
14 May 85 An AIM-120A AMRAAM air-to-air missile is test-fired successfully
29 June 85 First flight of Kawasaki T-4 (J)
12 Aug 85 A Japan Air Lines Boeing 747 crashes near Tokyo. 520 people are killed, the highest number ever in a single aircraft
19 Sept 85 First flight of Grumman Gulfstream IV (US)

28 Jan 86 The crew of seven of the Space Shuttle *Challenger* are killed in an explosion after lift-off
15 Feb 86 First flight of Beechcraft 2000 Starship I (US)

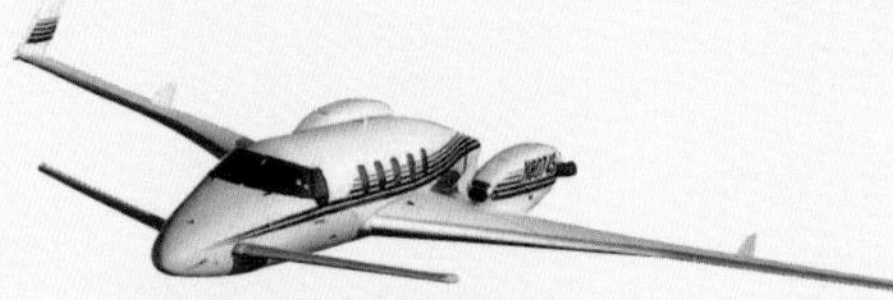

Beechcraft 2000 Starship I *(US) first flew 15 Feb 1986*

24–25 March 86 Libyan naval vessels are sunk by US aircraft after they threaten US Navy units
14 April 86 Nearly 100 USAF and US Navy aircraft from UK bases and carriers make a coordinated attack on Libyan targets
25 April 86 First flight of MiG-33 (Fulcrum-E) (USSR)
4 July 86 First flight of Dassault-Bréguet Rafale A (F)
6 Aug 86 First flight of BAe ATP (GB)

Dassault-Bréguet Rafale *(F) first flew 4 July 1986*

8 Aug 86 First flight of BAe EAP (GB)
23 Sept 86 First flight of Piaggio P.180 Avanti (IT)

Piaggio P.180 Avanti *(IT) first flew 23 Sept 1986*

17 Nov 86 First flight of Mil Mi-34 VAZ (Hermit) (USSR)
30 Nov 86 First flight of Fokker 100 (HO)
4 Dec 86 First flight of McDonnell Douglas MD-87 (US)
23 Dec 86 After a 9-day flight Jeanna Yeager and Dick Rutan complete the first unrefueled circumnavigation of the world in the Voyager Aircraft Inc *Voyager*
31 Dec 86 First flight of IAI Lavi (IS)

19 Feb 87 First flight of Boeing E-6A Hermes (US)
27 Feb 87 First flight of Airbus A320-200 (INT)
9 March 87 First flight of Yakovlev Yak-41 (Freestyle) (USSR)
30 April 87 First flight of Promavia Jet Squalus (B)
10 July 87 First flight of Westinghouse Airships *Skyship 500HL* (US)
2 Sept 87 First flight of American Blimp Corp ABC GA 42 (US)
9 Oct 87 First flight of EH Industries EH 101 Merlin (GB/IT)

EH Industries EH 101 Merlin *(GB/IT) first flew 9 Oct 1987*

28 Oct 87 First flight of US Lighter Than Air Corp LTA 138-S (US)

16 April 88 First flight of McDonnell

McDonnell Douglas/BAe T45A Goshawk *(US/GB) first flew 16 April 1988*

Douglas/BAe T-45A Goshawk (US/GB)

28 June 88 First flight of Sukhoi Su-35/Su-37 (USSR)

3 July 88 US Navy guided-missile cruiser shoots down an Iran Air Airbus A300, in error

July 88 Ceasefire proposed in Iran-Iraq War

14 July 88 First flight of TBM International TBM 700 (INT)

28 Aug 88 Three pilots are killed together with 39 spectators, when three Aermacchi MB-339s of the Italian aerobatic team collide during a display at the Ramstein in West Germany

28 Sept 88 First flight of Ilyushin Il-96 (USSR)

Ilyushin Il-96 *(USSR) first flew 28 September 1988*

9 Dec 88 First flight of Saab JAS-39 Gripen (SW)

21 Dec 88 First flight of An-225 Mriya (Cossack) (USSR)

21 Dec 88 A Pan Am Boeing 747 is blown apart by a bomb. 16 crew, 243 passengers and 11 persons on the ground, are killed in the Scotish town of Lockerbie

2 Jan 89 First flight of Tupolev Tu-204 (USSR)

5 Jan 89 Two US Navy F-14 Tomcat fighters shoot down two Libyan MiG-23s over international waters, claiming they were hostile

9 March 89 First flight of Bell-Boeing V-22 Osprey (see overleaf) (US)

17 July 89 First flight of Northrop Grumman B-2A Spirit (US)

10 Jan 90 First flight of McDonnell Douglas MD-11 (US)

Saab JAS-39 Gripen *(SW) first flew 9 December 1988*

BELL-BOEING V-22 OSPREY first flight 19 March 1989

Powerplant: Two 4,588kW (6,150shp) Allison T406-AD-400 turboshafts
Primary role: Convertiplane transport
Dimensions: Span (proprotors turning) 84ft 7in (25.78m); length 57ft 4in (17.48m) overall
Payload: 24 troops/15,000lb (6,803kg)
Weights: Loaded 47,000lb (21,319kg) VTO, 60,500lb (27,443kg) STO
Speed: 363mph (584kph) max
Combat radius: 633 miles (1,017km)
Crew: 3
Production total (all marks): 360 ordered
Variants: MV-22B, CV-22B, HV-22B

Bell and Boeing combined forces in April 1982 with a view to producing the ultimate tilt-rotor aircraft, merging a helicopter's capability for vertical take-off and landing, hovering, and sideways and backwards flight with the speed and range of a fixed-wing craft when its rotors have tilted forward to act as turboprops. Bell took on the wing and engine nacelles, and Boeing built the fuselage. In 1986 the V-22 Osprey went into full-scale development aiming to meet the needs of all four US armed forces. The first flight took place in 1989. Engines are cross-linked to allow one swivelling unit to drive both proprotors in case of engine failure, and in-flight refuelling is possible from a Marine KC-130F Hercules. Design features include predominantly composite construction (for example graphite/epoxy solid laminate in the wings) and a dial-free flight deck. The fully automatic wing-stowing procedure takes 90 seconds, with the wing turning 90 degrees on a 'carousel'. The MV-22A is intended to be the Army/Marine Corps vehicle, the grey HV-22A is the Navy support craft, the SV-22A is the proposed anti-submarine model and the CV-22A is the designated USAF machine. The Ospreys entered active service with the US Marine Corp in 2005.

1 March 90 First flight of Beech 1900D Airliner (US)

29 March 90 First flight of Ilyushin Il-114 (USSR)

13 April 90 First flight of Sukhoi Su-34 (USSR)

16 June 90 First flight of Hawker 1000 (GB)

29 Sept 90 First flight of Lockheed Martin F-22 (see overleaf) (US)

10 Oct 90 Airtours International founded

21 Nov 90 First flight of Nanchang/ Pakistan Aeronautical K-8 Karakoram (INT)

9 Dec 90 First flight of Pan Atlantic Aerospace LEAP (CA)

GULF WAR

16 Jan–28 Feb 91 Intense air campaign waged by the Coalition forces against Iraq during the liberation of Kuwait sees extensive use of laser-guided bombs, stealth aircraft and cruise missiles

13 Feb 91 First flight of Swearingen Jaffe SJ30 (US)

NORTHROP GRUMMAN B-2A SPIRIT first flight 17 July 1989

Powerplant: Four 19,000lb (84.5kN) General Electric F118-GE-100 non-afterburning turbofans
Primary role: Long-range bomber
Dimensions: Wingspan 172ft (52.43m); length 69ft (21.03m) overall
Armament: 2 detachable Boeing rotary launcher assemblies with 16 AGM-129 ACMs or 16 AGM-69 SRAM IIs; or 16 B83 or 16 B61 freefall nuclear bombs; or up to 80 500lb (227kg) Mk 82
Weights: Empty 153,700lb (69,717kg); loaded 376,000lb (170,550kg)
Speed: Mach 0.81 (569mph/915kph)
Range: 5,075 miles (8,170km) unrefueled
Crew: 2/3
Production total (all marks): 21

A 'flying wing' with a huge span, the B-2 was funded in 1982 as a secret 'black' project by the USAF and first flew on 17 July 1990. Designed to carry a wide range of weaponry including cluster bombs, sea mines, fire bombs and deep-penetration bombs, the aircraft is of stealth design and includes a seamless, curved surface whose contours constantly change direction, eliminating radar 'hot spots' at the edges, and a jagged trailing edge. The turbofans exhaust above the trailing edges to hide the heat from the ground and reduce infra-red signature. The exhaust plume includes an injection of chloro-fluorosulphate to suppress contrails. However, the aircraft's radar-absorbent coating requires special facilities to maintain, limiting its service potential. The first production machine, *Spirit of Missouri*, entered service on 17 Dec 1993. By the end of the 1990s, nineteen B-2As were in service. B-2 development had cost $45 billion by 1997, and the intended production run of 133 was cut dramatically. Flying nonstop missions from the USA, the B-2 made its combat debut during the Kosovo campaign of 1999

LOCKHEED MARTIN F-22 first flight 29 September 1990

Powerplant: Two 35,000lb (15,875kg) Pratt & Whitney F119-0W-100 turbofans
Primary role: Tactical fighter
Dimensions: Wingspan 44ft 6in (13.56m); length 62ft 1in (18.92m) overall
Armament: One 20mm M61A2 6-barreled cannon, four 5,000lb (2,268kg) capacity wing pylons, eight AMRAAM, two AIM-9M Sidewinder and four AIM-120A or six AIM-120C; stealth missiles carried in one under-fuselage and two intake bays
Weights: Empty 31,670lb (14,365kg); loaded 55,000lb (24,950kg)
Speed: 921mph (1,483kph) max at sea level
Range: 2,000 miles (3,220km)
Crew: 1
Production total (all marks): 339 planned
Variants: 2 prototypes; F-22A single-seater

The F-22 was developed to meet a 1981 USAF requirement for a new advanced tactical fighter with ground-attack capability to replace the F-15. The first flight by the prototype took place on 29 September 1990. A low radar cross-section and stealth are achieved through airframe design, avionics and internal missile carriage. A low-maintenance fighter with a beyond-visual-range attack capability, the F-22 is remarkably manoeuvrable, test flights having demonstrated a 60-degree angle of attack. The first operational squadron is the US 27th Fighter Squadron which reached operational capability in December 2005. Current plans are for 180+ to enter service with the US Air Force.

***McDonnell Douglas C-17 Globemaster III** (US) first flew 15 Sept 1991*

27 Apri 91 First flight of Eurocopter Tiger (Tigre) (INT)

29 April 91 First flight of Atlas Aviation ACE (SA)

10 May 91 First flight of Bombardier Canadair CRJ-X (CA)

26 June 91 First flight of Westinghouse Airships Sentinel S1000 (US)

Aug 91 First flight of Bell 430 (US & CA)

15 Sept 91 First flight of McDonnell Douglas C-17 Globemaster III (US)

21 Oct 91 First flight of Airbus A340 (INT)

6 Dec 91 First flight of Dornier 328 (G)

12 Dec 91 First flight of Daewoo KTX-1 Yeo-Myung (SK)

15 April 92 First flight of McDonnell Douglas AH-64D Longbow Apache (US)

15 June 92 First flight of Learjet 60 (US)

2 Nov 92 First flight of Airbus A330 (INT)

18 Dec 92 First flight of McDonnell Douglas MD 900 Explorer (US)

4 March 93 First flight of Dassault Falcon 2000 (F)

5 Feb 93 First flight of Lindstrand Balloons AS300 (GB)

11 March 93 First flight of Airbus A321 (INT)

15 May 93 First flight of Embraer EMB-312 H/ALX Super Tucano (BR)

18 May 93 First flight of Aero L-139 Albatross 2000 (CH)

16 Oct 93 First flight of Kubicek AV-1 (CH)

1993 Nato begins air patrols and air-strikes in support of peacekeeping forces in Bosnia-Herzegovina. An F-16 and a Sea Harrier are shot down

21 Dec 93 First flight of Cessna Citation XI (US)

19 Feb 94 First flight of Eurocopter EC 135 (INT)

***Dassault Falcon 2000** (F) first flew 4 March 1993*

EUROFIGHTER TYPHOON first flight 27 March 1994

Powerplant: Two 13,488lb (6,117kg) EJ200 twin-spool turbofans
Primary role: Close air combat
Dimensions: Wingspan 35ft 11in (10.95m); length 52ft 4½in (17.07m)
Armament: AIM-120 AMRAAM/ Meteor/ASRAAM/BGT IRIS-T; three Paveway III LGBs plus a TIALD designator/Storm Shadow/Brimstone
Weights: Empty 21,495lb (9,750kg)
Speed: Mach 2
Range: (Combat) over 1,000 nautical miles
Crew: 1 or 2
Production total (all marks): 640 expected

The Eurofighter consortium was formed in June 1986 by Britain, Germany and Italy, joined later by Spain, with the aim of producing an air superiority fighter by the end of the century. Specifications decided in September 1987 implied a light, twin-turbofan single-seater, a mix of AAMs for both close combat and beyond visual range, with air-to-surface as a secondary role, a low radar cross-section and a high supersonic performance. The name Typhoon

27 March 94 First flight of Eurofighter Typhoon (INT)
13 May 94 First flight of 21st Century Airships SPAS 13 (CA)
12 June 94 First flight of Boeing 777 (US)
22 June 94 First flight of Antonov An-38 (USSR)
13 Sept 94 First flight of SATIC Airbus A300-600ST Beluga (INT)
22 Nov 94 First flight of McDonnell Douglas MD 600N (US)
16 Dec 94 First flight of Antonov An-70/An-77 (USSR)

***Boeing 777** (US) first flew 12 June 1994*

was decided in 1998. Highly manoeuvrable with relaxed stability, the aircraft is a close-coupled canard delta with the centre of gravity aft. The first flight was made by the prototype DA.1 on 27 March 1994, followed by DA.2 on 6 April that year. The first flight by a two-seater was that of DA.6 on 31 August 1996. The Eurofighter Typhoon is in service with four nations; Britain, Germany, Italy and Spain. Austria has ordered 15 and 74 aircraft have also been ordered by Saudi Arabia.

1995 First flight of Kamov Ka-62 (USSR)
28 Jan–12 Feb 95 Combat breaks out between Ecuador and Peru. Two Peruvian Su-22s and an A-37 are shot down by Ecuadorian Mirage F1s and Kfirs. Helicopters of both sides are also lost
Early 1995 First flight of Agusta A119 Koala (IT)
31 March 95 First flight of Grob Strato 2C (G)
May 95 First flight of MiG-AT 821 (USSR)
1 May 95 First flight of Lindstrand Balloons HS 110 (GB)
3 May 95 First flight of Gippsland Aeronautics GA-8 Airvan (AUS)
31 May 95 First flight of Schweizer RU-38A (US)
1 June 95 First flight of Dassault Falcon 900EX (F)
9 June 95 First flight of Eurocopter EC-120 (INT)
11 Aug 95 First flight of Embraer EJR-145 (BR)
25 Aug 95 First flight of Airbus A319 (INT)

***Airbus A319** (INT) first flew 25 Aug 1995*

***Grumman Gulfstream V** (US) first flew 22 Sept 1995*

22 Sept 95 First flight of Grumman Gulfstream V (US)
7 Oct 95 First flight of Bombardier Learjet 45 (US)

1996 First flight of MiG-110 (USSR)
1996 First flight of Yak-77 (USSR)
29 Feb 96 Cessna Citation Excel (US)
April 96 First flight of Cessna 172R & SP Skyhawk (US)
July 96 First flight of Lancair Colombia 300 (US)
10 October 96 A Greek Mirage 2000 firing a R550 Magic 2 shot down a Turkish F-16D over the Aegean Sea, the only confirmed air-to-air kill of an F-16.
13 Oct 96 First flight of Bombardier Global Express (CA)
26 Oct 96 First flight of PZL Zwidnik SW-4 (PO)
16 Nov 96 First flight of VisionAire Vantage (US)

25 Sep 97 First flight of Sukhoi S-37 Berkut (USSR)
11 Dec 97 First flight of Bell 427 (US)
25 Dec 97 First flight of Galaxy Aerospace (ITI) Galaxy (IS)

1998 First flight of Aviaspetstrans (Myasishchev) Yamal (USSR)
20 Jan 98 First flight of Fairchild Aerospace 328JET & 428JET (G)

23 Jan 98 AEA Explorer (AUS)
Feb 98 First flight of AASI Jetcruzer 500 (US)
28 Feb 98 First Flight of Northrop Grumman Global Hawk (UAV) (US)
24 March 98 First flight of Chengdu CAC J-10 (CH)

Opposite page: Embraer EJR-135 *(BR) first flew 4 July 1998*

19 June 98 First flight of Luscombe Sparton (US)
4 July 98 First flight of Embraer EJR-135 (BR)
30 Oct 98 First flight of Boeing Business Jet (US)
Late 98 First flight of Ayres LM 200 Loadmaster (US)
Dec 98 First flight of Sikorsky S-92 Helibus (US)
16 Dec 98 Operation 'Desert Fox', four nights of air strikes by US and British aircraft on Iraqi military sites because of Saddam Hussein's non-cooperation with UN weapons inspectors
22 Dec 98 First flight of Raytheon Premier I (US)

Unveiled early 1999 First flight of MiG 1.42 /1.44 MFI multirole aircraft (USSR)
1999/2000 First flight of Tupolev 334 & 354 (USSR)
21 Mar 99 Bertrand Piccard & Brian Jones make the first non-stop balloon flight around the world in the *Breitling Orbiter 3*

KOSOVO WAR

24 March–9 June 99 1st Nato air campaign which successfully removes Serbian ground forces from Kosovo. NATO loses F-117 as well as an F-16. Six MiG-29s were shot down and other aircraft destroyed on the ground

2000 Concorde withdrawn from service
2000 First flight of Fairchild Aerospace 528JET 728JET & 928JET (INT)
2000 First flight of Chichester Miles Leopard (US)
2000 During the course of the two-year border war between Ethiopia and Eritrea, Ethiopia has lost at least 5 MiG 29s and 2 MiG 23s to Eritrea
25 July 00 Air France Concorde crash at Paris
18 Sept 00 First flight of Boeing X-32 Joint Strike Fighter (US)
16 Dec 00 First flight of X-35 Joint Strike Fighter (US)
4 Jan 01 First flight of Hindustan Aeronautics Tejas Light Combat Aircraft (IND)
16 Feb 01 British and US aircraft strike Iraqi air-defense positions in support of no-fly zones
28 March 01 Israeli combat helicopters attack Palestinian bases of Yasser Arafat's bodyguard in Gaza City and the West Bank
1 April 01 A US Navy surveillance P-3 Orion collides with a Chinese fighter over the South China Sea. The fighter crashes and the pilot is reported missing, but the US aircraft manages to land
26 April 01 Zeppelin NT receives type certification.
19 May 01 at 10:25 am the 1st series Zeppelin, with the call sign D-LZZR, makes her maiden flight from Friedrichshafen over the Bodensee
11 August 01 First flight of Raytheon's Hawker Horizon 4000 (US)
11 September 01 ('9/11') Muslim terrorist group al-Qaeda hijack four United Airline 757 airliners. Two crash into the World Trade Center, New York; another into the Pentagon; and the fourth crashes into a field in Pennsylvania when passengers and flight crew attempt to retake control of the aircraft from the hijackers

Hinustan Aeronautics Tejas *(IND) first flew 4 Jan 2001*

WAR IN AFGHANISTAN

7 Oct 01 Operation 'Enduring Freedom' (part of the 'War on Terrorism'). Early combat operations including a mix of strikes from land-based B-1 Lancer, B-2 Spirit and B-52 Stratofortress bombers; carrier-based F-14

Tomcat and F/A-18 Hornet fighters; and Tomahawk cruise missiles launched from both US and British ships and submarines

26 Oct 01 Joint Strike Fighter contract awarded to the X-35 for the USA and Britain

15 Jan 02 First flight of Airbus A318 (INT)

11 Feb 02 First flight of Airbus A340-500 (INT)

Summer 02 Dassault Rafale enters service with French Navy

1 July 02 First flight of Pilatus PC-21 (SWI)

11 July 02 First flight of Adam A500 (US)

1 February 03 The United States Space Shuttle *Columbia* disintegrates on re-entry, killing all seven astronauts

6 March 03 First flight of Bell/Augusta BA 609 (US)

7 March 03 First flight of HAL HJT-36 (IND)

GULF WAR: Liberation of Iraq

20 March 03 Operation 'Iraqi Freedom':" large-scale attack by US and British warplanes in support of the land assault

20 May 03 First flight of SpaceShipOne (US)

28 July 03 First flight of Adam A700 AdamJet (US)

24 October 03 Concorde makes its last scheduled commercial flight

2004 Dassault Rafale enters service with French Air Force

27 March 04 NASA's X-43 pilotless plane breaks world speed record for an atmospheric engine by briefly flying at 7,700 kilometres (4,780 miles) per hour (seven times the speed of sound)

5 May 04 Air France and Netherlands-based KLM (Royal Dutch Airlines) merge and are now known as Air France-KLM

29 May 04 First flight of Aceair AERIKS 200 (SWI)

15 July 04 First flight of Aermacchi M-346 (IT)

20 July 04 First flight of Aerocomp Comp Air Jet (US)

29 Jan 05 Non-stop flights between mainland China and Taiwan begin for the first time since 1949

5 March 05 Steve Fossett completes the first non-stop, solo circumnavigation of the world in the Virgin Atlantic *GlobalFlyer*, completing the trip in 67 hours and 2 minutes.

27 April 05 First flight of Airbus A380 (INT) 'Superjumbo'

2–3 July 05 Steve Fossett and Mark Rebholz recreate the first direct crossing of the Atlantic by the British John Alcock and Arthur Whitten-Brown on June 14, 1919 in a Vickers Vimy bi-plane

4 Oct 05 SpaceShipOne successfully makes her 3rd flight into space and proves to be a plausible option for space tourism, thus winning the Ansari X-Prize

16 Nov 05 NASA's X-43 reaches a record speed of Mach 10 (7,000 mph, 11,200 km/h)

15 Dec 05 F-22 Raptor enters sevice with USAF

31 March 06 Eurofighter Typhoon begins to enter squadron service with RAF, Luftwaffe, Italian and Spanish Airforces

15 December 06 First flight of F-35 Lightning II Joint Strike Fighter (US)

25 October 07 First commercial flight of the Airbus A380 from Singapore to Sidney with Singapore Airlines

17 Jan 08 A British Airways Boeing 777 crash-lands at London's Heathrow airport. All 136 passengers and 16 crew survive the crash-landing on the south runway

2008 Boeing 787 Deamliner expected to make its first flight (US)

2008 Airbus A400M military transport expected to make its first flight (INT)

14 May 08 Swiss Yves Rossy demonstrates flying up to 186mph with a jet-engine-powered wing strapped to his back, the nearest humankind has yet come to being a true 'birdman'

FIGHTER ACES

This is a selection of the many hundreds of fighter aces. The expression 'Fighter Ace' is defined as a pilot who has shot down five or more enemy aircraft. Enormous scores have been attributed to the Luftwaffe in WW2; many factors are involved in this. German pilots flew many more sorties than their opponents and as the war progressed and their opponents became more numerous, the Germans were in an ever increasing 'target rich' environment.

Mohammed Alam
Pakistan: 1965 Indo-Pakistan War
In one day he scored 5 of his total of 9 victories.

Douglas Bader
Britain: WWII.
Both legs amputated before the War. His total was 20 confirmed and 4 shared, with 18 probables and damaged. Shot down and captured by the Germans in 1941.

Albert Ball
Britain: WWI.
44 victories. Ball was the first British ace idolized by the public. Killed in flying accident while on patrol.

Heinz Bär
Germany: WWII.
A total of 220 victories which included 16 victories while flying the Me 262, making him the top-scoring 'jet ace' of WWII. Died in an air crash in 1957.

William 'Billy' Avery Bishop
Canada: WWI.
72 victories. Because Bishop flew many of his patrols alone, most of his victories were never witnessed.

Oswald Boelcke
Germany: WWI.
40 victories. First German ace. Killed in midair collision with another German aircraft.

Albert Ball *Richard Bong*

Richard Bong
USA: WWII.
USAAF's and America's leading fighter ace with 40 victories, all in Pacific theatre.

Gregory 'Pappy' Boyington
USA: WWII.
28 victories. Top-scoring US Marine pilot, all against the Japanese.

Randall 'Duke' Cunningham
USA: Vietnam.
Navy pilot with 5 victories. First US ace of the Vietnam War.

René Paul Fonck
France: WWI
75 victories. Highest- scoring ace for the Allies.

Giora Epstein
Israel: Six-Day War, War of Attrition and October War. 17 victories

Francis 'Gabby' Gabreski
USA: WWII and Korea
28 victories in WWII, becoming top-scoring USAAF ace in the European theatre. In Korea he flew F-86 Sabres. Korean score was 6 victories and one shared.

Adolf Galland
Germany: WWII
104 victories, all gained against the Western Allies.

Hermann Wilhelm Göring
Germany: WWI
22 victories. Commanded von Richthofen's élite JG 1 on 8 July 1918. Became head of the Luftwaffe in WWII.

Georges Marie Ludovic Jules Guynemer
France: WWI
53 victories. Guynemer was France's most beloved ace. Flew over 600 aerial combats, surviving being shot down 7 times, but eventually was shot down and killed.

Erich Hartmann
Germany: WWII
The highest-scoring ace of all, with 352 victories. Hartmann survived World War 2 without a scratch, even though shot down many times.

Max Immelmann
Germany: WWI
15 victories. Laid the foundation for single-seat fighter tactics in WWI. Killed in action.

Tetsuzo Iwamato
Japan: WWII
94 victories. Top-scoring Japanese ace. Many

Erich Hartmann Robin Olds

of his victories were shared or only probables.

James Edgar 'Johnnie' Johnson
Britain : WWII
34 victories plus 7 shared. Top scoring British ace of WWII.

Lidiya 'Lilya' Litvak
USSR: WWII
Soviet Union's most prolific female fighter pilot with 12 victories. She was killed in the same engagement in which she achieved her final two victories.

Adolf Gysbert 'Sailor' Malan
South Africa: WWII
27 victories, 7 shared and 7 probables. His 'Ten Rules of Air Fighting' were distributed to all RAF and also some American fighter units.

Edward Corringham 'Mick' Mannock
Britain: WWI
61 victories. Revered by his men and proved to be one of the greatest flight leaders of the war.

David McCampbell
USA: WWII
34 victories, Top-scoring US Navy ace of WWII. Killed in action.

Joe McConnell
USA: Korea
16 victories. The top-scoring ace of the Korean War. A test pilot after the war, he died in a flying accident.

James Thomas Byford 'Mac' McCudden
Britain : WWI
57 victories. Within days of receiving his aviator's certificate, his talents as a pilot proved so extraordinary that he became an instructor. One of 3 brothers to serve with the RFC. Both he and his brother John, also an ace, were killed.

Werner Mölders
Germany: Spanish Civil War and WWII.
14 victories in Spain and 101 in WWII. He died in a flying accident in 1941.

Nguyan Van Coc
North Vietnam: Vietnam War
9 victories. Included in the total were 2 drones.

Edward 'Butch' O'Hare
USA: WWII
12 victories, first US Navy ace. Became an 'ace in a day'. Killed in action. Chicago's O'Hare Airport is named after him.

Robin Olds
USA: WWII and Vietnam
12 victories in WWII. A full colonel 20 years later, he commanded the 8th Tactical Fighter Wing in Vietnam, adding 4 MiGs to his total of 16 victories.

Manfred Albrecht Freiherr von Richthofen
Germany: WWI
80 victories. Probably the most famous ace ever. The British referred to him as the 'Red Baron'. The highest-scoring ace of WWI. Killed in action.

Edward 'Eddie' Vernon Rickenbacker
USA: WWI
26 victories, the highest scoring US ace of WWI.

Richard 'Steve' Ritchie
USA: Vietnam
5 victories. Top-scoring US Air Force pilot of the Vietnam War.

Indra Lal 'Laddie' Roy
India: WWI
This 19-year old was credited with his 10 victories during a 2-week period, before being shot down in flames and killed.

Saburo Sakai
Japan: China and WWII
Survived to end the war with 64 victories to his name.

Bob Stanford Tuck
Britain: WWII
His final confirmed score was 27 victories, but it could possibly have been more.

Ernst Udet
Germany: WWI
Highest-scoring German ace to survive WWI, with 62 victories. Luftwaffe Quartermaster-General in WWII. Commited suicide during WWII.

Werner Voss
Germany: WWI
48 victories. Killed during a legendary dogfight with 7 S.E.5as, having downed two and damaged the rest.

AVIATORS, INNOVATORS AND PIONEERS

Ader, Clément (1841–1925)
Recognized by many as being the first man to fly a powered aeroplane. Made a flight of 165ft at Armainvillers, France, on 9 October 1890 in his steam-powered *Éole*'; preceding the Wright Brothers' achievement by some thirteen years, this, however, was more in the nature of a 'hop' than a controlled, sustained flight. Subsequent machines, *Avion II* and *Avion III*, were failures, and work on further machines was cancelled by a sceptical French Army in 1898.

Alcock, Sir John (1892–1919)
Pioneer aviator. With W. Brown achieved first non-stop aerial crossing of the Atlantic. Came third in 1914 London-to-Manchester air race, just three years after attaining pilot's certificate. Served in RNAS during World War I, winning DSC in Aegean before being taken prisoner by Turks. Involved with Vickers Ltd after war. With Brown, flew a converted Vimy bomber from Newfoundland to Ireland on 14–15 June 1919. Both men knighted for their achievement, which preceded Lindbergh's often more celebrated flight by eight years. Killed 18 December 1919 in Vickers Viking at Cote d'Evrard, France, attempting to land in thick fog.

Antonov, Oleg (1906–1984)
Built his first glider at the age of 18 and continued his work at the Leningrad Polytechnic Institute. In the 1930s became Chief Designer at the Moscow Glider Factory. Joined Yakovlev (q.v.) in 1938 to work on light aircraft and subsequently moved to Saratov, where he was was involved in designing the A-7 troop-carrying glider. After the Second World War he set up his own design bureau at Novosibirsk, then moved to Kiev. A string of famous transport aircraft – An-2, An-10, An-12, An-22, An-24, An-124 An-225 – was produced by the bureau throughout the postwar years.

Balbo, Italo (1896–1940)
During the First World War Balbo served with the Italian Army and in 1926 Benito Mussolini surprisingly made him Secretary of State for Air (he had no background of aviation). Very quickly learned to fly and in 1933 led a formation of 24 SM.55X flying boats on a transatlantic flight to Lake Michigan and back. Rapidly became the best known pilot in Italy and as part of his work set about transforming the Regia Aeronautica. At the beginning of the Second World War was appointed Governor of Libya but continued flying duties. Shot down by 'friendly fire' in 1940.

Barnwell, Frank S. (1880–1938)
Served as a shipbuilding apprentice and then joined an engineering firm near Stirling, where he and his brother built a number of gliders and aeroplanes. Became Chief Draughtsman for the British & Colonial Aeroplane Company in 1911, and over the ensuing years produced a number of outstanding military aircraft designs, including the M.1 monoplane fighter and the Bristol F.2B Fighter. Took up a technical commission in the Royal Australian Air Force 1921–3 but returned to Bristols (as the British & Colonial Aeroplane Co had been renamed) and was responsible for the design of a number of front-line RAF aircraft, including the Bulldog fighter and the Blenheim bomber. On 2 August 1938 he was killed in a light aircraft of his own design.

Batten, Jean (1909–1982)
New Zealander; went to England in 1932 to learn to fly. In May 1934 flew 10,500 miles from Lympne

Oleg Antonov

to Darwin in 14 days 22 hours 30 minutes – the women's record for a solo flight from England to Australia. The following year made the reverse flight in 17 days 16 hours 15 – the first England – Australia solo flight by a woman. In 1935 also became the first woman to fly solo from England to South America, and in 1936 she made the first direct England–New Zealand flight.

Bell, Alexander Graham (1847–1922)
Inventor of the telephone but also founded the Aerial Experiment Association (AEA) of Nova Scotia and Hammondsport, New York. In 1908 Bell's *June Bug* won the Scientific American Trophy for the first public flight in the United States. The company was wound up in 1909, but Bell's work on gliders, aeroplanes and kites continued.

Bell, Lawrence Dale (1894–1956)
Joined the Glenn L. Martin company in 1912 and rose to become vice-president and general manager. Left the company in January 1925 and three years later joined Consolidated. Formed Bell Aircraft in 1935 and during World War II produced the P-39 Airacobra and Kingcobra fighters and the jet-powered P-59 Airacomet and, after the war, the rocket-powered X-1 (the first aircraft in the world to exceed the speed of sound in level flight). Future development concentrated on helicopters, the company producing the well-known JetRanger, Iroquois and HueyCobra types.

Bellanca, Giuseppe Mario (1886–1960)
A Sicilian aircraft designer who in 1910 emigrated to the United States, where he founded a flying school at Mineola, Long Island. He became a consulting engineer at the Wright Aeronautical Corporation in the 1920s, and was responsible for test-bed aircraft for Wright's radial engines. Formed own company, Columbia Aircraft in 1927, specialising in high-wing monoplanes. His Bellanca Aircraft Corporation was formed later that year and continued in existence until the 1980s.

Birkigt, Mark (1878–1953)
Founder of the Hispano-Suiza company and initially concentrated on building motor cars, but in World War I developed his interest in aero engines and developed a number of reliable designs, particularly the V8 powerplants for the French SPAD and British S.E.5a single-seaters. Later developments saw Hispano concentrate on aircraft cannon, the 20mm weapon becoming one of the most widely used armaments during World War II and afterwards.

Bishop, Ronald Eric (1903–1989)
Apprenticed to the de Havilland Company and rose to become the firm's design director. Was responsible for many designs, including the famous twin-engined Mosquito and Hornet, the Vampire (one of the earliest jet fighters) and the Comet jet-powered passenger airliner; the current Nimrod maritime reconnaissance aircraft was developed from the last-named.

Blackburn, Robert (1885–1955)
Founder of the Blackburn Aeroplane & Motor Company, which became one of the most famous names in aviation. From early beginnings in 1909, the company went on to specialize in a whole range of naval aircraft and, in the inter-war years, flying boats. Notable designs included the Dart, Ripon and Baffin torpedo-bombers, the World War II Skua fighter-bomber and, perhaps the company's greatest achievement, the postwar Buccaneer carrier-based strike bomber.

Blériot, Louis (1872–1936)
Famed as the first aviator to cross the English Channel (July 1909), Blériot had for many years prior to taking up aviation been a designer and producer of motor-car headlamps. He invested the

Louis Blériot

money made from this venture into aircraft production, and with the Voisin brothers (q.v.) produced a number of experimental (and largely unsuccessful) aeroplanes prior to his epic Channel crossing. He gave up flying shortly afterwards, although his company, the Société Blériot Aéronautique, continued in existence for some years afterwards.

Bloch, Marcel (1892–1986)
One of the most illustrious names in French aviation history. His early years were spent working in an aeronautical laboratory and later at the Maurice Farman factory but during World War I he teamed up with Henri Potez and produced first aeroplane propellers and then complete aircraft. Avions Marcel Bloch was formed in the 1930s, and a number of front-line fighter designs were produced, including the MB.152. After the war the company changed its name to Dassault, which went on to become one of the most important European aircraft concerns, responsible for the famous Mirage family of delta-winged jets.

Boeing, William E. (1881–1956)
A timber merchant who set up Pacific Aero Products in 1916, renamed the Boeing Airplane Company the following year. Produced a range of outstanding fighter aircraft between the wars (F4B/P-12 family) but just before World War II began to concentrate on heavy bombers, of which the B-17 was the outstanding example and mainstay of the USAAF throughout the conflict. The B-29 Superfortress followed, and afterwards the jet-powered B-47 and B-52, the latter of which is still in service today. Airliners have also been a major consideration for Boeing, from the prewar Model 247 to today's 747 and subsequent types.

Boelcke, Oswald (1891–1916)
One of the most skilled and famous fighter pilots of World War I. Developed a series of 'rules' for air combat, known as his 'Dicta', which became the standard teaching aids for all aspiring German fighter pilots. Holder of the Iron Cross and Pour le Mérite. Killed in a flying accident in October 1916.

Branker, Sir William Sefton (1877–1930)
One of the leading champions of civil aviation until his death in the *R101* airship disaster. Served in South Africa and India following his commissioning into the Royal Artillery in 1896, learned to fly in 1913 and held a number of important administrative positions during World War I.

William E. Boeing

Oswald Boelcke

Cayley's 1837 design for a dirigible

Bréguet, Louis (1880–1955)
An aeroplane designer and builder from 1907, responsible for the famous Bréguet XIV reconnaissance aircraft of World War I. Founder of Compagnie de Messageries Aériennes, which later evolved into Air France. The company merged with the Dassault concern in 1971. Current aircraft from the Bréguet stable include the Jaguar fighter-bomber, produced in collaboration with Britain.

Bulman, Paul Ward Spencer (1896–1963)
Known familiarly as 'George' Bulman. One of the leading test pilots of the interwar years, first with the Royal Aircraft Establishment at Farnborough and then with Hawker Aircraft at Kingston. Became a director of Hawkers but relinquished his post in 1945 to set up his own business.

Byrd, Richard Evelyn (1888–1957)
One of the great polar aviators. Was awarded the Congressional Medal of Honor for a flight over the North Pole, although it was later discovered that Byrd's and Floyd Bennett's Fokker Trimotor had in fact failed to reach its destination. Attempts to cross the Atlantic involved Byrd planning the 1919 flight by Curtiss NC flying boats and a failure to beat Lindbergh for a solo crossing in 1927. During the 1930s he turned his attention to the South Pole and carried out many pioneering explorations there.

Camm, Sir Sydney (1893–1966)
Trained as a carpenter and joined the Martinsyde company prior to World War I. Became Senior Draughtsman for Hawker Aircraft in 1923 and quickly rose to become Chief Designer. Was responsible for some of the most famous British aircraft of the interwar, World War II and postwar years, including the Hart family, Hurricane, Typhoon, Sea Hawk, Hunter and Harrier. Became Hawker Siddeley's Director of Design.

Caudron, Gaston and René (1882–1915; 1884–1959)
Brothers who set up their own aircraft company and flying school in France and produced a number of outstanding early designs, specialising in twin-boom aeroplanes. Production of leading aircraft types continued during World War I and afterwards, but the company was wound up shortly after World War II. The C.714 and derivatives (lightweight fighters) were the last important types to be produced.

Cayley, Sir George (1773–1857)
Regarded as the 'Father of the Aeroplane', founded the science of aeronautics and designed the earliest aerodynamically sound heavier-than-air machine, both powered and unpowered, although unmanned. In 1849 one of his aeroplanes managed

to carry a child aloft. A prolific inventor, he was also responsible for such important innovations as artificial limbs and the caterpillar tractor.

Cessna, Clyde (1880–1954)
A farmer and mechanic who ran his own motor-car business before building his own aircraft (based on a Blériot fuselage) and learning to fly. In 1925 helped establish Travel Air in association with Walter Beech. Founded his own aircraft company in 1927, and his name is now synonymous with classic light aircraft.

Chadwick, Sir Roy (1893–1947)
Personal assistant to A. V. Roe in 1911 and joined the latter's firm when that was formed in 1913. Rose throughout the World War I years to become the firm's Chief Designer by 1919 and subsequently was involved in all the designs. His most famous creation was the Avro Lancaster bomber. Killed in the crash of the prototype Tudor airliner in August 1947.

Chanute, Octave (1832–1910)
A civil engineer by training but developed his interest in aviation and wrote *Progress in Flying Machines*, published in 1894. His main contribution to aeroplane development was in the field of hang-gliding, and he was responsible for the Pratt system of truss bracing. Became a close friend of the Wright Brothers, introducing the latters' work to European aviation enthusiasts just as they were becoming involved in their early flights.

Cierva, Juan de la (1895–1936)
Builder of gliders and powered aeroplanes but more famously the inventor and developer of the gyroplane concept, a machine with conventional thrust but also a rotorhead. Moved from Spain to England in 1925 and collaborated with A. V. Roe in producing a series of autogyros. Formed the Cierva Autogyro Company in 1926, many of the designs being license-built overseas. Killed in an airliner crash in 1936.

Clark, Virginus E. (1886–1948)
An engineer at the United States Naval Academy who joined NACA in 1917 and designed and developed improved aerofoils, notably the so-called 'Clark Y' (used on Lindbergh's *Spirit of St Louis*). Other claims to fame were the development of low-drag engine cowlings for aircraft and the invention of Duramold, a wood/plastic compound for use in aircraft production.

Coanda, Henri (1886–1972)
A Romanian who went to The School of Aeronautics in Paris and in 1910 demonstrated, statically, an aircraft with a ducted turbine screw, considered by some to be the first example of a jet aeroplane. Joined the British & Colonial Aeroplane Company (Bristol) in 1912 and worked in the design office before returning to Romania two years later. Discovered the 'Coanda Effect', in which air tends to 'stick' to a curved surface.

Cobham, Sir Alan (1894–1973)
Learned to fly in the RFC, which he joined from the Royal Artillery in 1917, and following World War I took up the management of aviation tours, first with Berkshire Aviation Tours and then in 1921 with the de Havilland Aeroplane Hire Service. He pioneered route-finding for Imperial Airways and subsequently organized a series of 'Circuses', bringing air displays to the British public. His final legacy was that of inflight refuelling, which he pioneered in Britain.

Cochran, Jacqueline (1906–1980)
Famed as the first woman to fly an aircraft through the sound barrier, piloting an F-86 Sabre in 1953. Her original career was as a beautician, but she learned to fly in 1932 and quickly took up competitive flying, winning the Bendix Trophy in 1938. Was instrumental in establishing the Women's Air Force Service Pilots (WASPs) organisation for internal ferrying of aircraft during the World War II years.

Cody, Samuel Franklin (1867–1913)
An American who is best remembered for being the first to make a controlled flight in Britain, flying his own aircraft, the British Army Aeroplane No 1. He had moved to England in the early 1890s after running a successful series of 'Wild West' shows in his home country (whence his nickname), and joined the War Office. After his flight he went on to design and build his own aircraft. Killed when one of these, *Waterplane*, broke up in flight.

Cornu, Paul (1881–1944)
A French car salesman whose interest in vertical take-off led to his designing model helicopters in the early years of the twentieth century, followed by a full-size man-carrying machine in 1907. The

latter had twin rotors and was powered by a 24hp Antoinette engine, and it reportedly rose a short distance into the air near Lisieux, France, in November 1907. Its viability has since been questioned.

Costes, Dieudonné (1896–1973)
A World War I pilot (8 victories) who later became Bréguet's Chief Pilot and achieved the first crossing of the South Atlantic when he flew from Senegal to Brazil in 1928 and the first non-stop flight from Paris to New York two years later. He made a large number of other record-breaking flights, including one from Paris to Siberia.

Cunningham, John (1917–)
Known as 'Cat's Eyes Cunningham' for the legendary reputation he built up as a night fighter pilot during World War II (20 victories). He was also the first British pilot to down an enemy aircraft at night. After the war he became de Havilland's Chief Test Pilot and as such had much to do with the revolutionary Comet jet airliner, taking it for its maiden flight and later completing a circumnavigation of the world.

Curtiss, Glenn Hammond (1878–1930)
A bicycle manufacturer who joined Alexander Graham Bell's (q.v.) Aerial Experiment Association and began designing aeroplanes for that company, including the famous *June Bug*, which he flew successfully in 1908. Best known as the man responsible for the world's first practical flying boats and for the JN 'Jenny' training aircraft of World War I. His own company was set up before World War I and continued producing outstanding aircraft (including the well-known 'Hawk' fighter series) until after World War II.

Samuel Franklin Cody

De Havilland, Sir Geoffrey (1882–1965)
Founder of one of the world's best-known aircraft manufacturing companies, which created such outstanding aircraft as the Moth series of light biplanes, the multi-role Mosquito of World War II, the DH 108 single-seat jet (the first British aircraft to fly faster than sound) and the Comet jet passenger liner. His first aircraft was produced in 1908, and his reputation quickly advanced, so much so that he was taken on in an official capacity as the designer and test pilot for the Royal Aircraft Factory at Farnborough, producing such well-known types as the B.E.1 and F.E.2. Prior to founding his own company he designed further successful aircraft for Airco, including the D.H.2 fighter and D.H.4 and D.H.9 bombers.

Delagrange, Léon (1873–1910)
A sculptor and self-taught pioneering pilot who bought an aircraft from the Voisin brothers (q.v.) and undertook a tour of Europe, becoming the first person to fly in Italy and the first to take a female passenger aloft. He made a record-breaking flight in a Blériot in 1909, flying 124 miles in just over 2 hours. Died in an accident when his Blériot broke up in flight.

Deperdussin, Armand (d.1924)
Responsible, with his designer Louis Béchereau, for a series of early monoplanes, one of which won the Gordon Bennett Trophy in 1912 and another of which, fitted with floats, became the first ever Schneider Trophy winner the following year. Despite these successes his company never really prospered. He was arrested for embezzlement in 1913 but was leniently treated. However, he committed suicide in 1924.

Doolittle, James (1896–1993)
One of the most illustrious names in US aviation history. In 1922 made the first non-stop flight across the United States and three years later

James Doolittle

won the Schneider Trophy in a Curtiss seaplane. He also set a new world air speed record in 1931 and became the first pilot to make a fully instrumented landing. His most famous legacy is the so-called 'Doolittle Raid' of 1942, organising a raid on Japan by carrier-based Mitchell bombers. He later commanded the US Fifteenth and Eighth Air Forces.

Dornier, Claudius (1884–1969)
Designer of a successful series of seaplanes and flying boats in World War I, which work continued after the war in Switzerland, culminating in the well-known Wal and Do X. His company returned to Germany in the 1930s and produced the Do 17 series of medium bombers and, postwar, a number of successful civil aircraft.

Douglas, Donald Wills (1892–1981)
Founded the company which has produced some of the world's outstanding passenger airliners, including the prewar DC-3, many of which are still in service today. Other achievements include the manufacture of very effective torpedo-bombers for the US Navy; in 1924 two World Cruisers (redesigned DT torpedo-bombers) flew almost 29,000 miles for the first ever round-the-world flight. After World War II his company produced a series of passenger transports – DC-6, 7, 8, 9 and 10 – which enjoyed large sales, and also a number of front-line military aircraft, including the piston-engined A-1 Skyraider and A-3 Skywarrior and A-4 Skyhawk attack bombers.

Dufaux, Armand and Henri (1883–19??; 1879–19??)
As with many pioneers, these two Swiss brothers were originally bicycle and motorcycle engineers, but they turned their attention to model helicopters and in 1905 demonstrated one in Paris. A larger helicopter/glider was demonstrated five years later, whereupon the brothers turned their attention to fixed-wing designs, one of which was flown along Lake Geneva in 1910.

Du Temple, Félix (1823–1890)
French aviation pioneer who produced successful clockwork- and steam-powered model flying machines as early as the mid 1850s, one of which featured one of the first types of retractable undercarriage. Take-off was achieved in a larger, man-carrying monoplane in 1874, but the flight was neither sustained nor controlled.

Earhart, Amelia (1898–1937)
Perhaps the most famous female aviator of all time, she was the first woman to cross the Atlantic (albeit as a passenger) in 1927 but then established flying records in her own right. She was the first woman to fly from coast to coast and back across the United States and in 1932 the first to cross the Atlantic. She died in unknown circumstances in 1937 while attempting a circumnavigation of the globe in a Lockheed Electra.

Edwards, Sir George (1908–)
Joined Vickers Aviation in 1928 and helped develop the company's military aircraft under Chief Designer R. K. Pierson, including the geodetic Wellesley and Wellington. He himself became Chief Designer in 1945 and was responsible for the outstanding VC2 Viscount airliner, one the earliest applications of turboprop power. Became Chairman of the British Aircraft Corporation (which included the Vickers concern) in 1963, serving until 1975.

Ellehammer, Jacob Christian Hansen (1871–1946)
A Danish inventor who built and tested an unmanned aircraft as early as 1905–06 and a larger triplane, which successfully took off on many occasions from 1907. Further experimental aeroplanes were built.

Esnault-Pelterie, Robert, (1881–1957)
French pioneer who built gliders from 1904 and a powered monoplane, the REP 1, in 1907, followed by the REP 8 the next year; the latter made many demonstration flights. One of his innovations was the introduction to aircraft of wingtip control surfaces.

Etrich, Dr Igo (1879–1967)
Austrian engineer who evolved a series of Taube monoplanes with bird-like wings. These were adopted by the Rumpler company in Germany, and many aircraft with Etrich's hallmark served in the First World War, chiefly in the reconnaissance role.

Fabre, Henri (1882–1984)
Early French pioneer who in 1910 developed and built the first successful seaplane. Modifications to the design led to several more flights, but Fabre was unable to secure financial backing and he subsequently abandoned his work to concentrate on the design and development of aeroplane floats.

Amelia Earhart

Fairey, Sir Richard (1887–1957)
Joined J. W. Dunne in 1911 and assisted in the building of tailless aeroplanes, then joined Short Brothers, becoming their Chief Engineer. Set up his own company in 1915, heralding the design and manufacture of a line of successful, mainly naval aircraft until well after World War II. Among the well-known Fairey products were the Fairey III series, the immortal Swordfish biplane and, postwar, the Gannet anti-submarine/AEW aircraft and the world speed record-breaking FD2 research jet.

Farman, Henry and Maurice (1874–1958; 1877–1964)
Among the foremost aviation pioneers, who started off as ballooning enthusiasts and then went on to found their own company. Henry made the first one-kilometre closed-circuit flight in Europe, and his boxkite-type biplane was very successful. The company produced many innovative designs, including the well-known Longhorn and Shorthorn types.

Fedden, Sir Roy (1885–1961)
A motor-car engineer in his early career, Fedden went on to oversee the production of license-built aero-engines for the Brazil-Straker company. The latter was taken over by Bristol in 1920 and he, as Technical Director, was responsible for the Mercury and Hercules radial engines of the 1930s and 1940s. During the latter part of World War II he was a technical adviser to the Ministry of Aircraft Production.

Flettner, Anton (1885–1961)
German inventor of the Flettner tab (for easing the pilot workload on control surfaces) and famed also for his work on early helicopters. Work on autogyros in the 1930s led to the development of, first, the Fl 265, the world's first effective helicopter, and then the Fl 282, the world's first production helicopter. Moved to the USA after World War II to work for the US Navy.

Focke, Dr Heinrich Karl Johann (1890–1979)
German World War I pilot who in 1924 founded, with Georg Wulf, the Focke-Wulf company, which

went on to produce many outstanding machines, including the Fw 200 airliner/reconnaissance aircraft and the Fw 190 series of fighters and fighter-bombers. However, Focke was ejected from the company by the Nazis and went on to found Focke-Achgelis, concentrating on the design and production of rotorcraft, one of which, the FA 223 Drache, attained production status.

Fokker, Anthony (1890–1939)
Dutch designer who built his first aircraft in 1910 and subsequently established his own company at Johannisthal in Germany. Responsible for some of the most outstanding German aircraft of World War I, including the Eindecker series, the D.VII biplane and the immortal Dr.I triplane, mount of the 'Red Baron'. After the war the company moved to the Netherlands and continued to produce transport and fighter aircraft, including the record-breaking F.VII long-distance monoplane. The name is still well established today as a manufacturer, products including the Friendship and Fellowship passenger airliners.

Folland, Henry Philip (1889–1954)
Worked with Geoffrey de Havilland in the Design Office at the Royal Aircraft Factory at Farnborough and took over from him when he left. Was responsible for the S.E.5. After joining Nieuport in 1917 he moved to the Gloucestershire Aircraft Company (Gloster) three years later and produced a series of successful single-seat fighters, including the Gamecock and Gladiator. Postwar founded his own company, the most famous product of which was the Gnat lightweight fighter/trainer.

Anthony Fokker

Gouge, Sir Arthur (1890–1969)
Started career as a mechanic for Short Brothers but rose to become Chief Designer in 1926 and General Manager in 1929. Inspired the design of such classic flying boats as the Empire class and the Sunderland. Postwar joined Saunders-Roe and guided the design of the company's huge Princess flying boat.

Grade, Hans (1879–1946)
First German to make a flight in his home country, in February 1909. Established his own company, Hans Grade Fliegerwerke, in 1911 but this was quickly absorbed by the larger concern Aviatik.

Grahame-White, Claude (1879–1959)
Purchased a Blériot aeroplane during a visit to France in 1909 and taught himself to fly. Founded a flying school at Brooklands and then set up the London Aerodrome at Hendon, now the site of the Royal Air Force Museum. Built his own aircraft after leaving the RNAS in 1915. He devoted his energies to property after World War I.

Gurevich, Mikhail (1893–1976)
Co-founder of Mikoyan i Gurevich (MiG), one of Soviet Russia's foremost aviation design bureaux, producing such important postwar military jets as the MiG-15, 17, 19, 21, 25 and 27. He graduated as an engineer in 1923 and in 1931 became vice-president in the Kochyerigin company, working on such aircraft as the TSh-3 close attack aircraft. The MiG design bureau was established in 1942 and produced a number of important World War II fighters, notably the MiG-3.

Handley Page, Sir Frederick (1885–1962)
An electrical engineer by training who became fascinated by the possibilities opening up in the aviation world in the early 1900s and formed, in 1909, his own company. Handley Page specialized in large bombers and transport aircraft, including the giant O/400 of World War I, the H.P.42 passenger transport biplane of the 1930s, the Halifax heavy

bomber of World War II and the Hastings transport and Victor nuclear bomber of the postwar era.

Hargrave, Lawrence (1850–1915)
Inventor of the boxkite, the basic structure for many pioneering aeroplanes. An Englishman who moved to Australia to study engineering and began producing models powered by compressed air and, later, built a prototype rotary engine. His full-size gliders were a partial success, but his efforts to develop a piloted powered aircraft were unsuccessful.

Hawker, Harry (1889–1921)
An Australian émigré with an enthusiasm for engineering who travelled to Britain and joined the Sopwith company in 1912. Quickly became the company's test pilot and had a considerable input into their aircraft design. Attempted an Atlantic crossing with Lt Cdr Mackenzie Grieve in 1919 but had to ditch and was rescued. Killed in July 1921 when testing a Nieuport Goshawk.

Heinemann, Edward Henry (1908–1991)
Joined Douglas as a draughtsman in 1926, moved to Northrop and then back to Douglas again and became involved in the Design Office. Rose quickly to prominence and was responsible for the majority of Douglas's military aircraft in the war and early postwar years, including the SBD Dauntless, the F3D Skyknight and the A-4 Skyhawk lightweight attack bomber.

Heinkel, Ernst (1888–1958)
A builder of early boxkite-type aircraft who was taken on, in succession, by LVG, Albatros and Hansa-Brandenburg before setting up his own company in 1922, specialising in training and fighter aircraft, seaplanes and flying boats. The company produced a number of innovative and outstanding aircraft, including the He 176 (the world's first rocket-propelled aircraft), the He 178 (the world's first turbojet-powered aircraft), the He 111 (mainstay of the Luftwaffe bomber force during the early war years) and the He 219 Uhu night fighter.

Howard Hughes

Henson, William Samuel (1812–1888)
Built experimental models of gliders in 1840 and followed these with a blueprint for a steam-powered aeroplane two years later. Formed the Aerial Steam Transit Company in 1843, which led to widespread speculation about the imminence of an 'aerial steam carriage'. Tests followed, but these were unsuccessful, and although his partner John Stringfellow (q.v.) carried on the work Henson retired from the aviation scene.

Hinkler, Herbert (1892–1933)
An Australian who served with the RNAS during World War I and then moved to Avro as a test pilot. He made a number of pioneering flights, including one from Croydon to Riga non-stop (1,200 miles) and a solo flight from England to Australia. He also made the first solo crossing of the South Atlantic. He was killed while attempting another England–Australia flight.

Horikoshi, Jiro (1903–1982)
Graduate of the University of Tokyo; joined Mitsubishi in 1927 and swiftly rose to become Chief Designer. Was responsible for the Type 96 ('Claude') fixed-wheel fighter and later the immortal A6M Zero ('Zeke') fighter and the J2M Raiden ('Jack').

Horten, Reimar and Walter (1915–1993; 1913–)
Designers and builders primarily of tailless gliders ('flying wings'), culminating in the powered, single-seat Ho IX (Gotha 229). The Go 229 V2 was fitted with turbojets and briefly flew in this form, attaining a speed of nearly 600mph, although the war's end put a stop to plans for mass-production of the type.

Hughes, Howard (1905–1976)
Well known for his eccentricity, Hughes learnt to fly in 1927 and took up air racing, establishing his own company for the purpose. He gained a new world speed record in 1931 flying his H-1 at 352.1mph, and in 1938 he beat the round-the-

world record, flying a Lockeed Super Electra, in a time of just over 91 hours. After World War II he built the H-4 flying boat ('Spruce Goose'), the world's largest aircraft, and flew it once.

Ilyushin, Sergei Vladimirovich (1894–1977)
Joined the Russian Army in 1917 and qualified as a pilot, then graduated as a designer, joining the Soviet Air Force administration, which he eventually headed. Joined the Central Design Bureau and devoted his work to long-range bomber design, working on the TsKB-56 twin-engined bomber, the TsKB-26 long-range bomber and, the most famous of his creations, the TsKB-57 Shturmovik, better known as the Ilyushin Il-2 (the most widely produced aircraft in history). Postwar his company designed and produced the Il-28 twin-jet bomber and a number of successful airliners.

Johnson, Amy (1903–1941)
Joined the London Aeroplane Club in 1928 and quickly became a qualified mechanic and pilot. In 1930 flew solo from England to Australia in a D.H.60 Moth in 19 days, and in 1933 flew from Wales to the USA in a D.H.84 Dragon. Flew for the Air Transport Auxiliary in World War II but was drowned when her aircraft ditched in the Thames Estuary in 1941.

Johnson, Clarence ('Kelly') (1910–1990)
Joined Lockheed in 1933 and went on to be Chief Research Engineer for the company. Was responsible for such outstanding aircraft as the P-38 Lightning twin-boom fighter, the Constellation passenger transport, the widely exported F-104 Starfighter, the triple-sonic SR-71 reconnaissance jet and much else at 'Skunk Works'.

Junkers, Hugo (1859–1935)
While other aircraft designers were concentrating on wood and fabric materials for their creations, Junkers, an engineer by training, devoted his energies to producing all-metal aeroplanes, his first, the Junkers J.1, utilising thin sheet iron for its construction. Other all-metal aircraft followed, and after World War I his company produced a number of successful all-metal airliners with corrugated skinning, notably the Ju 52/3m trimotor, mainstay of the Luftwaffe's transport fleet during World War II. The company also produced two of the most famous aircraft of the war, the Ju 87 Stuka dive-bomber and the Ju 88 twin-engined bomber.

Kartveli, Alexander (1896–1974)
A Russian who emigrated to France following the Revolution and worked for the Blériot and Fokker companies before finally moving to the USA and taking up a position with the Seversky company. His first important project as design leader was the P-35 fighter, forerunner of the famous P-47 Thunderbolt, produced after the company had been renamed the Republic Aircraft Corporation. Postwar he was responsible for the design of the F-84 and F-105 front-line fighters.

Kingsford Smith, Sir Charles (1897–1935)
Served in the Royal Flying Corps during World War I and afterwards joined Western Australian Airways. Made a number of pioneering flights, including the first transpacific flight when he flew his Fokker F.VII *Southern Cross* from the USA to Australia. Died when his Altair aircraft came down near Burma while on an England–Australia flight.

Koolhoven, Frederik (1886–1946)
Became a pilot in 1910 and joined Deperdussin two years later, soon taking charge of the British division of the company. Became Chief Designer for Armstrong Whitworth in 1913 and was responsible for the F.K. 3 and F.K.8. Joined British Aerial Transport in 1917 and then in 1920 moved

Clarence 'Kelly' Johnson

back to the Netherlands, forming his own company in 1934.

Lanchester, Frederick William (1868–1946)
Perhaps better known for his pioneering work in the motor-car industry but also made a significant contribution to the theory of flight, building model gliders which established the principles of lift and drag. Was later a government adviser on aeronautics and a consultant to the Wolseley and Daimler motor-car manufacturers.

Langley, Samuel Pierpont (1834–1906)
Native of Massachusetts. Conducted experiments with aerofoils, models powered by rubber and later steam engines (known as 'Aerodromes'). Tried to develop a manned aeroplane with the aid of a $50,000 grant but his work ended in failure and he became disillusioned.

Lavochkin, Syemyen Alexeivich (1900–1960)
Studied engineering in Moscow and joined the Central Design Bureau (TsKB) and later the Bureau of New Design (BNK). Joined with V. P. Gorbunov and M. I Gudkov in 1938 to establish a separate bureau and produced the LAGG-1, the first of a successful series of fighters culminating in the La-11. Postwar the bureau designed and built the first Soviet jet to be equipped with an afterburner (La-150M) and the first with swept wings (La-160), but it closed in 1960.

Charles Lindbergh

Le Bris, Jean-Marie (1808–1872)
An early glider pioneer who based his designs on the albatross. He attempted to launch his creations from carts drawn by horses, and managed to get airborne for a short distance. He was killed in a fight.

Levavasseur, Léon (1863–1921)
Originally a student of art but then drawn into engineering. Built an aeroplane in 1903; it failed, but its engine, named *Antoinette*, was remarkably advanced for its day and was the forerunner of a successful series. Founded the Société Antoinette with Ferdinand Ferber and continued to design monoplanes.

Lilienthal, Otto (1848–1896)
Universally recognized as a truly great aviation pioneer. Prussian-born and the author of *Bird Flight As the Basis of Aviation*, he experimented with hang gliders from 1890, culminating in the No 11 monoplane glider of 1894. So successful were they that they were manufactured for other pioneers worldwide. He died when a glider he was flying crashed.

Lindbergh, Charles Augustus (1902–1974)
Leaned to fly in 1922, joining, in succession, a flying circus, the US Army Air Corps and an airmail company. When a prize for the first New York–Paris non-stop flight was offered, he arranged backing and persuaded Ryan to build the *Spirit of St Louis* monoplane, achieving worldwide fame when he achieved his ambition on 20–21 May 1927. He fell into disfavour during the early years of World War II because of his strong opinions that the US should keep out of the conflict. After the war he joined Pan American Airways in an advisory capacity.

Lippisch, Alexander Martin (1894–1976)
A sailplane enthusiast who later turned his talents to designing tailless aircraft and rocket engines, culminating in the futuristic Me 163 point-defence interceptor of the latter years of World War II. Before joining Messerschmitt in 1939 he had worked for DFS. He emigrated to the US after the war, continuing his research in the field of supersonic aircraft.

Loughead (Lockheed), Allan Haines (1889–1969)
Formed, with his brother, the Alco Hydro-Aeroplane Company in 1913 and, more successfully, Loughead Aircraft in 1916, re-established as the Lockheed Aircraft Company in 1926. From that point fortunes grew only slowly, and the company was acquired by an investment group in 1932 and re-launched as the Lockheed Aircraft Corporation, which went on to produce such outstanding aircraft as the wartime P-38 Lightning and the post-war Constellation airliner and SR-71 Mach 3 reconnaissance aircraft, as well as a series of big transports. Allan had been forced to leave his company, however, in 1929, although he continued his work on aircraft design and manufacture.

Loening, Grover Cleveland (1888–1976)
Holder of the first US Master's degree in aeronautical science. Joined the Queen Aircraft Corporation in 1911 and in 1914 became Chief Aeronautical Engineer for the US Army at San Diego. Founded his own manufacturing business in 1917, specialising in amphibians (for example, the OL series), although he left the company when it was merged with Curtiss-Wright and established the Grover Loening Aircraft Company. However, this venture was less successful.

McDonnell, James Smith (1899–1980)
Gained a degree in aeronautical engineering in 1925 and worked for numerous organisations throughout the 1920s and 1930s until founding his own company, the McDonnell Aircraft Corporation, in 1938. This concern rapidly grew, designing and producing the FD/FH (the US Navy's first carrier jet), the F2H Banshee and the hugely successful F4F/F-4 Phantom II series.

Maxim, Sir Hiram Stevens (1840–1916)
An American who came to live in England in 1881 and persuaded backers to contribute funds to the design of a huge aeroplane driven by a pair of steam engines. This was tested on a rig but, although it rose into the air the absence of an effective control system caused it to slip and become badly damaged. Thereafter, money lacking, his design slipped into obscurity, although the machine gun which he invented was of course very widely produced.

Messerschmitt, 'Willy' Emil (1898–1978)
One of the best-known names in aviation history, and responsible for the classic Bf 109 fighter and the world's first operational jet fighter, the Me 262. He began by building and testing gliders in 1913 and went on to establish his design company in 1923, the actual aircraft being manufactured by BFW from 1926 until 1938. Helped form Messerschmitt-Bölkow-Blohm in West Germany in 1969.

Mikoyan, Artyem Ivanovich (1905–1970)
A graduate of the Frunze Military Academy and the Zhukovski Air Force Academy, joining Polikarpov and finally establishing, with Mikhail Gurevich (q.v.), the Mikoyan i Gurevich bureau. A long series of classic fighters ensued, beginning with the MiG-1 and MiG-3 of World War II, through the early Mig-9 and famous MiG-15 jets, to today's MiG-25, -27 and -29.

Mil, Mikhail Leontyevich (1909–1970)
An autogyro and helicopter specialist who founded the bureau which bears his name in 1947, having previously worked with Kamov's Deputy Chief Designer. His company produced the widely exported Mi-8, the gigantic V-12 and the current Mi-24 'Hind' helicopter gunship.

James McDonnell

Mitchell, Reginald Joseph (1895–1937)
One of the most prominent aircraft designers in history, he joined Supermarine after working his apprenticeship with a locomotive manufacturer and quickly became the company's Chief Designer. He was responsible for the S.6 series of seaplanes that won the Schneider Trophy outright for Britain in 1931, a number of successful amphibians and flying boats, and the immortal Spitfire fighter of World War II.

Mollison, James Allan (1905–1959)
Commissioned with the RAF in 1923, he learned to fly and on leaving in 1928 joined the Australian Aero Club in Adelaide and then Australian National Airways. Set records for solo Australia–England (1931), England–Cape Town (1932) and Atlantic east-to-west (1932) flights. Married Amy Johnson (q.v.)

Morane, Léon and Robert (1885–1918; 1886–1968)
These two brothers formed, with Gabriel Borel and Raymond Saulnier, the Société Anonyme des Aéroplanes Morane-Borel-Saulnier in 1911, although Borel quickly departed, establishing Morane-Saulnier. This rapidly grew into one of the most successful French aviation companies, producing front-line aeroplanes through World War I and the interwar years, and specialising in the 1930s in parasol-wing aircraft. The MS. 406 single-seat fighter marked the culmination of the design effort up to World War II; light aircraft were produced after the war.

Mozhaiskii, Alexander Fedorovich (1825–1890)
A Russian naval cadet with a background in engineering, he became interested in manned flight and began to design a series of kites in the 1870s. A large steam powered monoplane was designed and built in the late 1870s, but when take-off was attempted with a mechanic on board in 1884 it crashed shortly after leaving the ground.

Niéport (Nieuport), Édouard de (1875–1911)
A French engineer, he established his own company producing electrical components for internal-combustion engines and then in 1908 set up his own aviation manufacturing business. This failed, but a new venture two years later went on to become the famous SA des Établissements Nieuport and produced a series of successful monoplanes and, later, such outstanding biplanes as the 17 and 24. The company went out of business in 1934.

North, John Dudley (1893–1968)
Chief Engineer of the Grahame-White company from 1912, manager of Austin's aviation division until 1917 and from then on Chief Designer and later Managing Director of Boulton and Paul Aircraft. His legacies include the Overstrand biplane bomber and the Defiant turret fighter, and he was also involved in the design of the ill-fated *R101* airship.

Northrop, John Knudson (1895–1981)
Joined with the Loughead brothers (q.v.) in 1916 and seven years later went to work for Douglas on their World Cruiser aircraft. Moved again, this time to help found the Lockheed Corporation, in 1927. Formed the Northrop Corporation in 1932, which became the wholly independent Northrop Aircraft in 1939. Postwar, the company produced such front-line aircraft as the F-89 Scorpion and the T-38/F-5 trainer/fighter series, but more innovative has been the company's contribution to the concept of flying wings, significantly the XB-35 and current B-2 bomber.

Ohain, Hans von (1911–1998)
A pioneer whose contribution to the development of aviation is often forgotten, as he worked on turbojet propulsion in the 1930s and bench-tested a successful engine in September 1937 under the auspices of Ernst Heinkel. This led directly to the He 178, the world's first turbojet aircraft. After the war he emigrated to the USA, becoming Chief Scientist at the Aero Propulsion Laboratory.

Pemberton Billing, Noel (1881–1948)
Aircraft constructor who built a small aerodrome at Fambridge in Essex in 1909. Won a bet with Frederick Handley Page that he could learn to fly in a day, won, and with the proceeds (£500) set up his own company to build flying boats. Helped plan the RNAS attack on the Zeppelin sheds at Friedrichshafen in World War I, but soon afterwards gave up serious aircraft design to enter Parliament. His company evolved into the well-known Supermarine Aviation Works.

Pilcher, Percy Sinclair (1876–1899)
One of the most celebrated early British aviation

pioneers, he built a number of hang gliders in 1895–96, joining forces with Hiram Maxim (q.v.). He studied the work of Otto Lilienthal (q.v.) and decided to try to improve on his designs by adopting a triplane layout and fitting an engine to his next creation. This, however, never flew owing to Pilcher's death when one of his earlier gliders crashed while he was piloting it.

Platz, Reinhold (1886–1966)
A skilled welder who joined Fokker in 1912, bringing his metalworking techniques to the company. As a result, Fokker became convinced of the advantages of steel tube construction for their aircraft, and this method was incorporated into the military monoplanes and biplanes for which the company became renowned. He was quickly made Chief Designer, and led the team which produced the legendary Dr.I triplane and D.VII biplane fighters.

Polikarpov, Nikolai Nikolayevich (1892–1944)
From 1916 worked under Sikorsky (q.v.), assisting in the design of the S-16 fighter and the Ilya Muromets bomber. Later went to the Duks factory and supervized the licence-building of SPAD S.VIIs and D.H. 4s and 9s and the design of the indigenous and highly successful U-2 trainer. Later, as Chief Designer for the Central Construction Bureau, he was responsible for the I-15 biplane and I-16 monoplane fighters.

Post, Wiley (1898–1935)
Lost an eye while drilling for an oil company but learned to fly and became the personal pilot for F. C. Hall, an oil magnate. Hall then financed a circumnavigation by Post, with Harold Gatty as navigator, and the pair completed the flight in June 1931 in a Lockheed Vega, *Winnie Mae*, in just over 8 days, 15 hours and 51 minutes. Two years later Post completed a solo circumnavigation in the same aircraft.

Potez, Henri Charles Alexandre (1891–1981)
Educated at the École Supérieure d'Aéronautique and on the outbreak of World War I found himself working alongside Marcel Dassault in a technical capacity. The pair quickly became friends and in 1916 set up the Société d'Études Aéronautiques to produce their own aircraft, although this venture was wound up in 1919. Potez then started his own business, and this flourished for many years, notable designs including the 630 series of long-range fighters.

Pulawski, Zygmunt (1901–1931)
One of Poland's foremost designers, he was educated at Warsaw Technical University and later moved to France to work for Bréguet. On his return he joined PZL, the State Aircraft Factory as designer and was responsible for a successful series of fighter aircraft, beginning with the gull-winged P.1, progressively developed into the nimble P.11.

Roe, Sir Alliott Verdon (1877–1958)
One of the great names in British aviation history. A marine engineer whose primary interest was aviation, building his first aeroplane in 1907. In 1910 he produced the first of a number of triplanes and set up his own company, and two years later began the design of the 504 series – a hugely successful and widely exported biplane. The company grew into the famous Avro concern, producing the Lancaster heavy bomber in World War II and the Vulcan strategic bomber of the postwar years.

Rohrbach, Adolf Karl (1889–1939)
Worked successively for the Blohm und Voss shipyard, the Zeppelin works (where he met Claude Dornier) and the Staaken concern (where he became Chief Designer). He was responsible for the innovative E.4/20, a four-motor design of all-metal construction which flew in 1920 and is generally considered to be the forerunner of the modern passenger transport aircraft

Santos-Dumont, Alberto (1873–1932)
A Brazilian who went to France in 1891 and took up ballooning. His interest developed into the design and construction of dirigibles, and in one of these he flew round the Eiffel Tower in 1901. He progressed to aeroplane design and in 1906 his *14bis* made the first sustained powered flight in Europe. His later *Demoiselle* was also a successful design, but in 1910 he was diagnosed as having multiple sclerosis and he returned home. He committed suicide in 1932.

Saulnier, Raymond (b.1881)
An engineer who was employed by the Blériot company in 1908, working on the Blériot XI which made the first cross-Channel flight in 1909. Formed his own company, but when this failed went into business with Léon and Robert Morane (q.v.) and Gabriel Borel (q.v.); when the latter left the Morane-Salunier company was formed, pro-

ducing a series of monoplanes and front-line fighters up to World War II.

Seguin, Laurent and Louis (1883–1994; 1869–1918)
Louis joined with his half-brother Laurent in 1905 to build motor-car engines, and the pair, and their company Société des Moteurs Gnome, progressed to the design of a wholly new concept – the rotary engine – for use in aeroplanes. The first rotary was produced in 1908, and the concept quickly found widespread favour because of its lightness and the fact that it required no radiator. Development continued apace, and large numbers of World War I aeroplanes were so equipped.

Seversky, Alexander Prokofiev de (1894–1974)
A mechanical engineering graduate, he joined the Baltic Naval Air Service in 1915 but lost a leg when he crashed his aircraft. Went to the US in 1917 and remained there, not wishing to return to his native country because of the Revolution. Employed by the US Government, he developed a new bomb sight and then went on to establish the Seversky Aero Corporation (later renamed Republic Aviation)

Igor Sikorsky

Short, Horace Leonard, Albert Eustace and Hugh Oswald (1872–1917; 1975–1932; 1883–1969)
Eustace and Oswald learned to fly balloons and quickly set up their own manufacturing business; in 1908, with the increasing interest in heavier-than-air craft, they switched to aeroplane design and manufacture, whereupon Horace joined them. They specialized in seaplanes, among which were the World War I Types 184, 827/830 and 320; and on 27 July 1914 Short Seaplane No 121 made the first airborne torpedo drop in history. The company continued to flourish, producing the Stirling heavy bomber and the outstanding Sunderland flying boat of World War II. Postwar the company designed and manufactured aircraft of more modest dimensions, including the S.C.1 vertical take-off jet and the Skyvan light passenger transport.

Sikorsky, Igor Ivanovich (1889–1972)
A graduate of the Kiev Polytechnical Institute who built a prize-winning aeroplane, the S-6, in 1912 and was immediately offered the position of Chief Aeroplane Designer at the Russo-Baltic Wagon Works. He had a considerable input into the Ilya Mouramets bomber of World War, I but after the Revolution he emigrated to the USA and set up the Sikorsky Aero Engineering Corporation, specialising in waterborne aircraft. However, the helicopter had always been his primary interest, and his company eventually concentrated on these craft, quickly becoming renowned throughout the world.

Sopwith, Sir Thomas Octave Murdoch (1888–1989)
Originally a balloonist, he transferred his interests to heavier-than-air craft and in 1912 set up the Sopwith Flying School. The Sopwith Aviation Company was soon established, and the firm's Tabloid aeroplane won the 1914 Schneider competition. This gave impetus to a series of very successful military aircraft such as the Pup and Camel fighters. After World War I the company was hit by the slump and the majority of its assets were taken over by the newly established H. G. Hawker Engineering Company (later Hawker Aircraft), of which Sopwith became joint Managing Director.

Sperry, Elmer and Lawrence (1860–1930; 1892–1923)
Elmer invented a gyroscopic stabilizer, which his son Lawrence demonstrated successfully in 1914

in a Curtiss flying boat. Elmer went on to develop a directional gyro system and a drift indicator for blind flying (first achieved in 1929). A further contribution from the son was the invention of a retractable undercarriage before his untimely death in a crash into the English Channel while on a promotional tour of Europe.

Stout, William Bushnell (1880–1956)
Aviation editor of the *Chicago Tribune* and then founder of the magazine *Aerial Age*. In 1919 he set up Stout Engineering Laboratories, building an advanced monoplane known as the Batwing. The Stout Metal Airplane was formed in 1922 and work began on the design of large cantilever monoplanes, culminating in the famous 4-AT Trimotor of 1928. By this time, however, Stout had sold his company to Henry Ford.

Stringfellow, John (1799–1883)
The partner of William Henson (q.v.), he continued the work undertaken when the latter left for the USA, constructing a steam-powered monoplane in 1848 and a triplane in 1868. Neither machine managed to fly successfully, however.

Sukhoi, Pavel Osipovich (1898–1975)
A designer at the Tupolev bureau from 1920 who led the team producing the ANT-5 sesquiplane and the ANT-25 and -27 long-range aircraft and, later, the Su-2 reconnaissance bomber for the Soviet Air Force. He set up his own design bureau in 1938, but it was not until after World War II that his designs found great favour: he was a pioneer in jet propulsion, and despite his bureau being closed down from 1949 to 1953 it went on to produce some of the Soviet Union's outstanding combat aircraft of the postwar era.

Sir Thomas Sopwith

Tank, Kurt Waldemar (1898–1983)
Student of electrical engineering at Berlin Technical High School, where his interest in gliders led him to found the Akaflieg flying club. After five years with Rohrbach (q.v.) he joined Messerschmitt in 1929 but by 1931 was with Focke-Wulf, where in 1931 he became Technical Director. His lasting legacy is the Fw 190 fighter and fighter-bomber series. Postwar he designed aircraft for Argentina and India.

Trippe, Juan Terry (1899–1981)
A bomber pilot, he spent a year in banking and then established, in succession, Long Island Airways, Colonial Air Transport and AVCO in order to win contracts for the US Mail Service. Finally, in 1927 he founded Pan American Airways, guiding that company to the forefront of the US passenger/transport industry.

Tupolev, Andrei Nicolayevich (1888–1972)
A mechanical engineer at the Duks factory, he co-founded the TsAGI (Central Aero and Hydrodynamic Institute) in 1918 and in 1922 was made chairman of a commission organising the production of all-metal aircraft in the Russian republic, guiding the design of the ANT-2. He became Chief Engineer of the GUAP (Chief Administration of the Aviation Industry) but was arrested in 1937, accused of passing secrets to the Germans. He was rehabilitated in 1943 and from then concentrated on the design of large, long-range military and civil aircraft, beginning with the Tu-4 (B-29 copy) and culminating in the Tu-144 supersonic passenger transport.

Verville, Alfred Victor (1890–1970)
Joined Glenn Curtiss in 1914 and helped design the Jenny and other aircraft, subsequently joining the Air Service Engineering Division, a government department. He went to Europe to study aircraft designs on that continent and returned, inspired, to design the VCP series, the racing version of

which won the 1920 Pulitzer Prize. His later R-3 monoplane won the 1924 Pulitzer competition. He set up his own company in 1928 but this survived for four years only.

Vinci, Leonardo da (1452–1519)
The earliest known serious student of aviation. Taking birds as his inspiration, he investigated their flight characteristics and endeavoured to design a series of ornithopters, although it is now known that he misconstrued their wing movements. He also produced sketch designs for a primitive helicopter and devized a workable parachute and glider.

Voisin, Gabriel and Charles (1880–1973; 1888–1912)
Gabriel's interest in kites led to an interest in gliders and he became the engineer in Le Syndicat de l'Aéronautique under Ernest Archdeacon. His brother joined him to form Les Frères Voisin, concentrating on pusher biplanes. Production continued throughout World War I, when over 10,000 Voisins were sold to various air arms.

Whitcomb, Richard Travis (1921–)
Engaged in 1943 by NACA to investigate the problems of supersonic flight and its associated problems of airflow he was awarded the Collier Trophy for his discovery of the area rule principle. He also led the development of the supercritical wing and of winglets, reducing drag and thus improving performance in fast jets.

Whittle, Sir Frank (1923–96)
Trained as a pilot with the RAF and then joined the CFS as an instructor. Meanwhile he was studying the principles of gas-turbine propulsion and patented an engine based on these principles. Despite official apathy he persisted, set up his Power Jets company in 1936 and designed a workable jet engine. An Air Ministry contract led to the W.1 engine and its incorporation into the Gloster E.28/39, which flew at Cranwell on 15 May 1941, becoming the first British jet aircraft to do so. Whittle continued for some time as a technical adviser to the Ministry and later in life emigrated to the USA.

Wright, Wilbur and Orville (1867–1912; 1871–1948)
Designers and builders of the world's first aircraft capable of sustained flight under power and under control, an event which took place at Kittty Hawk in North Carolina on 17 December 1903. Their initial *Flyer* was developed in 1905 into the *Flyer III*, the first aeroplane capable of withstanding prolonged and repeated flights. There followed a series of designs based on the original – the Model A of 1908, for example, being the world's first military aeroplane. The brothers' ideas and layouts were widely imitated around the world, but their business was constantly hampered by battles over patents.

Yakovlev, Alexander Sergeyevich (1906–1989)
An experimenter with gliders who built his first powered aeroplane in 1926 and as a result was officially admitted into the Zhukovski Air Force Academy. He joined Polikarpov (q.v.) in 1931 but within three years had moved on to establish his own bureau, concentrating on sports and light aircraft. He turned to military aircraft and thus evolved the Yak-1/3/9/ series of fast lightweight fighters. His entry into the field of jet aircraft postwar was not initially successful, although the Yak-25 and -28 all-weather fighters saw widespread Soviet service.

Orville Wright

Aircraft and Weaponry

GUNS

At first pilots and observers armed themselves with handguns and rifles on their aircraft. Then these began to be replaced by pivot-mounted machine-guns. But the breakthrough came with the development of the synchronizer gear, making it possible to fire the machine gun through the propeller arc without damaging the propeller and therefore aiming the aircraft at the target rather than just the gun. The beginnings of the first fighters – or scouts, as they were first known – was born, the first aircraft designed purely for combat. Most fighters carried one or two rifle-calibre machine-guns, in various configurations. The bombers had one or more

***Left:** A typical World War I mounting of twin Spandau machine guns on a Fokker Dr. I.*

***Left:** A B-17 'Flying Fortress' displaying part of its considerable defensive armament. Four .50 calibre machine guns can be seen here.*

***Right:** US Navy aviation ordnancemen load an 20mm M61A1 rotary Gatling cannon on to an F/A-18C Hornet.*

defensive positions, all with pivot-mounted machine-guns.

Until the early 1930s aircraft achieved marginally higher speeds and a slight increase in armament, with basically the same biplane design. The new fighters now developed were completely different, both in shape, speed and capability. The eight-gun rifle-calibre armament of the Spitfire and Hurricane and the two 20mm cannon and twin machine-gun armament of the Messerschmitt Bf 109 were typical. Bombers began to mount multiple power-operated multi-gun turrets, fitted with rifle-calibre guns.

As the war progressed, heavier and heavier armament was being mounted for both bombers and fighters. By the end of the War the four 20mm cannon armament of most RAF fighters, six and eight .50 calibre machine-guns of USA and the 20mm and 30mm armament of the Luftwaffe were fitted. Crude air-to-air unguided rockets also began to be deployed, but without much success. The bombers began to carry more and heavier defensive weaponry, with remote control turrets in addition to the normal manual equivalent.

The first two generations of jet fighters mounted the sort of conventional armament that had been carried during the later war years, USA generally adopted either a six .50-calibre or four 20mm configuration. The British aircraft were armed with four 20 or 30mm cannon and the USSR a combined mix of 37mm and 23mm. By the 1960s the rotary Gatling-type cannon firing up to 6,000 rounds per minute was being mounted on aircraft.

Though still useful, as proven during the Vietnam War, the gun was increasingly being relegated to back-up the ever-increasing efficiency of missile-armed combat aircraft.

MISSILES

The Sidewinder air-to-air missile was developed in the very early 1950s, the first being successfully tested on 11 September 1953. It was first to see combat on 24 September 1958 in a skirmish between F-86Fs of the Formosan Air Force and Communist Chinese MiGs – it was claimed that four of the MiGs were brought down. Guided simply by an enemy aircraft's heat signature, the missile is steered by a combination of its fins and an infra-red sensitive cell onto the target aircraft. No AAM has ever been easier to integrate with a fighter, since it does not need an airborne radar to help guide it to its target. Missiles of very similar design and performance are the Russian Atol and the French Magic.

Medium- and long-range air-to-air missiles are typified by the US Sparrow and Phoenix missiles, which are guided by the onboard radar of their attacking aircraft. Having acquired a target on radar and established that it is an enemy aircraft, the radar is then locked on in attack mode and a missile launched. Radar contact has to be maintained, or illuminated, by the radar during the missile's flight until the target is hit or has escaped. The medium-range Sparrow was a contemporary of the shorter-range Sidewinder; and the long-range Phoenix was first deployed in 1974.

The advanced medium-range air-to-air missile, the AMRAAM, has been developed to replace missiles such as the Sparrow. It has its own built-in active radar seeker that allows it to locate its target independently and then attack it, leaving the launch aircraft free to manoeuvre away.

Air-Launched Cruise Missiles equipped with either nuclear or conventional high-explosive warheads can be launched by such aircraft as the B-52 and the B-1B.

Anti-ship missiles have made their mark in recent decades, most dramatically during the Falklands War with the Argentine Exocet attacks, and again during the Iran-Iraq tanker wars. The Harpoon first saw action with the US Navy in clashes against the Libyan Navy during the 1980s. There are numerous missiles of this type, varying in size from the Russian 4½ ton long-range Raduga Kh-41 Moskit with its 150-mile range, to the lightweight Sea Skua, capable of being mounted on light helicopters. Anti-ship missiles generally have an average range of between 30 and 60 miles. Early types used visual guidance such as TV datalinking, but more

***Above:** The AMRAAM (out-board) and Sidewinder (centre) AA missiles can be seen on this F-16 fighter. The anti-radar Harm missile (inboard) completes the attack profile for this formidable aircraft.*

Above: *A view of a French Super Entendard aircraft being launched from the flight deck of the French aircraft carrier* Foch. *Mounted on the aircraft's right wing pylon is an AM-39 Exocet air-to-surface missile.*

modern missile are generally guided to their targets by on-board active radar guidance.

The destruction of hostile radars and radar-controlled AAA and SAM sites is critical to modern air warfare. Shrike and Harm missiles are typical of this type of air-launched weapon dedicated to anti-radar attack. During the mid-1960s the Shrike began to be used during the Vietnam War. Its successor, Harm, was to see successful action during the raids on Libya in 1986 and then intensive use during the Coalition's War against Iraq and later use by NATO in Kosovo. Guided by the enemy's radar transmissions, these types of missiles home in on and destroy such sites.

Above: An AGM-86 air-launched cruise missile (ALCM) has greatly enhanced the B-52 bomber's capabilities. The missile has seen action against Iraq in 1991, 1998 and 2003 as well as Serbia in 1999

BOMBS

Varying in size from the hand-held grenade of the pre-WWI period to the 10-ton Grand Slam of WWII, conventional bombs have ranged greatly in size and type. The most common sizes over the past 50 years have usually been in the 500lb to 1000lb range. During WWII small incendiary bombs were also dropped in massive quantities, raining down and razing European and Japanese cities to the ground. In the late stages of the War napalm began to be used; it was subsequently widely used in the Korean and Vietnam Wars. There are also cluster bombs (now controversial) which separate in mid-air and eject a number of submunitions (bomblets) scattering over a wide area; these are intended to kill enemy personnel and destroy vehicles.

Dating back to the later stages of WWII, the Luftwaffe had notable successes with their Fritz X anti-ship guided glide-bomb. The laser-guided bomb was first seen in use during the Vietnam War. But not until the Allied wars against Iraq, Kosovo and in Afghanistan did the laser-guided bomb see deployment in large numbers. It was to bring a new level of accuracy and destructive power to appropriately equipped air forces. All that is necessary is to fit a guidance system to a conventional bomb with a controllable flying surface, and it is estimated its efficiency can increase as much as 100-fold.

The only atomic bombs dropped in action, those of Hiroshima and Nagasaki, were dropped by means of a conventional bomb run. On bomb release, the B-29 made a rapid descent turn to 155 degrees away from the aiming point. The bomb exploded at a pre-set height when the aircraft was at a safe distance, approximately 11 miles away from the target. This became the established means of delivery for such bombs during the 1950s. Various other forms of attack, such as Loft bombing, Toss bombing and Low-level Laydown techniques can be also be employed.

Right: *German ground crew fuze a bomb before it is loaded on to a Me 262 ground-attack fighter during World War Two.*

Below: *A U.S. Air Force A-10C Thunderbolt II drops a GBU-12 Paveway II 500 lb. laser guided bomb.*

Above: *During the early part of World War I aviators dropped bombs over the side of their aircraft.*

WA
WEAPONS
SCHOOL
AF810977

Above: *Colonel Paul W. Tibbets, Jr., pilot of the B-29 'Enola Gay', the plane that dropped the atomic bomb on Hiroshima, waves from his cockpit before the take-off, 6 August 1945.*

Above: *A B-1B Lancer bomber releases a payload of Mk 82 retard bombs. Up to 84 of these weapons can be carried in the aircraft's stores bays. Other types of conventional bombs, cluster bombs and mines may be carried.*

Right: *A US Navy F-14A Tomcat firing a long-range AIM-54 Phoenix missile. The missile has a maximum speed of Mach 5, a range of 100+ miles and a warhead of 135 lb of high explosive. Its guidance is semi-active and active radar homing. It first entered service in 1974 and retired in from US service in 2004. It has also seen service with the Iranian air-force claiming a number of kills during the Iran-Iraq War of 1980–8.*

NK
202
NAVY

Further Reading

AAF – The Official Guide to the Army Air Forces (A Directory, Almanac and Chronicle of Achievement), New York, 1944
Aart van der, D. *Aerial Espionage,* Shrewsbury, 1985
Air Ministry (comp.) *The Rise and Fall of the German Air Force (1933 to 1945),* London, 1948
Air Ministry. *The Air Offensive against Germany,* London, 1941
Air Ministry. *The Battle of Britain August-October 1940,* London, 1941
'Aireview' (comp.) *General View of Japanese Military Aircraft in the Pacific War,* Tokyo, 1956
Alcock, Sir John, and Brown, Sir Arthur Whitten. *Our Transatlantic Flight,* London, 1969
Alexander, Jean. *Russian Aircraft Since 1940,* London, 1975
Allen, Oliver *The Airline Builders,* Alexandria, Va., 1981
Allward, M. *Hurricane Special,* London, 1975
Anderson, W. *Pathfinders,* London, 1946
Anderton, D. A. *B-57 and RB-57F,* Windsor, 1973
—*Strategic Air Command,* London, 1975
Andrade, J. M. *US Military Aircraft Designations and Serial, Since 1909,* Leicester, 1979
—*Latin-American Military Aviation,* Leicester, 1982
—*Spanish and Portuguese Military Aviation,* Leicester, 1977
—*US Military Aircraft Desiginations and Serials since 1909,* Leicester, 1979
Andrews, C. F. *Vickers Aircraft since 1908,* London, 1969
Angle, G. D. ed. *Aerosphere – 1939,* New York, 1940
Armitage, M. I. and Mason, R. A. *Air Power in the Nuclear Age, 1945–82 Theory and Practice,* London, 1983
Armitage, M. *The Royal Air Force: An Illustrated History,* London, 1993
Arthur, Max, *There Shall Be Wings; The RAF from 1918 to the Present,* London, 1993
Austin, A. B. *Fighter Command,* London, 1941
Ballard, J. *The United States Air Force in Southeast Asia: Fixed Wing Gunships,* Washington, 1982
Banks, Air Commodore F. R. *Aircraft Prime Movers of the Twentieth Century,* New York, 1970
Banks, Howard. *The Rise and Fall of Freddie Laker,* London, 1982
Barker, R. *The Ship-Busters (The Story of the R.A.F. Torpedo-Bombers),* London, 1957
—*The Thousand Plan (The Story of the First Thousand Bomber Raid on Cologne),* London, 1965
—*The RAF at War* Alexandria, Va., 1981
Barnes, C. H. *Bristol Aircraft since 1910,* London, 1970
—*Shorts Aircraft since 1910,* London, 1967
Barron, John. *MiG Pilot,* New York, 1980
Bartlett, Donald L., and James B. Steele. *Empire: The Life, Legend and Madness of Howard Hughes,* New York, 1979
Bartz, K. *Swastika in the Air,* London, 1956
Bathie, William W. *Fundamentals of Gas Turbines,* New York, 1984
Beaman, J. R. *Last of the Eagles,* Greensboro, N. C. 1976
—*The Unknown Mustangs,* Greensboro, 1975
Beaubois, H. *Airships (An Illustrated History),* London, 1974
Becker, Beril. *Dreams and Recollections of the Conquest of the Skies,* New York, 1967
Bell, D. *Air War over Vietnam.* Vols. I–IV, London, 1982
Bender, Marylin, and Selig Altschul. *The Chosen Instrument,* New York, 1982
Benes, B. *Wings in Exile,* London, 1942
Ben-Porat, Yeshayahu, Eitan Haber, and Zeev Schiff. *Entebbe Rescue,* New York, 1977
Bentley, G. *RNZAF, A Short History,* Wellington, 1969
Berg, A. Scott. *Lindbergh,* New York, 1998
Berger, C. *The United States Air Force in Southeast Asia,* Washington, 1977
Berlin Airlift. HMSO, London, 1949
Bernstein, Aaron. *Grounded: Frank Lorenzo and the Destruction of American Airlines,* New York, 1990
Berry, P., Dunstall, T., Ford, M. and Whittle, J. A. (comp.) *The Douglas DC4,* Brentwood, 1967
Biddle, Wayne. *Barons of the Sky,* New York, 1991
Boyne, Walter J. ed., *The Smithsonian Book of Flight,* London, 1987
Birdsall, S. *Hell's Angels (B-17 Combat Markings),* Canoga Park, Calif., 1969
—*Log of the Liberators,* Garden City, N.Y., 1973
—*The B-17 Flying Fortress,* Dallas, 1965
—*The B-24 Liberator,* New York 1969
Bishop, E. *Mosquito: Wooden Wonder,* London, 1971
Blue, A. G., Borelli, G., Borgiotti, A., Gori, C., and Pini, G. *North American P-51 Mustang 1940–45 (le Macchine e la Storia),* Modena, 1973
Borden, Norman E. *Air Mail Emergency 1934,* Freeport, 1968
Borovik, Y. *Israeli Air Force* (Warbirds No. 23), London, 1984
Botting, Douglas. *The Giant Airships,* Alexandria, Va., 1981
Bowen, Ezra. *Knights of the Air,* Alexandria, Va., 1980
Bowers, P. M. *Boeing Aircraft since 1916,* London, 1966
Bowman, G. *War in the Air,* London, *1956*
Bowyer, C. *Hurricane at War,* London, 1974
—*Mosquito at War,* London, 1973
—*Sunderland at War,* London, 1976
Bowyer, M. J. F. *Fighting Colours (RAF Fighter Camouflage and Markings 1937–1969),* London, 1969
—*Bombing Colours (RAF Bomber Camouflage and Markings 1937–1973),* Cambridge, 1973
—*2 Group R.A.F.,* London, 1974
Boyd, A. *The Soviet Air Force since 1918,* London, 1977
Boyne, Walter J. *Messerschmitt 262: Arrow to the Future,* Washington, D.C., 1980
—*The Aircraft Treasures of Silver Hill,* New York, 1982
—*Clash of Wings: Air Power in World War II,* New York, 1994
—and Donald S. Lopez, eds. *The Jet Age,* Washington, D.C., 1979
Bozung, J. H. (ed.) *The 5th over the Southwest Pacific,* Los Angeles, 1947
—(ed.) *The 8th sees England,* Los Angeles, 1946
—(ed.) *The 9th sees France and England,* Los Angeles, 1947
—(ed.) *The 12th over the Mediterranean,* Los Angeles, 1946
—(ed.) *The 15th over Italy,* Los Angeles, Calif., 1947
Braham, Wg Cdr J. R. D. *Scramble,* London, 1961

Branson, A. and Birch, N. *The Tiger Moth Story,* London, 1965
Braybrook, R. *Battle for the Falklands (3): Air Forces,* London, 1982
—*Falklands – The Air War,* Middlesex, 1986
Brenner, Melvin A., James O. Leet, and Elihu Schott, *Airline Deregulation,* Westport, 1985
Brent, W. A. *Rhodesian Air Force: A Brief History 1947–1980,* Kwambonambi, 1987
Brickhill, Paul. *The Dam Busters,* New York, 1955
Brindley, J. F. *French Fighters of World War Two* (Vol 1), Windsor, 1971
Brookes, A. J. *Photo Reconnaissance,* London, 1975
Brooks, Peter W. *The Modern Airliner,* Manhattan, Kans., 1982
—*Zeppelin: Rigid Airships, 1893–1940,* Washington, D.C., 1992
Broughton, J. *Thud Ridge,* New York, 1969.
—*Going Downtown, the War against Hanoi and Washington,* New York, 1988
Brown, David. *Carrier Fighters 1939–1945,* London 1975
—*Carrier Operations in World War II* (Vol 1: The Royal Navy), London, 1968
—*Carrier Operations in World War II* (Vol 2: The Pacific Navies December 1941 to February 1943), London, 1974
—*The Seafire,* London, 1973
—Shores, Christopher; and Macksey, Kenneth. *The Guinness History of Air Warfare,* London, 1976
Brown, D. L. *Miles Aircraft since 1925,* London, 1970
Brown, J. A. *A Gathering of Eagles* (Vol II: *The Campaigns of the South African Air Force in Italian East Africa June 1940–November 1941*), Cape Town, 1970
—*Eagles Strike* (Vol IV: *The Campaigns of the South African Air Force in Egypt, Cyrenaica, Libya, Tunisia, Tripolitania and Madagascar 1941–1943*), Cape Town, 1974
Bruce, J. *British Aeroplanes 1914–1918,* New York, 1969
—*Britain's First Warplanes,* London, 1987
Buckingham, W. A. *Operation Ranch Hand: Air Force and Herbicides in Southeast Asia 1961–1971,* Washington, 1982
Burnet, Charles. *Three Centuries to Concorde,* London, 1979
Bushby, J. *Air Defence of Great Britain,* London 1973.
Caidin, M. *Black Thursday (The Flying Fortress attack on Schweinfurt. October 14, 1943),* New York, 1960
—*Flying Forts (The B-17 in World War II),* New York, 1968
—*The Ragged, Rugged Warriors (The Heroic Story of the Early Air War against Japan in the Far East and Pacific),* New York, 1966
Cameron, I. *Wings of the Morning,* London, 1962
Campbell, Christopher. *Aces and Aircraft of World War I,* London, 1981
Caoimh, F, *The Aviation Book: The World's A–Z,* London, 2006
Caras, R. A. *Wings of Gold (The Story of United States Naval Aviation),* New York and Philadelphia, 1965
Carpenter, D. B. and Mayborn, M. *Ryan Guidebook,* Dallas, 1975
Carter, C. J. (ed.). *Sixty Squadron.* Private, 1967
Chant, C, *Pioneers of Aviation,* (Grange Books PLC) 2001
Charles, M. *Berlin Blockade,* London, 1959
Chassin, L. M. *Aviation Indochine,* Paris, 1954
Chaturvedi, M. S. *History of the Indian Air Force,* New Delhi, 1978
Cheshire, Gp Capt Leonard, VC. *Bomber Pilot,* London, 1943
Chilton, C. E. (ed.) *Coastal Command's War Record 1939–1945,* Northwood, 1957
Chinnery, P. *Air War Vietnam,* London, 1987
—*Life on the Line, Stories of Vietnam Air Combat,* London, 1988
Christienne and Lissarangue, *A History of French Military Aviation,* Paris, 1986
Clausburg, K. *Zeppelin,* Munich, 1959
Clayton, D. C. *Handley Page – An Aircraft Album,* London, 1970
Coffey, Thomas. *Iron Eagle: The Turbulent Life of General Curtis LeMay,* New York, 1986
Cole, C. and Cheesman, E, *The Air Defence of Britain 1914–1918,* London, 1984
Coleman, Ted. *Jack Northrop and the Flying Wing,* New York, 1988
Collier, R. *The Battle of Britain,* London, 1962
—*Bridge Across the Sky,* London, 1978
—*Eagle Day,* London, 1966
Collison, T. *Flying Fortress (The Story of the Boeing Bomber),* New York, 1943
Combs, V/Adm. J. S. *United States Naval Aviation 1910–1960,* Washington, 1960
Committee (ed.) *Destiny Can Wait – The Polish Air Force in the Second World War,* London, 1949
Conradis, H. *Design for Flight (The Kurt Tank Story),* London, 1960
Constant, Edward. *The Origins of the Turbojet Revolution,* Baltimore, 1980
Cooper P. J, *Farnborough: 100 Years of British Aviation,* Shepperton, 2004
Costello, John, and Hughes, Terry. *Concorde,* London, 1976
Craig, J. F. *The Messerschmitt Bf 109,* New York, 1968
Craven, W. F. and Cate, I. L. (ed.) *The Army Air Forces in World War II,* (Vols 1–7), Chicago, 1948-1958
Crickmore, Paul F. *Lockheed SR-71 Blackbird.* London, 1986
—*Lockheed SR- 71, The Secret Missions Imposed,* London, 1993
Crocker, D, *Dictionary of Aviation,* London, 2007
Crossfield, A. Scott, with Clay Blair Jr. *Always Another Dawn: The Story of a Rocket Test Pilot.* New York, 1960
Crouch, Tom D. *The Bishop's Boys: A Life of Wilbur and Orville Wright.* New York, 1989
—*The Eagle Aloft: Two Centuries of the Balloon in America,* Washington, D.C., 1983
Cuneo, J. *Winged Mars* Vol I: *The German Air Weapon 1870–1914,* Harrisburg, 1942
—*Winged Mars* Vol II: *The Air Weapon 1914-1916,* Harrisburg, 1947
— Cutlack, F. *The Official History of Australia in the War of 1914–1918* Vol VIII: *The Australian Flying Corps in the Western and Eastern Theatres of War 1914–1918,* Sydney, 1933
Cunningham, Bob; Simons, Bob; McKinney,. Jim; and Smith, Robert, *Tumult in the Clouds,* Forth Worth, 1990
Cynk, J. B. *History of the Polish Air Force 1918–1968,* Reading, 1972

FURTHER READING

—*Polish Aircraft 1893–1939*, London, 1971
Daley, Robert. *An American Saga: Juan Trippe and His Pan Am Empire*, New York, 1980
Davenport, William Wyatt. *Gyro! The Life and Times of Lawrence Sperry*, New York, 1978
Davies, R. E. G. *A History of the World's Airlines*, London, 1964
—*Airlines of the United States since 1914*. London, 1972
—*Pan Am: An Airline and its Aircraft*. New York, 1987
Davilla, J. J. and Soltan, A. M. *French Aircraft of the First World War*, Stratford, Conn., 1997
Davis, L. *MiG Alley*, Carrollton, 1978
—*Air War Over Korea*, Carrollton, 1982
—*Gunships: A Pictorial History of Spooky*, Carrollton, 1982.
—*Wild Weasel: The SAM Suppression Story*, Carrollton, 1986
Davies, P. E. and Thornborough, A. M. *The Harrier Story*, London, 1996
Deichmann, Gen.d.Flieger a.D.P. *German Air Force Operations in Support of the Army* (USAF Historical Studies: No.163), New York, 1962
Delear, F. J. *Igor Sikorsky – His Three Careers in Aviation*, New York, 1969
Delve, Ken. *Combat Missions From the Cockpit*, London, 1990
—*D-Day: The Air Battle*, London, 1994
—and Jacobs, P. *The Six-Year Offensive: Bomber Command in World War Two*, London, 1992
Dempster, Derek D. *The Tale of the Comet*, New York, 1958
—*Dependable Engines … since 1925*. East Hartford, Conn., 1990
Dial, J. F. *United States Camouflage WWII (T. O. No. 07–1–1)*, Arlington, Texas, 1964
Dick, R and Patterson, D, *Aviation Century: The Golden Age*, Erin, Ontario, 2004
—*50 Aircraft that Changed the World*, Erin, Ontario, 2007
Dienst, J. and Hagedorn, D. *North American F-51 Mustang in Latin American Air Force Service*, Arlington, 1985
Dietrich, Noah, and Bob Thomas. *Howard: The Amazing Mr. Hughes*, Greenwich, 1972
Doll T. E., Jackson, B. R. and Riley, W. A. *Navy Air Colors – 1945–1985*, Carrollton, Calif., 1985
—*Flying Leathernecks in World War II*, Fallbrook, Calif., 1971
—*U.S. Navy Markings WWII – Pacific Theatre*, 1967
Donahue, A. G. *Tally-Ho! Yankee in a Spitfire*, London, 1941
Donovan, F. *Bridge in the Sky*, New York, 1986
Dornbusch, C. E. (comp.) *Unit Histories of the United States Air Forces*, Hampton Bays, N.Y., 1958
Dorr, R. *Air War Hanoi*, London, 1988
—*Air War South Vietnam*, London, 1990
—*US Bombers of World War Two*, London, 1989
—*US Fighters of World War Two*, London, 1991
Drendel, L. *Air War over Southeast Asia: A Pictorial Record*. Vols. 1–3, Carrollton, 1982–84
—*… and Kill MiGs*, Carrollton, 1974
—*USAF Phantoms in Combat*, Carrollton, 1987
Dressel, J. and Griel, M. *Fighters of the Luftwaffe*, London, 1993
—*Bombers of the Luftwaffe*, London, 1994
Durkota, A., Darcey, T. and Kulikov, V. *The Imperial Russian Air Service: Famous Pilots and Aircraft of World War One*, Mountain View, Calif., 1995
Drum, Gen.d.Flieger a.D.K. *Airpower and Russian Partisan Warfare* (USAF Historical Studies: No. 177), New York, 1962
Dugan, J. and Stewart, C. *Ploesti (The Great Ground-Air Battle of 1 August 1943)*, London, 1963
Dunn, Maj. Peter M. *Flying Combat Aircraft of the USAAF/USAF*, Iowa, 1986
Duval, G. R. *American Flying Boats*, Truro, 1974
—*British Flying-boats and Amphibians 1909–1952*, London, 1966
—*British Flying-boats (A Pictorial Survey)*, Truro, 1973.
Dwiggins, Don. *The Complete Book of Airships – Dirigibles, Blimps and Hot Air Balloons*. Blue Ridge Summit, Pa., 1980
—*The SST: Here It Comes Ready or Not*. Garden City, N.Y., 1968
Eddy, Paul, Elaine Porter, and Bruce Page. *Destination Disaster*, New York, 1976
Ege, Lennard. *Balloons and Airships*, New York, 1974
Eglin, Roger, and Berry Ritchie. *Fly Me, I'm Freddie!* New York, 1980
—*Eight Decades of Progress*, Lynn, 1990
Emde, H. *Conquerors of the Air (The evolution of aircraft 1903–1945)*, London, 1968
Emde, Heimer, and Carlo Demand. *Conquerors of the Air*, New York, 1968
English, M, *Aviation Photography*, (Photographers' Institute Press/PIP) 2005
Evans, A. A. W/Cdr. *Memorable Prangs*, London, 1949
Fahey, J. C. *U.S. Army Aircraft (Heavier-than-Air) 1908–1946*, New York, 1946
Fails, W. R. *Marines and Helicopters 1962–1973*, Washington, 1978
Fairlie, Gerard, and Elizabeth Cayley *The Life of a Genius*, London, 1965
Farley, E. J. *U.S. Army Air Force Fighter Planes P-1 – F-107*, Los Angeles, 1961
Feist, U. and Francillon, R. J. *Luftwaffe in World War II*, Fallbrook, Calif., 1968
Finch, Volney C. *Jet Propulsion– Turbojets*, Palo Alto, 1948
Flanagan, D. N. and Oishi, Y. *Color Schemes of Japanese Aircraft in World War II*, Takatsuki/Shiga, 1964
Flintham, Victor. *Air Wars and Aircraft*, London, 1989
Francillon, R. J. *American Fighters of World War Two* (Vol. 1), Windsor, 1968
—*U.S. Army Air Forces in the Pacific*, Fallbrook, Calif., 1969
—*Imperial Japanese Navy Bombers of World War Two*, Windsor, 1969
—*Japanese Aircraft of the Pacific War*, London, 1970
—*The Royal Australian Air Force & Royal New Zealand Air Force in the Pacific*, Fallbrook, Calif., 1970
—*Grumman (Eastern) TBF (TBM) Avenger* (Profile No. 214), London, 1970
—*Tonkin Gulf Yacht Club*, London, 1988
—*Vietnam Air Wars*, London, 1988
Francis, D. *Mr. Piper and his Cubs*, Ames, Iowa, 1973
Franks, Norman. *Aircraft Versus Aircraft*, London, 1998
Franks, N. and Bailey, F. *Over the Front*, London, 1992

—and Guest, R. *Above the Lines,* London, 1993
Frederick, John H. *Commercial Air Transportation,* Homewood, 1961
Fredette, R. *The First Battle of Britain 1917–1918,* London, 1966
Freeman, R. A. *American Bombers of World War Two,* Windsor, 1973
—*Camouflage and Markings of the United States Army Air Force 1937–1945,* London, 1974
—*Mustang at War,* London, 1974
—*Republic Thunderbolt,* London, 1978
—*The Mighty Eighth: Units, Men and Machines (A History of the US 8th Army Air Force),* London, 1970
—*The Mighty Eighth: Warpaint & Heraldry,* London, 1997
—*The Mighty Eighth in Colour,* London, 1991
—*B-17 Fortress at War,* London, 1977
—*The Ninth Air Force in Colour,* London, 1995
—*B-26 Marauder at War,* London, 1991
—*The Royal Air Force of World War Two in Colour,* London, 1992
—*The Fight for the Skies,* London 1998
Fricker, J. *Battle for Pakistan: The Air War of 1965,* Shepperton, 1975
Fry, G. L. *The Debden Eagles (4th Fighter Group in World War II),* USA, 1970
Futrell R. F. *The United States Air Force in the Korean War,* Washington, 1983
—*The United States Air Force in Southeast Asia: the Advisory Years to 1965,* Washington, 1981
—*Aces and Aerial Victories, The United States Air Force in Southeast Asia 1965–1973,* Washington DC, 1976
Galland, Adolf. *The First and the Last,* New York, 1954
Garbett, M. and Goulding, B. *Lincoln at War,* Shepperton, 1979
Gardner, R, *From Bouncing Bombs to Concorde: The Authorised Biography of Aviation Pioneer Sir George Edwards OM,* Stroud, 2005
Garfield, B. *The Thousand-Mile War (World War II in Alaska and the Aleutians),* Garden City, N.Y., 1969
Garrison, Paul. *How the Air Traffic Control System Works,* Blue Ridge Summit, Pa., 1980
Gauvreau, Emile, and Lester Cohen. *Billy Mitchell,* New York, 1942
Gerber, Albert B. *Bashful Billionaire,* New York, 1967
Gero, D, *Aviation Disasters: The World's Major Civil Airliner Crashes Since 1940* (4th Edition), Stroud, 2006
Gething, M. J. *Sky Guardians: Britain's Air Defence 1918–1993,* London, 1993
Geisenheyner, M. E. A. *Lehmann – Zeppelin-Kapitän,* Frankfurt, 1937
Gibbs-Smith, Charles H. *Aviation: An Historical Survey from its Origins to the End of World War II,* London, 1970
—*Ballooning.* London, 1948
—*The Invention of the Aeroplane (1799–1909).* New York, 1965
—*Aviation: An Historical Survey,* London, 1970
Gilbert, Glen A. *Air Traffic Control: The Uncrowded Sky.* Washington, D.C., 1973
Gillison, D. *Royal Australian Air Force 1939–1942,* Canberra, 1962
Gillispie, Charles C. *The Montgolfier Brothers and the Invention of Aviation,* Princeton, NJ., 1983
Glines, Carroll V. *The Saga of the Air Mail,* Princeton, 1968
—*Doolittle's Tokyo Raiders,* Princetown, N.J., 1964
—and Moseley, W. F. *The DC-3 (The Story of a Fabulous Airplane),* Philadelphia and New York, 1966
Godden, J. *Harrier: Ski-jump to Victory,* Oxford, 1983
Godson, John. *The Rise and Fall of the DC-10,* New York, 1975
Golley, John, Sir Frank Whittle, and Bill Gunston. *Whittle: The True Story,* Shrewsbury, 1987
Goote, Th. *Peter Strasser, der F.d.L.,* Frankfurt, 1938
Gordon, J. *... of Men and Planes* (Vol II: Fighters, World War II), Ottawa, 1968
—*... of Men and Planes* (Vol III: RCAF, RCN, Canadian Army (Air)), Ottawa, 1968
—*The R.C.A.F. Overseas (The First Four Years),* Toronto, 1944
—*The R.C.A.F. Overseas (The Fifth Year),* Toronto, 1945
Goulding, J. and Moyes, P. *RAF Bomber Command and its Aircraft 1936–1940,* London, 1975
Green, W. (ed.). *The Indian Air Force and its Aircraft,* London, 1982
—*Augsburg Eagle (The Story of the Messerschmitt 109),* London, 1971
—*The Warplanes of the Third Reich,* London, 1970
—*Warplanes of the Second World War: Fighters* (Vol. 1, 2, 3 & 4), London, 1960–61
—*Warplanes of the Second World War: Flying Boats* (Vol. 5), London 1962
—*Warplanes of the Second World War: Floatplanes* (Vol. 6), London, 1962
—*Warplanes of the Second World War: Bombers and Reconnaissance Aircraft* (Vol 7, 8 & 9), London 1967–68
—*Famous Fighters of the Second World War.* Abingdon, 1977
—*The World's Fighting Planes,* London, 1964
—*Famous Bombers of the Second World* War, London, 1975
—*Famous Fighters of the Second World War,* London, 1975
and Swanborough, G. *The Complete Book of Fighters,* London, 1994
—and Fricker, J. *The Air Forces of the World,* London 1958
Gregory, Col H. F. *The Helicopter, or Anything a Horse can do,* London, 1948
Griehl, M. and Dressel, J. *Zeppelin! The German Airship Story,* London, 1990
Griffin, G. *Gabriele D'Annunzio – The Warrior Bard,* London, 1935
Griffin, J. A. *Canadian Military Aircraft Serials and Photographs,* Ottawa, 1969
Griffith, H. *R.A.F. in Russia,* London, 1942
Gropman, A. L. *Airpower and the Airlift Evacuation of Kham Du,* Washington, 1979
Gruenhagen, R. W. *Mustang (The Story of the P-51 Fighter),* New York, 1969
Gruss, R. *Les Flottes de l'Air en 1938,* Paris, 1938
Guedalla, P. *Middle East 1940–1942 (A Study in Air Power,* London, 1944
Gunston, W. *Night Fighters (A Development & Combat History),* Cambridge, 1976
—(ed.) *Chronicle of Aviation,* London, 1992
—*General Dynamics F-111,* London, 1978

FURTHER READING

—*Night Fighters, A Development and Combat History*, Cambridge, 1976
—*Fighters of the Fifties*, Cambridge
—*The Encyclopedia of the World's Combat Aircraft*, London, 1976
—*Fighters of the Fifties*, Osceola, Wis., 1981
—*Israeli Air Force*, London, 1982
—*Spy Planes*, London, 1983
—*Modern Fighting Helicopters*, London, 1986
—and Spick, M. *Modern Air Combat*, London 1983
Gupta, S. C. *History of the Indian Air Force 1933–45 (Official History of the Indian Armed Forces in the Second World War 1939–45)*, New Delhi, 1961
Gurney, G. *Journey of the Giants (The Story of the B-29 – the weapon that won the war in the Pacific)*, New York, 1961
—*The War in the Air (A Pictorial History of World War II Air Forces in Combat)*, New York, 1962
Haddow, G. and Grosz, P. *The German Giants – The Story of the R-planes 1914–1919*, London (2nd ed.), 1969
Hager, A. R. *Wings for the Dragon (The Air War in Asia)*, New York, 1945
Hall, A. W. *American Fighters of World War 2*, Cambridge, 1976
—*RAF Fighters in World War 2*, London, 1975
—and Taylor, E. *Avro Anson Marks I, III. IV, & X*, New Malden, 1972
Hall, J. and Nordhoff, C. (ed.), *The Lafayette Flying Corps*, Vols. I, and II Cambridge, 1920
Hall, R. Cargill. *Lightning Over Bougainville*, Washington, D.C., 1991
Halley, J. J. *Famous Fighter Squadrons of the R.A.F.* (Vol. 1), Windsor, 1971
—*Famous Maritime Squadrons of the R.A.F.*, Windsor, 1973
—*Royal Air Force Unit Histories* (Vol 1: Nos. 1 to 200 Squadrons), Brentwood, 1969
—*Royal Air Force Unit Histories* (Vol 2: Nos. 201 to 1435 Squadrons), Brentwood, 1973
Hallion, Richard, ed. *The Hypersonic Revolution: Case Studies in the History of Hypersonic Technology*, 3 vols. Washington, D.C., 1998
—*Legacy of Flight: The Guggenheim Contribution to American Aviation*. Seattle, 1977
—*On the Frontier: Flight Research at Dryden, 1946–1981* NASA SP-4222. Washington, D.C, 1984
—*The Wright Brothers: Heirs of Prometheus*, Washington, D.C.: National Air and Space Museum, 1978
Halperin, Merav and Lapidot, Aharon. *G-Suit: Combat Reports from Israel's Air War*, London, 1990
Hammond, Paul. *Super Carriers and B-36 Bombers: Appropriations, Strategy, and Politics*, New York, 1963
Hanle, Paul A. *Bringing Aerodynamics to America*, Cambridge, Mass., 1982
Hardy, M. J. *The Lockheed Constellation*, New York, 1973
—*Sea, Sky and Stars, An Illustrated History of Grumman Aircraft*, London, 1987
Harlin, E. A. and Jenks, G. A. *Avro – An Aircraft Album*, London, 1973
Harris, Sir A. *Bomber Offensive*, London, 1947
Hartney, H. *Up And At 'Em*, Harrisburg, Pa. 1940
Harvey, Derek. *The Viscount*, London, 1958
—*The Comet*, London, 1959
Harvey, F. *Air War–Vietnam*, New York, 1967
Hastings, Max. *Bomber Command*, London, 1979
Hatch, A, *Glenn Curtiss: Pioneer of Aviation*, (The Lyons Press) 2007
Haute van, A. *French Air Force. Vol. 2: 1941–1974*, London, 1975
—*Pictorial History of the French Air Force* (Vol 1: 1909–1940 & Vol 2: 1941–1974), London, 1974–75
Hegener, H. *Fokker: The Man and the Aircraft*, Letchworth, 1961
Heinkel, Ernst. *Stormy Life*, New York, 1956
Heppenheimer, T. A. *Hypersonic Technologies*, Arlington, Va., 1993
—*Hypersonic Technologies and the National Aerospace Plane*. Arlington, Va.: Pasha, 1990
—*A Brief History of Flight*, New York, 2001
—*Turbulent Skies*, New York, 1995
Herington, J. *Air War against Germany and Italy 1939–1943* (Australia in the War of 1939–1945, Series 3 (Air) Vol III), Canberra, 1954
—*Air Power over Europe 1944–1945* (Australia in the War of 1939–1945, Series 3 (Air) Vol IV), Canberra, 1963
Heron, S. D. *History of the Aircraft Piston Engine*, Detroit, 1961
Hess, W. N. *Fighting Mustang (The Chronicle of the P-51)* New York, 1970
—*Pacific Sweep (The 5th and 13th Fighter Commands in World War II)*, Garden City, N.Y., 1974
Heziet, Vice Admiral Sir Arthur. *Aircraft and Sea Power*, New York, 1970
Hildebrandt, E, *Anytime Baby! Hail and Farewell to the US Navy F-14 Tomcat*, Shepperton, 2006
Hitchcock, T. H. *Messerschmitt '0-Nine' Gallery*, Acton, Mass., 1973
Hoare, J. *Tumult in the Clouds (A Story of the Fleet Air Arm)*, London, 1976
Hodgson, J. E. *The History of Aeronautics in Great Britain*, London, 1924
Hoeppner, E. von, *Deutschlands Krieg in der Luft*, Leipzig, 1921
Hopkins, C. K. *SAC Tanker Operations in the Southeast Asia War*, SAC, Offutt AFB, 1979
Horsley, T. *Find, Fix and Strike*, London, 1945
Horwitch, Mel. *Clipped Wings: The American SST Conflict*, Cambridge, Mass., 1982
Houghton, G. W. *They Flew through Sand (The Western Desert Notes of an R.A.F. Officer)*, London, 1942
Howard, C. and Whitley, J. *One Damned Island After Another – The Saga of the Seventh (Air Force)*, Chapel Hill, N.C., 1946
Howard, Fred. *Wilbur and Orville: A Biography of the Wright Brothers*, New York, 1987
Howard-Williams, J. *Night Intruder*, Newton Abbott, 1976
Hubbard, K. and Simmims, M. *Operation Grapple: Testing Britain's First H-Bomb*, Shepperton, 1985
Hughes, Thomas Parke. *Elmer Sperry, Inventor and Engineer*. Baltimore, 1971
Hunt, L. *Twenty-One Squadrons (The History of the Royal Auxiliary Air Force 1925–1957)*, London, 1972
Imrie, Alex. *The Fokker Triplane*, London, 1992
Ingells, Douglas J. *The Plane That Changed the World*. Fallbrook, Calif., 1966

—*Tin Goose*. Fallbrook, Calif., 1968
—*L-1011 Tristar and the Lockheed Story*. Fallbrook, Calif., 1973
Inoguchi, R., Nakajima, T., and Pineau, R. *The Divine Wind (Japan's Kamikaze Force in World War II)*, London, 1959
Ishoven, A. van. *Messerschmitt Aircraft Designer*, London, 1975
Irving, David. *The Rise and Fall of the Luftwaffe*, London 1976
Jablonski, E. *Air War* (Vols I–IV), New York, 1971-1972
—*Flying Fortress (The Illustrated Biography of the B-17s and the Men Who Flew Them)*, Garden City, N.Y., 1965
Jackson, A. J. *Avro Aircraft since 1908*, London, 1965
—*Blackburn Aircraft since 1909*, London, 1968
—*British Civil Aircraft since 1919* (Vols 1–3), London, 1973–1974
—*De Havilland Aircraft since 1915*, London, 1962
Jackson, K. *Berlin Airlift*, Wellingborough, 1988
Jackson, R. *Air War over France 1939–40*, London, 1974
—*Before the Storm (The Story of Bomber Command, 1939–1942)*, London, 1972
—*Storm from the Skies (The Strategic Bomber Offensive, 1943–1945)*, London, 1974
—*Strike from the Sea*, London, 1970
—*The Red Falcons*, Brighton, 1970
—*Airships*, Garden City, N.Y., 1973
—*Hawker Hurricane*, Poole, 1987
—*Hawker Tempest and Sea Fury*, Poole, 1989
Jakab, Peter L. *Visions of a Flying Machine: The Wright Brothers and the Process of Invention*. Washington, D.C., 1990
James, D. N. *Gloster Aircraft since 1917*, London 1971.
—*Hawker – An Aircraft Album*, London, 1972
—*Westland Aircraft Since 1915*, London, 1991
Jarrett, P. *Percy Pilcher and the Challenge of Flight*, Edinburgh. 2001
—*Ultimate Aircraft*, London, 2000
—*Another Icarus*, London, 1987
Jenkins, Dennis. *Messerschmitt 262 Sturmvogel*, North Branch, Minn., 1996
Johnson, Clarence 'Kelly,' and Maggie Smith. *Kelly: More Than My Share of It All*. Washington, D.C., 1989
Johnson, F. (ed.) *R.A.A.F. over Europe*, London, 1946
Jones, H. *The War in the Air*, Vol II, Oxford, 1928
—*The War in the Air*, Vol IV, Oxford, 1934
—*The War in the Air*, Vol VI, Oxford, 1937
—*The War in the Air*, Appendices, Oxford, 1937
Jones, L. S. *US Fighters 1925 to 1980s*, Fallbrook, Calif., 1975
—*US Bombers B-1 (1928) to B-1 (1980s)*, Fallbrook, Calif., 1974
Jones, O. L. *Organization, Mission and Growth of the Vietnamese Air Force, 1949–1968*, Hickam AFB, 1968.
Josephy, Alvin M., ed. *The American Heritage History of Flight*, New York, 1962
Joubert de la Ferté, Air Chief Marshal Sir P. *Birds and Fishes (The Story of Coastal Command)*, London, 1960
Jupter, I. P. *US Civil Aircraft* (Vol 6), Fallbrook, Calif., 1974
Kaplan, Ellen, ed., *In the Company of Eagles*, East Hartford, Conn., 1990
Karman, Theodore von, and Lee Edson. *The Wind and Beyond: Theodore von Karman*, Boston, 1967
Kasulka, H. *USN Aircraft Carrier Units 1946–1956 and 1957–1963*, Carrollton, 1985
Kealy, J. D. F. and Russel, E. C. *A History of Canadian Naval Aviation 1918–1962*, Ottawa, 1965
Keats, John. *Howard Hughes*, New York, 1966
Kelly, Fred G. *The Wright Brothers: A Biography*, New York, 1989
Kennett, Lee. *A History of Strategic Bombing*, New York, 1982
Kent, Richard J., Jr. *Safe, Separated and Soaring: A History of Federal Civil Aviation Policy 1961–1972*, Washington, D.C., 1980
Kerrebrock, Jack L. *Aircraft Engines and Gas Turbines*, Cambridge, Mass, 1977
Kilduff, Peter. *Richthofen: Beyond the Legend of the Red Baron*, London, 1993.
—*The Red Baron Combat Wing*, London, 1997
—*The Illustrated Red Baron*, London, 1999
—*Germany's First Air Force 1914–1918*, London, 1991
—*Germany's Last Knight of the Air*, London, 1979
—*Over the Battlefront*, London, 1996
Kinert, Reed. *Racing Planes and Air Races*. Vols. I–XII. Fallbrook, 1969–76
King, H. F. *Armament of British Aircraft 1909–1939*, London, 1971
Kirschner, Edwin J. *Aerospace Balloons from Montgolfier to Space*, Fallbrook, Calif., 1985
Kleinheins, P. *Die Grossen Zeppelin*, Düsseldorf, 1985
Knäusel, H. G. *LZ1, der Erste Zeppelin*, Bonn, 1985
Knight, Geoffrey. *Concorde: The Inside Story*, London, 1976
Kohri, K., Komori, I., Naito, I. *The Fifty Years of Japanese Aviation 1910–1960* (2 Vols), Tokyo, 1961
Komons, Nick A. *The Cutting Air Crash*. Washington, D.C., 1973
—*Bonfires to Beacons: Federal Civil Aviation Policy Under the Air Commerce Act, 1926–1938*, Washington, D.C., 1978
—and Joseph Garonzik. *Aviation's Indispensable Partner Turns 50*, Washington, D.C., 1986
Kuter, Laurence S. *The Great Gamble: The Boeing 747*, University of Alabama, 1973
Ky, N. C. *Twenty Years and Twenty Days*, New York, 1976
Lamb, Cdr Charles. *War in a Stringbag*, London, 1977
Lambermont, P. and Pirie, A. *Helicopters and Autogyros of the World*, London, 1958
Lamberton, W. *Fighter Aircraft of the 1914–1918 War*, Letchworth, 1960
—*Reconnaissance and Bomber Aircraft of the 1914–1918 War*, Letchworth, 1962
Langsdorff, W. von (ed), *Flieger am Feind*, Gütersloh, 1934
Larkins, W. T. *US Marine Corps Aircraft 1914–1959*, Concord, Calif., 1959
Lawrence, W. J. *No. 5 Bomber Group R.A.F. (1939–1945)*, London, 1951
Lawson, T. D. *30 Seconds over Tokyo*, London, 1943
Leary W. M. *Perilous Mission: Civil Air Transport and CIA Covert Operations in Asia*, Tuscaloosa, 1984
Lee, A. *The German Air Force*, London, 1946
—*The Soviet Air Force*, London, 1950
—(ed.) *The Soviet Air & Rocket Forces*, London, 1959

FURTHER READING

Lee, D. *Eastward: A History of the Royal Air Force in the Far East 1945–1972,* London, 1944
Lee, D. L. *Flight from the Middle East,* London, 1980
Lehmann, Ernst. *Zeppelin.* New York, Green, 1937.
LeMay, General Curtis E., and MacKinlay Kantor. *Mission with LeMay,* Garden City, N.Y., 1965
Levine, Alan J. *The Strategic Bombing of Germany, 1940–1945,* Westport, Conn., 1992
Levine, Isaac Don. *Mitchell: Pioneer of Air Power,* New York, 1958
Lewis, P. *Squadron Histories: R.F.C., R.N.A.S., and R.A.F. 1912–1959,* London, 1959
—*The British Bomber since 1914,* London, 1967
—*The British Fighter since 1912,* London, 1967
Lewis, Peter. *British Aircraft 1909–1914,* London, 1962
Lindbergh, Charles. *The Spirit of St. Louis,* New York, 1953
Littauer, R. and Uphoff, N. *The Air War in Indochina,* Boston, 1971
Lloyd, Air Marshal Sir H. *Briefed to Attack (Malta's Part in African Victory),* London, 1949
Lloyd, F. H. M. *Hurricane – The Story of a Great Fighter,* Leicester, 1945
Loftin, Laurence K. *Quest for Performance,* NASA SP-468. Washington, D.C., 1985
Lord, Walter, *Incredible Victory,* New York, 1967
Lumsden, A. *Wellington Special,* London, 1974
Luukkanan, E. *Fighter over Finland,* London, 1963
M.O.I. (Air Min.) *There's Freedom in the Air (The Official Story of the Allied Air Forces from the Occupied Countries),* London, 1944
MacClure, V. *Gladiators over Norway,* London, 1942
MacDonald, H. *Aeroflot: Soviet Air Transport since 1923,* London, 1975
Mackworth-Praed, Ben, ed. *Aviation, the Pioneer Years,* London, 1990
Macmillan, Capt. N. *The Royal Air Force in the World War* Vols I–IV, London, 1942–1950
Macmillan, N. *Offensive Patrol – The Story of the RNAS, RFC and RAF in Italy,* London, 1973
Manchester, William. *The Glory and the Dream,* Boston, 1974
Manning, G, *Military Aircraft of the 1960s,* Shepperton, 2004
Mansfield, Harold. *Billion Dollar Battle,* New York, 1965
—*Vision: A Saga of the Sky,* New York, 1986
Marsh, L. O. *Polish Wings over Britain,* London, 1943
Mason R. *Chickenhawk,* London, 1953
Mason, F. K. *Battle over Britain,* London, 1969
—*British Fighters of World War Two* (Vol 1), Windsor, 1970
—*Hawker Aircraft since 1920,* London, 1961
—*The Gloster Gladiator,* London, 1964
—*The Hawker Hurricane,* London, 1962
Maurer, M. (ed), *The US Air Service in World War I,* Vol I, II, III & IV, Washington, DC, 1978–79
—*Air Force Combat Units of World War II,* New York, 1959
Maxtone-Graham, John. *The Only Way to Cross,* New York, 1972
Mayborn, M. and Pickett, B. *Cessna Guidebook* (Vol 1), Dallas, Texas, 1973
Maynard, Crosby. *Flight Plan for Tomorrow: The Douglas Story,* Santa Monica, 1962
McCarthy, J. R. and Allison G. B. *Linebacker II: A View from the Rock,* Washington, 1979
McCravy, J. R. and Sherman, D. E. *First of the Many (A Journal of Action with the Men of the Eighth Air Force),* New York, 1944
McCudden, James, VC. *Flying Fury,* London, 1939
McDaniel, W. H. *The History of Beech,* Wichita, Kansas, 1971
McDowell, E. R. *The P-40 Kittyhawk,* New York, 1968
McGregor, Ken. *'Beam Dream.' The Saga of the Air Mail Service, 1918–1927,* ed. Dale Nielson. Washington, D.C., 1962
McIntyre, Ian. *Dogfight: The Transatlantic Battle over Airbus,* Westport, Conn., 1992
McKee, Alexander. *The Friendless Sky: The Story of Air Combat in World War I,* New York, 1964
McRuer, Duane, Irving Ashkenas, and Dunstan Graham, *Aircraft Dynamics and Automatic Control.* Princeton, 1973
Melhorn, Charles M. *Two-Block Fox.* Annapolis, Md., 1974
Merrick, K. A. *Luftwaffe Colors* (Vol 1, 1935–1940), Melbourne, 1973
Mersky P. B. and Polmar, N. *The Naval Air War in Vietnam,* Annapolis, 1981
Mesko, J. *Airmobile: The Helicopter War in Vietnam,* Carrollton, 1984
Messenger, Charles. *'Bomber' Harris and the Strategic Bombing Offensive, 1939–1945,* London, 1984
Mets, D. R. *Land-Based Air Power in Third World Crisis,* Maxwell AFB, 1986
Middlebrook, M. *The Nuremberg Raid 30–31 March 1944,* London, 1973
—*The Battle of Hamburg,* London, 1980
—*The Berlin Raids,* London, 1968
Mikesh R. C. *Flying Dragons: The South Vietnamese Air Force,* London, 1988
—C. *B-57 Canberra at War 1954–1972,* Shepperton, 1980
Miller, Jay *The X-Planes, X-1 to X-29,* Marine on St. Croix, Minn., 1983
—*Lockheed F-117 Stealth Fighter,* Arlington, 1992
Miller, Ronald, and David Sawers. *The Technical Development of Modern Aviation.* New York, 1970
Millor, J. *Lockheed U-2,* Austin, 1983
Millot, B. *Divine Thunder (The Life and Death of the Kamikazes),* London 1971
Mills, S. E. *Arctic War Birds (Alaska Aviation of WWII),* Seattle, 1971
Mizrahi, J. V. *Knights of the Black Cross,* Granada Hills, Calif., 1972
—*U.S. Navy Dive and Torpedo Bombers,* Northridge, Calif., 1967
—*Carrier Fighters* (Vols 1 and 2), Northridge, Calif., 1969
—(ed.) *North American B-25 (The Full Story of World War II's Classic Medium),* Hollywood, 1965
Mondey, D. *Pictorial History of the US Air Force,* London, 1971
—*Westland,* London, 1982
Monks, N. *Fighter Squadrons (The Epic Story of two Hurricane Squadrons in France),* Sydney, 1941
Moolman, Valerie. *The Road to Kitty Hawk,* Alexandria, Va., 1980
Morgan, E. B. and Shacklady, E. *Spitfire: The History,* Stamford, 1987; new edition 2000
Morgan, L. *The Douglas DC-3,* Dallas, 1964

—*The P-47 Thunderbolt,* Dallas, Texas, 1963
Morris, A. *First of the Many,* London, 1968
Morrison, W. H. *Hellbirds (The Story of the B-29s in Combat),* New York, 1960
Morzik, Genmaj. a.D. F. *German Air Force Airlift Operations* (USAF Historical Studies: No. 167), New York, 1961
—*The Focke-Wulf 190: A Famous German Fighter,* Letchworth, 1965
—H. J. *The Messerschmitt 109: A Famous German Fighter,* Letchworth, 1963
Moss, Sanford A. *Superchargers for Aviation,* New York, 1942
Moyes, P. J. R. *Bomber Squadrons of the R.A.F. and their Aircraft,* London, 1964
—*British Bombers of World War Two* (Vol 1), Windsor, 1968
—*Royal Air Force Bombers of World War Two* (Vol 2), Windsor, 1968
Mrazek, J. E. *The Glider War,* London, 1975
Munday, E. A. *Fifteenth Air Force Combat Markings 1943–1945,* London, 1963
Munson, K. *Aircraft of World War II,* London, 1962
—*Airliners between the Wars 1919–1939,* London, 1972
—*Bombers between the Wars 1919–1939,* London, 1970
—*Fighters between the Wars 1919–1939,* London, 1970
—*Flying-boats and Seaplanes since 1910,* London, 1971
—*Helicopters and other Rotorcraft since 1907,* London, 1973
—and Swanborough, G. *Boeing – An Aircraft Album,* London, 1972
Murphy, Michael E. *The Airline That Pride Almost Bought: The Struggle to Take Over Continental Airlines,* New York, 1986
Murray, Russ. *Lee Atwood … Dean of Aerospace.* El Segundo, Calif., 1980
Musgrove, G. *Pathfinder Force (A History of 8 Group),* London, 1976
Musgrove, Gordon. *Operation Gomorrah: The Hamburg Firestorm Raids,* New York, 1981
Nalty B. C. *Air Power and the Fight for Khe Sanh* Office, Washington, 1973
—Watson, G. M. and Neufeld, J. *An Illustrated Guide to the Air War over Vietnam: Aircraft of the Southeast Asia Conflict,* London, 1981
Nance, John J. *Splash of Colors: The Self-Destruction of Braniff International,* New York, 1984
—*Blind Trust,* New York, 1986
Narracott, A. H. *Unsung Heroes of the Air,* London, 1943
Naval Airship Training and Experimental Command (comp.) *They Were Dependable – Airship Operations in World War II,* Lakehurst, N.J., 1946
Naylor, J. L., and E. Ower. *Aviation: Its Technical Development,* Philadelphia, 1965
Nemecek, Vaclav. *The History of Soviet Aircraft from 1918,* London, 1986
Netherwood, G. *Desert Squadron (The Royal Air Force in Egypt and Libya),* Cairo, 1944
Neumann, Gerhard. *Herman the German.* New York, 1984
Nevin, David. *Architects of Air Power,* Alexandria, Va., 1981
Nicholl, G. W. R. *The Supermarine Walrus,* London, 1966
Nichols, J. B. and Tillman, B. *On Yankee Station: The Naval Air War over Vietnam,* Shrewsbury, 1987
Nijboer, D, *Graphic War: The Secret Aviation Drawings and Illustrations of World War II,* Erin, Ontario, 2005
Nolan, Michael. *Fundamentals of Air Traffic Control,* Belmont, Calif., 1990
Nordeen L. O. *Air Warfare in the Missile Age,* London, 1985
Norman, Aaron. *The Great Air War,* New York, 1968
—*Pedigree of Champions: Boeing since 1916,* Seattle, 1985
Nowarra, H. *Marine Aircraft of the 1914–1918 War,* Letchworth, 1966
—Duval, O. R. *Russian Civil and Military Aircraft 1884–1969,* London, 1971
Nozawa, T. *A Pictorial History of Aviation in Japan 1910–1960,* Tokyo, 1960
—(ed.) *Encyclopedia of Japanese Aircraft 1900–1945* (Vols 1–5), Tokyo
Oakes, Claudia M. comp. *Aircraft of the National Air and Space Museum,* Washtington DC, 1981
O'Connor, M. *Air Aces of the Austro-Hungarian Empire 1914–1918,* Mesa, Arizona, 1986
O'Connor, N. *Aviation Awards of Imperial Germany and the Men Who Earned Them,* Vol II: *The Aviation Awards of the Kingdom of Prussia,* Princeton, 1990
—Vol III: *The Aviation Awards of the Kingdom of Saxony,* Princeton, 1993
—Vol IV: *The Aviation Awards of the Kingdom of Württemberg,* Princeton, 1995
Odgers, G. *Air War against Japan 1943–1945,* Canberra, 1957
—*The Royal Australian Air Force (An Illustrated History),* Sydney, 1965
Okumiya, M. Horikoshi, J., and Caidin, M. *Zero! (The Story of the Japanese Navy Air Force 1937–1945),* London, 1957
O'Leary, M. *US Sky Spies since World War I,* Poole, 1986
Oliver, D. *British Combat Aircraft in Action Since 1945,* Shepperton, 1987
Orlehar, Christopher. *The Concorde Story,* London, 1986
Oughton, J. D. *Bristol – An Aircraft Album,* London, 1973
Owen, Kenneth. *Concorde: New Shape in the Sky,* London, 1982
—*Pedigree of Champions: Boeing since 1916,* Seattle, 1985
—*The Pratt & Whitney Aircraft Story,* East Hartford, Conn., 1950
Owen, R. *The Desert Air Force,* London
Pace, S, *Boeing B-29 Superfortress,* Marlborough, 2003
Peacock, L. T . *Boeing B-47 Stratojet,* London 1987
—*Strategic Air Command,* London, 1988
Pearcy jr., A. A. *The Dakota,* London, 1972
Pearcy, Arthur. *Fifty Glorious Years,* Shrewsbury, 1985
Peasley, B. J. *Heritage of Valor (The Eighth Air Force in World War II),* Philadelphia and New York, 1964
Pentland, G. *Aircraft & Markings of the R.A.A.F. 1939–45,* Melbourne, 1970
—and Malone, P. *Aircraft of the R.A.A.F. 1921–71,* Melbourne, 1971
Perlmutter, A. et al. *Two Minutes Over Baghdad,* London, 1981
Philpott, B. *Luftwaffe Camouflage of World War 2,* London, 1975
Pierson, J. E. *A Special Study of Electronic Warfare in*

SEA 1964–1968, San Antonio, 1973
Plocher, Genltn. H. *The German Air Force versus Russia, 1941, 1942, and 1943* (USAF Historical Studies: No. 153, 154, and 155), New York, 1965–1967
Polmar, N. *The Ships and Aircraft of the US Fleet*, London, 1981
Poolman, K. *Flying Boat (The Story of the Sunderland)*, London 1962
—*The Catafighters*, London, 1970
Postlewaite, M and Goss, C, *War in the Air: The World War Two Aviation Paintings of Mark Postlewaite*, Marlborough, 2005
Potgieter, H. and Steenkamp, W. *Aircraft of the South African Air Force*, Jane's, London, 1981
Powers, G. F. *Operation Overflight*, London, 1970
Prange, Gordon W. *At Dawn We Slept: The Untold Story of Pearl Harbor*, New York, 1981
Preston, Antony. *Aircraft Carriers*, New York, 1979
Preston, Edmund. *Troubled Passage: The Federal Aviation Administration during the Nixon–Ford Term 1973–1977*, Washington, D.C., 1987
Price, A. *Aircraft versus Submarine*, London, 1973
—*Spitfire at War*, London, 1974
—*The Spitfire Story*, London, 1995
—*Battle over the Reich*, London, 1973
—*Instruments of Darkness (The Struggle for Radar Supremacy)*, London, 1967
—*The Bomber in World War II*, London, 1976
—*German Air Force Bombers of World War Two* (Vols 1 and 2), Windsor, 1968–1969
—*World War II Fighter Conflict*, London, 1975
—*Blitz on Britain 1939–1945*, London, 1977
—*Sky Battles: Dramatic Air Warfare Action*, London, 1993
Pritchard, A. *Messerschmitt*, London, 1975
Pritchard, J. Laurence. *Sir George Cayley*, London, 1961
Rae, John B. *Climb to Greatness*, Cambridge, Mass., 1968
Raleigh, W. *The War in the Air*, several volumes, Oxford, 1922
Rashke, Richard. *Stormy Genius: The Life of Aviation's Maverick, Bill Lear*, Boston, 1985
Rawlings J. D. R. *Fighter Squadrons of the RAF*, London, 1969
—*Coastal, Support and Special Squadrons of the RAF*, London, 1982
—*Pictorial History of the Fleet Air Arm*, London, 1973
Rawnsley, C. F. and Wright, R. *Night Fighter*, London, 1957
Redding, J. M. and Leyshon, H. I. *Skyways to Berlin (with the American Flyers in England)*, London, 1943
Redding, Robert, and Yenne, Bill. *Boeing, Planemaker to the World*, London, 1983
Reed, A. and Beamont, R. *Typhoon and Tempest at War*, London, 1974
Reitsch, Hanna. *The Sky My Kingdom*, London, 1955
Reynolds, Clark. *The Carrier War*, Alexandria, Va., 1982
Reynolds, Quentin. *They Fought for the Sky*, New York, 1957
Rice, Berkeley. *The C-5A Scandal*, Boston, 1971
Richards, D. *Royal Air Force 1939–1945* (Vol I: *The Fight at Odds*), London, 1953
—and Saunders, H. St.G. *Royal Air Force 1939–1945* (Vol II: *The Fight Avails*), London, 1954
Richardson, Doug. *F-16 Fact File*, London, 1983
Ries K. *Markings and Camouflage Systems of Luftwaffe Aircraft in World War II* (Vols 1–4), Finthen b.Mainz, 1963–1969
—*Photo-Collection Luftwaffe Embleme 1935–1945*, Finthen b.Mainz, 1976
Roberts, L. *Canada's War in the Air*, Montreal, 1942
—*There shall be Wings (A History of the Royal Canadian Air Force)*, London, 1960
Robertson B. *Aircraft Camouflage and Markings 1907–1954*, Marluw, 1956
—*British Military Serials 1878–1987*, Leicester, 1987
—(ed.) *United States Army and Air Force Fighters 1916–1961*, Letchworth, 1961
—(ed.) *United States Navy and Marine Corps 1918–1962*. Letchworth, 1962
Robertson, B. *Beaufort Special*, London, 1976
—*British Military Aircraft Serials 1911–1971*, London, 1971
—*Spitfire – The Story of a Famous Fighter*, Letchworth, 1960
—*Lancaster – The Story of a Famous Bomber*, Letchworth, 1964
Robinson, A. (ed.). *Air Power: The World's Air Forces*, London, 1980
Robinson, D. H. *The Zeppelin in Combat 1912–1918*, Seattle, 1971
—*Giants in the Sky*, Seattle, 1973
—and Charles Keller. *Up Ship*, Annapolis, Md., 1982
Robinson, Jack E. *Freefall: The Needless Destruction of Eastern Air Lines and the Valiant Struggle to Save It*, New York, 1992
Rochester, Stuart I. *Takeoff at Mid-Century: Federal Civil Aviation Policy in the Eisenhower Years 1953–1961*, Washington, D.C., 1976
Rodrigo, Robert. *Berlin Airlift*, London, 1960
Rozenkranz, Keith. *Vipers in the Storm: Diary of a Fighter Pilot*, New York, 1999
Rubenstein, M. and Goldman, R. M. *To Join with the Eagles (Curtiss Wright Aircraft 1903–1965)*, New York, 1974
—*The Israeli Air Force Story*, London, 1979.
Rudel, H. U. *Stuka Pilot*, Dublin, 1952
Rummel, Robert W. *Howard Hughes and TWA*, Washington, D.C., 1991
Russell, W/Cdr. W. W. *Forgotten Skies (The Air Forces in India and Burma)*, London, 1945
Russell, D. A. (ed.) et al. *Aircraft of the Fighting Powers* (Vols 1–7), Leicester, 1940–1946
Rust, K. C. *The 9th Air Force in World War II*, Fallbrook, Calif., 1967
—*Fifth Air Force Story*, Temple City, Calif., 1973
—*Twelfth Air Force Story*, Temple City, Calif., 1975
Ryan, Cornelius. *The Last Battle*, New York, 1966
Sampson, Anthony. *The Seven Sisters*, New York, 1975
—*Empires of the Sky*, New York, 1984
Saunders, H. St.G. *Royal Air Force 1939–1945* (Vol III: *The Fight is Won*), London, 1954
Schlaifer, Robert, and S. D. Heron. *Development of Aircraft Engines and Fuels*, Boston, 1950.
Schliephake, H. *The Birth of the Luftwaffe*, London, 1971
Scutts, J. *Air War over Korea* (Warbirds No. 11), London, 1982
Scutts, J. *Wolfpack: Hunting MiGs over Vietnam*, Shrewsbury, 1988

Sekigawa, E. *Pictorial History of Japanese Military Aviation,* London, 1974
Serling, Robert J. *The Electra Story.* Garden City N.Y., 1963
—*Howard Hughes' Airline: An Informal History of TWA,* New York, 1983
—*The Jet Age.* Alexandria, Va., 1982
—*Legend and Legacy: The Story of Boeing and its People,* New York, 1992
—*The Probable Cause,* Garden City, N.Y., 1960
—*The Only Way to Fly: The Story of Western Airlines,* Garden City, N.Y., 1976
—*Eagle: The Story of American Airlines,* New York, 1985
Shacklady, E. *The Gloster Meteor,* London, 1962
Shamburger, P. and Christy, J. *The Curtiss Hawks,* Kalamazoo, Mich., 1972
Sharp, C. M. and Bowyer, M. J. F. *Mosquito,* London, 1967
—*DH, A History of de Havilland,* Shrewsbury, 1960
Shepherd, C. *German Aircraft of World War II,* London, 1975
Sherrod, R. *History of Marine Corps Aviation in World War II,* Washington, D.C., 1952
Shores, C. and Ring, H. *Fighters over the Desert,* London, 1969
—and Hess, W. M. *Fighters over Tunisia,* London, 1975
Shores, C. F. *Pictorial History of the Mediterranean Air War* (Vol III: Axis Air Forces 1940–1945), London, 1974
—*Pictorial History of the Mediterranean Air War* (Vol 1: RAF 1940–43), London, 1972
—*Pictorial History of the Mediterranean Air War* (Vol 2:RAF 1943–45), London, 1973
—*2nd T.A.F,* Reading, 1970
Shorrick, N. *Lion in the Sky (The Story of Seletar and the Royal Air Force in Singapore),* Singapore, 1968
Shostak, Arthur B., and David Skocik. *The Air Controllers' Controversy: Lessons from the PATCO Strike,* New York, 1986
Shurdiff, William. *S/SIT and Sonic Boom Handbook,* New York, 1970
Singh, P. *Aircraft of the Indian Air Force 1933–73,* New Delhi, 1974
Smallwood, William. *Strike Eagles: Flying the F-15E in the Gulf War,* London, 1998
—*Warthog: Flying the A-10 in the Gulf War,* London, 1995
Smith, Dean C. *By the Seat of My Pants,* Boston, 1961
Smith, Henry Ladd. *Airways,* Washington, D.C., 1991
—and Gallaspy, J. D. *Luftwaffe Camouflage & Markings 1935–45* (Vol.2), Melbourne, 1976
Smith, J. R. *Focke-Wulf – An Aircraft Album,* London, 1973
—*Messerschmitt - An Aircraft Album,* London, 1971
—and Kay, A. *German Aircraft of the Second World War,* London, 1972
Snow, Peter, and David Phillips. *The Arab Hijack War,* New York, 1971
Solberg, Carl. *Conquest of the Skies,* Boston, 1979
Sonokawa, K. (ed.) *The Japanese Naval Air Arm, photo illustrated,* Tokyo, 1970
Spaight, J. M. *The Battle of Britain 1940,* London, 1941
Spick, M. *American Spyplanes,* London 1986
—*The Ace Factor; Air Combat and the Role of Situational Awareness,* Shrewsbury, 1988
—*All-Weather Warriors,* London, 1994
—*American Spyplanes,* London, 1986
—*BAe/McDD Harrier,* London, 1991
—*F/A-18 Fact File,* London, 1984
—*Fighter Pilot Tactics,* Cambridge, 1983
—*Jet Fighter Performance, Korea to Vietnam,* London, 1986
—*Milestones of Manned Flight,* London, 1994
—*Luftwaffe Fighter Aces,* London, 1996
—*Allied Fighter Aces,* London, 1997
—*Complete Fighter Aces,* London, 1999
St. John, Peter. *Air Piracy, Airport Security and International Terrorism: Winning the War against Hijackers,* New York, 1991
Steiner, John E. *Jet Aviation Development: One Company's Perspective,* Seattle, 1989
Steipflug, Steve. *McDonnell Douglas, Douglas Aircraft Company, 1st Seventy-Five Years,* Long Beach, 1995
Stoff, J. *The Thunder factory: An Illustrated History of the Republic Aviation Corporation,* London, 1990
Streetly, M. *World Electronic Warfare Aircraft,* London, 1983
Stroud, J. *European Transport Aircraft since 1910,* London, 1966
— *Japanese Aircraft,* Letchworth, 1945
—*The Red Air Force,* London, 1943
Sturtivant, R. *The Squadrons of the Fleet Air Arm,* Tonbridge, 1984
—*The Swordfish Story,* London, 1993
Sunderman, J. F. (ed.) *World War II in the Air: Europe,* New York, 1963
— (ed.) *World War II in the Air: Pacific,* New York
Sutton, H. T. *Raiders Approach!,* Aldershot, 1956
Swanborough, F. G. and Bowers, P. M. *United States Military Aircraft since 1908,* London, 1963
—*United States Navy Aircraft since 1911,* London, 1968
—*North American – An Aircraft Album,* London, 1973
Tanner, J. (ed.) *British Aviation Colours of World War Two,* London, 1976
—(ed.) *The Hurricane II Manual,* London, 1976
—(ed.) *The Lancaster Manual,* London, 1977
—(ed.) *The Spitfire V Manual,* London, 1976
Tapper, O. *Armstrong Whitworth Aircraft since 1913,* London, 1973
Taylor, H. A. *Airspeed Aircraft since 1931,* London 1970
—*Fairey Aircraft since 1915,* London, 1974
—*Test Pilot at War,* London, 1970
Taylor, J. W. R. (ed.) *Combat Aircraft of the World,* London, 1969
—and Allward, M. F. *Spitfire,* Leicester, 1946
—*Westland 50,* London, 1965
Taylor, J. W. R. and Mondey, D. *Spies in the Sky,* Shepperton, 1972
Taylor, J. W. R. and Moyes, M. J. R. *Pictorial History of the R.A.F.* (Vol 2: 1939–1945), London, 1969
Taylor, J. W. R. et al. *Air Forces of the World,* London, 1979
—(ed.). *Jane's All The World's Aircraft,* London: annual editions
—*A History of Aerial Warfare,* London, 1974
—(ed.) compiled by H. F. King, *Jane's 100 Significant Aircraft 1909–1969,* London, 1970
Taylor, Michael, and Mondey, David, ed., *The Guinness Book of Aircraft Facts and Feats,* London, 1984

—*These Tremendous Years, 1919–1938,* London, 1938
—*The Japanese Army Wings of the Second World War* (pictorial), Tokyo, 1972
Thetford, Owen C. *British Naval Aircraft since 1912,* London, 1982
—*Aircraft of the Royal Air Force since 1918*, London, 1976
Thomas, C. and Chris Shores. *The Typhoon and Tempest Story*, London, 1988
Thomas, Gordon, and Witts, Max Morgan. *Ruin from the Air: the Atomic Mission to Hiroshima*, London, 1977
Thomas, Lowell, and Edward Jablonski. *Doolittle: A Biography,* Garden City N.Y., 1976
Thompson, H. L. *New Zealanders with the Royal Air Force* (Vols 1 and 2), Wellington, 1956
Thompson, J. *Italian Civil and Military Aircraft 1930–1945*, Los Angeles, 1963
Thornborough, A. J. *The Phantom Story,* London, 1994
—*Sky Spies: Three Decades of Airborne Reconnaissance*, London, 1993
Thorne, B. K. *The Hump (The Great Himalayan Airlift of World War II)*, Philadelphia and New York, 1965
Thorpe, D. W. *Japanese Army Air Force Camouflage and Markings World War II,* Fallbrook, 1968
Titler, M. *The Day the Red Baron Died,* New York, 1970
Titz, Z. *Czechoslovakian Air Force 1918–1970,* Reading, 1971
Toland, John. *Ships in the Sky: The Story of the Great Dirigibles,* Seattle, 1973
Townsend, P. *Duel of Eagles,* London, 1970
Trotti, J. *Phantom Over Vietnam*, New York, 1985
Tunbull, A. D., *History of United States Naval Aviation,* Yale University Press, 1949
—and Clifford, L. L. *History of United States Naval Aviation,* New York, 1972
Turner, P. St.J. *Heinkel – An Aircraft Album,* London, 1970
—and Nowarra, H. J. *Junkers – An Aircraft Album,* London, 1971
Underwood, J. W. *The Stinsons,* 1969
Urech, J. *The Aircraft of the Swiss Air Force since 1914,* Stäfa, Zurich, 1975
USAAF. *Target: Germany (The Official Story of the VIII Bomber Command's First Year over Europe),* Washington, D.C., 1944
Vaeth, J. Gordon. *Langley: Man of Science and Flight,* New York, 1966
Vergnano, P. *The Fiat Fighters 1930–1945,* Genoa, 1969
Vincent, C. *Canada's Wings* (Vol I: The Blackburn Shark), Stittsville, Ont., 1974
Wagner, R. *American Combat Planes (A History of Military Aircraft in the USA)*, London, 1961
Wallace, G. *RAF Biggin Hill,* London, 1957
Webber, B. *Retaliation: Japanese Attacks and Allied Countermeasures on the Pacific Coast in World War II,* Oregon, 1975
Webster, C. and Frankland, N. *The Strategic Air Offensive against Germany* (Vols 1–4), London, 1961
Weick, Fred E., and James R. Hansen. *From the Ground Up,* Washington, D.C., 1988
Weil, J. and Barker R. F. *Combat Aircraft of World War Two*, London, 1977
Werner, Johannes. *Knight of Germany*, London, 1933
Wescott, Lynanne, and Paula Degen. *Wind and Sand: The Story of the Wright Brothers at Kitty Hawk,* New York, 1983
Wheeler, Howard A. *Attack Helicopters, a History of Rotary-Wing Combat Aircraft*, London, 1987
Whittle, Sir Frank. *Jet: The Story of a Pioneer,* London, 1953
Winchester, J, *Biplanes, Triplanes & Seaplanes* (Aviation Factfiles), San Diego, 2004
—*Concept Aircraft: Prototypes, X-Planes, and Experimental Aircraft* (Aviation Factfile), San Diego, 2005
Willoughby, M. F. *US Coast Guard in World War I,* Annapolis, Md., 1957
Wilson, Andrew. *The Concorde Fiasco,* Baltimore, 1973
Wilson, John R. M. *Turbulence Aloft: The Civil Aeronautics Administration amid Wars and Rumors of Wars, 1938–1953,* Washington, D.C., 1979
Winchester, Clarence, ed. *Wonders of World Aviation,* London, 1938
Windrow, M. C. *German Air Force Fighters of World War Two* (Vols 1 & 2), Windsor, 1968–1970
Winton, John. *Air Power at Sea 1939–45*, London, 1976
—*Air Power at Sea 1945 to Today*, London, 1987
Winwar, F. *Wingless Victory – A Biography of Gabriele D'Annunzio,* New York, 1956
Wisdom, T. H. *Wings over Olympus (The Story of the Royal Air Force in Libya and Greece)*, London, 1942
Wise, D. and Ross, T. B. *The U-2 Affair*, London, 1963
Wise, S. *Canadian Airmen and the First World War,* Toronto, 1980
Wohl, Robert. *A Passion for Wings,* New Haven, 1994
Wolfe, Tom. *The Right Stuff,* New York, 1979
Wood, D. and Dempster, D. *The Narrow Margin,* London, 1961
Woodman, H. *Early Aircraft Armament – The Aeroplane and the Gun up to 1918,* London, 1989
Wooldridge, E. T. Jr. *The P-80 Shooting Star,* Washington, D.C., 1979
—*Winged Wonders: The Story of the Flying Wings,* Washington, D.C., 1983
Wordell, M. T. and Seiler, F. N. *Wildcats over Casablanca,* Boston, Mass., 1943
Wragg, David. *Airlift a History of Military Air Transport*, Shrewsbury, 1986
Wright, Alan J. *Airbus,* London, 1984
Wright, L. *The Wooden Sword (The Untold Story of the Gliders in World War II)*, London, 1967
Yakovlev, A. *The Aim of a Lifetime,* Moscow, 1972
Yeager, General Chuck, and Leo Janos. *Yeager: An Autobiography,* New York, 1985
Yeager, Jeana, Dick Rutan, and Phil Patton. *Voyager,* New York, 1987
Zuerl, W. *Pour le Mérite-Flieger,* Munich, 1938
Zumbach, J. *On Wings of War*, London, 1975

EDENDERRY
19 MAR 2020
WITHDRAWN